"Ruth Baer is an experienced clinician, internationally-renowned researcher, mindfulness practitioner, and brilliant teacher who combines warm humor, deep intelligence, and empathic gentleness of heart."

—**Mark Williams**, professor of clinical psychology, Wellcome Trust Principal Research Fellow at Oxford University, and coauthor of *Mindfulness: A Practical Guide to Finding Peace in a Frantic World* and *The Mindful Way Through Depression*

"This book is like a mindfulness walk. It seamlessly integrates the best of mindfulness training from the major evidence-based care approaches, giving it a sense of breadth of vision, as if you can see across vast distances on your walk. It gently and calmly steps through many domains of self-exploration (rumination, emotion, self-criticism, values, and so on) and yet it never wanders. Each step is small, but each step is purposive, as if you are being guided on your walk by a very wise person who knows where she is going but is willing to let you set your own pace in getting there. And when you are done, you feel alive and whole, as if you have come home, and you are simply happy to be there. This is a walk worth taking—and a book worth reading. Highly recommended."

—**Steven C. Hayes, PhD**, foundation professor of psychology at the University of Nevada and author of *Get Out of Your Mind and Into Your Life*

"Anyone who struggles with difficult emotions or gets trapped in rumination will benefit enormously from this book. Written by one of the leaders in the secular approach to mindfulness, this book guides readers through the different facets of mindfulness and explains how these can be used and practiced to help us find inner calmness, reduce self-criticism, and attain happier states of mind. Knowledgeable, accessible, and practical, this book will be of immense help to many people in how to deal with our rather chaotic, emotional minds.'

—**Paul Gilbert**, professor of clinical psychology at the University of Derby and author of *The Compassionate Mind* and *Overcoming Depression*

"*The Practicing Happiness Workbook*, Ruth Baer's latest book, is an open invitation to find out for yourself how mindfulness can add immeasurably to your quality of life. Written with a reassuringly supportive tone, this workbook moves seamlessly between the problems and the promises each of us encounters as it describes how awareness, willingness, and kindness can open truly new vistas of well-being."

—**Zindel V. Segal**, professor of psychiatry and psychology at the University of Toronto and coauthor of *The Mindful Way through Depression*

"Bringing attention to our experience with compassion, patience, and equanimity can be radically transformative. You will be in the hands of a gentle, authoritative guide as Ruth Baer draws on her extensive clinical, scientific, and personal experience to set out a path of mindfulness practice and inquiry. *The Practicing Happiness Workbook* is an accessible and practical guide to the transformative power of mindfulness in everyday life."

—**Willem Kuyken**, professor of clinical psychology, cofounder of the Mood Disorders Centre at the University of Exeter and the Exeter Mindfulness Network, and coauthor of *Collaborative Case Conceptualization*

"In this wise and compassionate book, Ruth Baer integrates up-to-date research, effective and contemporary mindfulness-based approaches, and her own deep knowledge and understanding of the psychology of human distress and mindfulness meditation practice. Lucid and compelling, the book offers a practical step-by-step guide to awareness, insight, and transformation through mindfulness, enlivened by vivid personal stories and delightful touches of humor. A pleasure to read."

—**Melanie Fennell**, author of *Overcoming Low Self-Esteem*

"This is one of the most carefully designed and written handbooks on mindfulness to date. The author is a senior mindfulness researcher who has sifted through the burgeoning scientific literature to present the essential psychology and practice of mindfulness in a palpable, jargon-free, and highly accessible manner. Strongly recommended for anyone, regardless of background or experience, who wishes to live a happier, less encumbered life."

—**Christopher Germer**, clinical instructor at Harvard Medical School and author of *The Mindful Path to Self-Compassion*

"For many, happiness is an elusive state. Each fleeting moment leaves us clamoring for more. Chasing after happiness can become an exhausting and discouraging enterprise, as our most familiar strategies often backfire. Fortunately, this book offers an extremely effective alternative. Drawing on her extensive experience practicing and researching mindfulness, Baer provides compassionate and practical advice to those seeking to enhance their sense of satisfaction and purpose. Full of extremely practical tools and engaging case examples, this book provides us with the guidance we need to truly enjoy all that life can offer."

—**Susan M. Orsillo**, professor of psychology at Suffolk University and coauthor of *The Mindful Way through Anxiety*

"*The Practicing Happiness Workbook* weaves together the rigor of science, the beauty of art, the wisdom of reflection, and decades of lived clinical experience to offer us one of the most compelling books on how to cultivate greater happiness and well-being in our lives. Ruth Baer lucidly and brilliantly offers a book that has the power to transform our individual and collective lives."

—**Shauna L. Shapiro**, professor of psychology at Santa Clara University and coauthor of *The Art and Science of Mindfulness: Integrating Mindfulness into Psychology and the Helping Professions*

"In *The Practicing Happiness Workbook*, Ruth Baer draws from decades of her own and others' research, as well as her personal experience, to provide concise, accessible tips for living a meaningful, satisfying life. She clearly illustrates the natural human habits or 'traps' that can interfere with our well-being, while providing simple, step-by-step guidance to promoting new habits that will enhance and expand readers' lives. Vignettes and worksheets bring concepts to life and help readers apply them immediately to their own lives. This book may be life-changing for those who have never practiced mindfulness. It provides valuable structure and guidance for those who have practiced but not yet seen the benefits they seek, and useful reminders even for seasoned practitioners. I highly recommend this workbook and plan to buy copies for many people I know."

—**Lizabeth Roemer**, professor of psychology at the University of Massachusetts in Boston, MA, and coauthor of *The Mindful Way through Anxiety*

THE PRACTICING HAPPINESS WORKBOOK

how mindfulness can free you from the **4** psychological traps that keep you stressed, anxious, and depressed

RUTH BAER, PhD

NEW HARBINGER PUBLICATIONS, INC.

Publisher's Note

This publication is designed to provide accurate and authoritative information in regard to the subject matter covered. It is sold with the understanding that the publisher is not engaged in rendering psychological, financial, legal, or other professional services. If expert assistance or counseling is needed, the services of a competent professional should be sought.

Distributed in Canada by Raincoast Books

"Exercise: One-Word Labeling of Sensations, Thoughts, Emotions, and Urges" adapted from MIND OVER MOOD: CHANGE HOW YOU FEEL BY CHANGING THE WAY YOU THINK by Dennis Greenberger and Christine Padesky. 1995. Copyright Guilford Press. Adapted with permission of The Guilford Press.

SOBER acronym from "Exercise: Practicing Acceptance and Willingness in Daily Life with Mindful Pausing" adapted from MINDFULNESS-BASED RELAPSE PREVENTION FOR ADDICTIVE BEHAVIORS: A CLINICIAN'S GUIDE by Sarah Bowen, Neha Chawla, and G. Alan Marlatt. 2011. Copyright and adapted with permission of The Guilford Press. Mindful pausing steps inspired by MINDFULNESS-BASED COGNITIVE THERAPY FOR DEPRESSION by Zindel V. Segal, J. Mark G. Williams, and John D. Teasdale. 2001. Copyright and used with permission of The Guilford Press.

"Exercise: The Mountain Meditation" adapted from "Mountain Meditation" from the book WHEREVER YOU GO, THERE YOU ARE by Jon Kabat-Zinn, Ph.D. Copyright © 1994 Jon Kabat-Zinn, Ph.D. Used by permission of Hyperion. All rights reserved.

"The Happiest Day", from HEROES IN DISGUISE by Linda Pastan. Copyright © 1991 by Linda Pastan. Used by permission of W. W. Norton & Company, Inc.

Cover design by Amy Shoup; Interior design by Michele Waters-Kermes;
Acquired by Catharine Meyers; Edited by Jasmine Star

Library of Congress Cataloging-in-Publication Data on file

Baer, Ruth A.
  The practicing happiness workbook : how mindfulness can free you from the four psychological traps that keep you stressed, anxious, and depressed / Ruth Baer, PhD.
    pages cm
  Includes bibliographical references.
  ISBN 978-1-60882-903-3 (pbk. : alk. paper) -- ISBN 978-1-60882-904-0 (pdf e-book) -- ISBN 978-1-60882-905-7 (epub) 1. Happiness. 2. Meditation--Therapeutic use. 3. Mindfulness-based cognitive therapy. I. Title.
  BF575.H27B333 2014
  158.1--dc23

                        2014000498

Printed in the United States of America

16   15   14

10   9   8   7   6   5   4   3   2

Contents

PART 4
Putting It All Together

Acknowledgments

Immersing myself in the leading research-based mindfulness programs has convinced me that each has important wisdom to contribute to people wishing to improve their lives. This book is heavily indebted to the following colleagues who pioneered the development and scientific study of mindfulness-based treatment approaches:

- Marsha Linehan for dialectical behavior therapy

- Jon Kabat-Zinn for mindfulness-based stress reduction

- Zindel Segal, Mark Williams, and John Teasdale for mindfulness-based cognitive therapy

- Steve Hayes, Kirk Strosahl, and Kelly Wilson for acceptance and commitment therapy

- Jean Kristeller for mindfulness-based eating awareness training

- Sue Orsillo and Liz Roemer for acceptance-based behavior therapy

- Alan Marlatt, Sarah Bowen, and Neha Chawla for mindfulness-based relapse prevention

I thank all of you for your innovative thinking, compelling research, insightful books, outstanding training workshops, and friendly support of my professional development. It has been a privilege to learn from you. Your influence pervades my work, this book, and how I've come to see the world.

I am also deeply indebted to the many other psychologists who have influenced my work through their inspiring research on topics included in this book, including David Barlow, Kirk Brown, Linda Carlson, Sona Dimidjian, Barbara Fredrickson, Paul Gilbert, Willem Kuyken, Sonja Lyubomirsky, Christopher Martell, Kristin Neff, Susan Nolen-Hoeksema, Carol Ryff, Shauna Shapiro, and Ed Watkins, among many others.

I thank my friend and colleague Martha Wetter, without whom I wouldn't have ventured into DBT, where I first encountered mindfulness. I thank Cindy Sanderson and Charlie Swenson for outstanding professional training in DBT and for inspiring my initial suspicions that mindfulness might be important in the world of scientific clinical psychology.

I am grateful to the teachers at my first professional mindfulness retreats and trainings, who accepted with understanding and patience my initial difficulties with intensive meditation and helped me find my way, especially Jon Kabat-Zinn, Zindel Segal, John Teasdale, Ferris Urbanowski, and Mark Williams. I thank the many teachers at the Insight Meditation Society in Barre, Massachusetts, who have shaped my practice and understanding of mindfulness: Guy Armstrong, Rebecca Bradshaw, Christina Feldman, Joseph Goldstein, Michael Liebenson Grady, Michele MacDonald, Susan O'Brien, Larry Rosenberg, Sharon Salzberg, and Steven Smith. I especially thank Sharon and Joseph for making the Insight Meditation Society an ideal environment for this purpose.

I am indebted to the students in my classes for doing their mindfulness homework in the spirit of interest, exploration, and open-mindedness, and for writing wonderful accounts of their experiences, some of which I adapted for this book. I also thank the many clients in the groups we run in our clinic for their courage and willingness to engage with the mindfulness practices and discover their benefits, even in the midst of stress and pain. Their progress inspires me to share what I've learned.

I thank Fritha Saunders at Constable and Robinson for inviting me to write this book and guiding me through the process, Melissa Valentine at New Harbinger Publications for insights about marketing, Jon Davies and Jasmine Star for copyediting, and Kathy Norrish for the beautiful illustrations. My heartfelt thanks to the Nonfiction Writing Class at the Carnegie Center for Literacy and Learning in Lexington, Kentucky, and to Neil Chethik, our teacher, for listening to many excerpts from this book, offering countless helpful suggestions, and cheering me on. I also thank Leslie Guttman, my editor at the Carnegie Center, who scrutinized every sentence and helped sustain my energy. I'm indebted to Richard Smith, my friend and colleague in the psychology department, who read most of the manuscript and offered valuable suggestions from the perspective of an accomplished academic who has written for the nonacademic audience.

I'm grateful to my wonderful graduate students for their support of this project—despite the time it took away from mentoring them—especially Jess Peters, for her outstanding leadership in the lab, Tory Eisenlohr-Moul, Paul Geiger, Laura Smart, Brian Upton, and Erin Walsh.

I thank my father, Donald Baer, for his many influences—especially his frequent, loving reminders that the primary benefit of a tenured faculty position is the chance to pursue one's deepest interests. I thank my mother, Ann Marshall-Levine, for her thoughtful enthusiasm for my work, and my sisters, Miriam and Deb, for their sustaining, unconditional love. I thank Trevor Stokes, my graduate school advisor and honorary member of the family, for his continuing friendship and support of my professional endeavors, even when I venture into strange territory. I thank the rest of my family and my other friends and colleagues for their love, encouragement, and unfailing confidence that I could write this book.

Most of all, I'm deeply grateful for the love and support of my husband, Terry Schoen, who makes the journey joyful no matter what the weather on the mountain.

Foreword

Why can't we be as happy as we'd like to be? It turns out that we often trap ourselves into ways of thinking and feeling that create persistent unease. If this were not bad enough, the very ways we try to escape entangle us even more. We brood about our past mistakes and worry about our ability to cope in the future. Clinical levels of depression and anxiety, or problems in controlling our emotions or impulses, can take over our lives. Happiness can seem very elusive indeed.

It's rare to find a book that would help virtually everyone who reads it and puts its advice into practice. The book you hold in your hand is just such a rarity. Ruth Baer has brought together a number of different approaches that have been proven by careful research to release those who suffer from some of the most common emotional difficulties from the traps that emotions can set. These approaches have also been found to bring about a transformation in life that allows peace and well-being to be felt deeply, sometimes for the first time in years.

How can this be? The secret is in the title. Note that it doesn't refer to the pursuit of happiness, the quest for happiness, or the goal of happiness, but to the *practice* of happiness. This is fundamental. As it turns out, happiness is not a goal to be pursued, but rather a by-product of a certain way of living your life. As one psychologist has expressed it, it involves getting "out of your mind and into your life" (Hayes 2005). The essence of the mindfulness and acceptance approach to daily living involves fully inhabiting your life by learning, day by day and moment by moment, to first notice and then turn toward the present, with all its joys and discontents, nostalgia and regrets, plans and worries, thoughts and imaginings. It's realizing that you have potentialities you never dreamed of, but that making them real involves learning, piece by piece, how to drop the myriad ways in which you try to protect yourself. By trying to avoid or suppress discomfort whenever it arises, you get into a habit of withdrawing from your life, and you can find that you've become a stranger to your best and wisest self. This book offers you the chance to come home to your life through mindfulness.

Mindfulness is one of many translations of an ancient word that means "lucid awareness" or "nonforgetfulness." Mindfulness training is the practice of remembering to wake up, moment by moment, to what is arising in the inner and outer world as best you can. Developing such awareness takes gentle but firm persistence, as the mind quite naturally acquires most skills by making most of our behaviors automatic and habitual.

Habits are normally useful. If we had to think deeply about how to balance when we walk or how to keep an automobile in the correct part of the highway, we'd have little energy or mental space to think of anything else. But habits are also hungry. Any behavior we repeat more than once is fair game—a suitable candidate for becoming a habit. This is not a problem in itself. What *is* a problem is that the part of the mind that is freed up when actions become habitual typically isn't employed to appreciate the present moment or think great or creative thoughts; rather, it drifts off into daydreams, brooding about the past, worrying about the future, ruminating about our unsolvable problems or those of others, or trying to work out the meaning of life. When your mind wanders about in this way, happiness seems to elude you. And if you then turn your attention to why you feel less happy than you'd like to, it can make you feel even worse. So you distract yourself as best you can and postpone happiness for another day—without realizing that happiness was right in front of you all along. While you were searching for the meaning of life, you missed out on the experience of being alive.

This is why happiness, seen narrowly as a goal to be pursued, is an illusion. Yet none of us is immune. It's an illusion that catches us in its snare again and again. We need a reliable guide to help us navigate this path, and Ruth Baer is just such a guide: an experienced clinician, internationally renowned researcher, mindfulness practitioner, and brilliant teacher who combines warm humor, deep intelligence, and empathic gentleness of heart. Expect a good read, and enjoy reading this book, but also expect Ruth to invite you to practice some new things as an experiment. This is where the action starts—and where you can begin to reclaim your life. I wish you well as you embark on this adventure in practicing happiness.

—Mark Williams
    Professor of Clinical Psychology and Wellcome Principal Research Fellow
    University of Oxford
    Author of *Mindfulness: An Eight-Week Plan for Finding Peace in a Frantic World* (2011)

PART 1

Introduction

CHAPTER 1

How This Book
Will Help You

Happiness is not a station you arrive at, but a manner of traveling.
—Margaret Lee Runbeck

If you fit any of the following descriptions, this book is intended for you:

- You feel there's too much stress in your life, and you're not sure what to do about it.

- You're troubled by worries, fears, and anxiety.

- You're sad, blue, and discouraged, and it's wearing you down.

- You do things you regret, like overeating, losing your temper, or watching too much TV.

- You regret *not* doing things, like not keeping up with your friends and family, not pursuing your goals at work, or not taking care of yourself.

- You wish you could find more meaning and satisfaction in life.

- You wish you could be happier.

This book is about mindfulness and how it will make you happier. Happiness has several definitions (Peterson, Park, and Seligman 2005). One emphasizes positive emotions and says that happy people feel more pleasure than pain. Another says that happiness comes from finding purpose and direction in life through satisfying work, caring for others, or contributing to your community, even when these activities are difficult and uncomfortable. A third perspective says that joys and sorrows come and go, and that real happiness comes from the inner strength to find peace of mind through life's inevitable ups and downs (Salzberg 2011).

Mindfulness is a type of awareness that focuses on the present moment with an attitude of friendly curiosity. No matter how you define happiness—pleasure and enjoyment, meaning and purpose, or inner strength and balance—mindfulness will help you find more of it. Research shows that mindfulness helps with all of the problems listed above (Brown, Ryan, and Creswell 2007; Keng, Smoski, and Robins 2011). People who practice mindfulness feel less depressed, anxious, and stressed. They learn to stay in touch with their true priorities, handle their problems more effectively, and find peace of mind. Their relationships are stronger. They feel more positive emotions and get more enjoyment from ordinary activities (Geschwind et al. 2011). Even their physical health improves.

You may find it hard to believe that present-moment awareness can have so many benefits. Maybe you're thinking that you're already aware of your present moments—painfully aware. Your present moments are filled with stress and difficulties. Why would you want to be *more* aware of them?

Usually, when we say we're aware of our problems, we mean that they're often on our minds or that we constantly think about them. Thinking about problems is great when it helps us solve them. But often we get trapped in our own thinking. Thoughts go round and round in our heads, problems remain unsolved, and we feel worse.

Then we try another strategy: *not* thinking about our problems. This is harder than it sounds. Thoughts about problems come into our minds whether we want them to or not. To get rid of the unwanted thoughts, we often go to great lengths to distract ourselves. We bury ourselves in work, watch endless TV, or eat, drink, or shop too much. This creates more problems that demand our attention. It's hard to avoid being aware of them.

Mindfulness is a distinctly different kind of awareness. It's nonjudgmental and compassionate, even when the present moment is stressful and difficult. Practicing mindfulness teaches us to recognize harmful patterns of thinking and reacting before they get worse. It prevents downward spirals into stress, anxiety, and depression. Mindfulness keeps us in touch with what really matters: our most important values and goals. It helps us manage our reactions to events and provides time to choose wisely what to do in upsetting situations. This leads to a greater sense of meaning and satisfaction.

This book explains what mindfulness is, how to be more mindful in ordinary life, and how mindfulness will help you. Practicing mindfulness doesn't eliminate pain and misfortune, but it will make you happier in several ways. It will put you in touch with simple pleasures and momentary joys that you may have been overlooking. It will show you how to find meaning and purpose by acting on your deepest values and most important goals even when it's stressful, difficult, or painful to do so. It will help you find inner strength and peace of mind in the midst of serious adversity. It will wake you up to the experience of being alive.

For a detailed understanding of how this works, it's best to read the whole book and practice the exercises. As an introduction, let's consider the case of Glenn. Before he learned mindfulness skills, Glenn was extremely troubled by anxiety in social situations. He was especially fearful of speaking in groups. You may or may not share this problem—it doesn't matter. The ways of thinking and reacting that got Glenn into trouble, and the mindfulness skills that freed him, can be applied to many other types of problems.

* *Glenn's Story* *

Glenn wakes up in the morning feeling nervous. His heart is racing and his stomach is tight. He knows why: This afternoon he has to lead a one-hour staff meeting. His boss is away and asked Glenn to chair the meeting. Glenn couldn't think of an acceptable reason to say no, so he agreed, despite his fear of speaking in groups.

Glenn lies in bed obsessing about the meeting: *What if I make a mess of things? I always get so nervous. What if my voice shakes? People will hear it. They'll know how insecure I am, and they'll think I'm incompetent. I can't believe I agreed to do this. It's going to be a disaster. Maybe I should call in sick. No, that would look suspicious. Why can't I handle things better? It's only a meeting. I shouldn't get so worked up. I'll never get anywhere if I can't cope with things like this.*

After dwelling on these thoughts for several more minutes, Glenn forces himself out of bed and goes to work, alternately obsessing about the meeting and telling himself not to think about it. He spends much of the day reviewing the agenda and looking at his notes, despite having fully prepared for the meeting the day before. He walks into the conference room at precisely 3 p.m. and explains that he'll chair the meeting in the boss's absence.

For about forty-five minutes, Glenn works his way through the agenda. His mouth is dry, but his voice sounds okay. He keeps his eyes on his notes much of the time, looking up only when necessary. Then he sees someone yawning and checking the clock. *People are bored*, he thinks. *I'm making a mess of this. I should stop before it gets any worse.* A wave of anxiety comes over him. He announces that time is running short, and the rest of the agenda will be dealt with at a future meeting. People look at him oddly but are happy to rush off. *They couldn't wait to get out of here*, Glenn thinks. *I'm obviously no good at this.*

For a moment, Glenn feels relieved that the meeting is over, but then worries creep in. *How will I explain to my boss that I didn't finish the agenda?* he wonders. *I'll just have to say there wasn't time. But what if someone tells him we stopped early? I can't believe I did that! I'm such an idiot.*

Psychological Traps

What went wrong? Glenn's fear of speaking in groups and his understandable desire to feel less anxious caused him to fall into several psychological traps: patterns of thinking, feeling, and reacting that seem reasonable—on the surface or in the short term—but make problems worse over time. These traps are introduced below. Each trap is discussed in more detail in later chapters.

Trap 1: Rumination

Glenn worried excessively about the meeting, brooding and stewing about it in unhelpful ways. Psychologists call this rumination. It's different from constructive thinking because it doesn't solve problems—it makes matters worse. If asked why he ruminated so much, Glenn would say it seemed necessary to be prepared. Yet he'd prepared the day before. Ruminating didn't help; in fact, the more he dwelled on the meeting, the more anxious he felt.

Trap 2: Avoidance

Glenn thought about calling in sick—an obvious form of avoidance that he decided against. Instead, he used a more subtle form of avoidance by keeping his eyes on his notes during much of the meeting. He was afraid of seeing boredom or impatience on his coworkers' faces. But this backfired because he didn't see when people looked sincerely interested. When he happened to catch someone yawning and checking the clock, he automatically assumed that everyone had been doing that all along.

Trap 3: Emotion-Driven Behavior

Emotion-driven behavior is often impulsive and rash. To escape from uncomfortable feelings, we act suddenly, without considering the long-term effects. Later, we wish we'd handled the situation differently. When Glenn noticed someone looking bored, he felt so anxious and discouraged that he quickly ended the meeting. For a moment he felt relieved, but then he regretted his behavior and began to worry about the consequences.

Trap 4: Self-Criticism

Criticism is helpful when it's constructive, but Glenn judged himself in vague and unreasonable ways. He called himself an idiot, thinking that he deserved criticism and needed it to improve. But he'd chastised himself about public speaking for years, and it only made the problem worse. It sapped his energy and motivation and kept him from developing his skills.

How Mindfulness Skills Helped Glenn

This was not the end of the story for Glenn. By practicing the following skills, Glenn learned how to use mindful awareness to cope with his anxiety and handle stressful situations effectively. The mindfulness skills are introduced briefly here and described in much greater detail throughout this book.

Nonjudgmental observation and labeling. Glenn learned to observe his present-moment experiences, including thoughts (*I'm making a mess of this*), bodily sensations (racing heart, tight stomach), emotions (anxiety, discouragement), and urges (to call in sick, to end the meeting early). Instead of ruminating, he learned to label these experiences by calling them what they are, telling himself, "Those are thoughts," or "I'm feeling an urge." He learned to be nonjudgmental in his observing and labeling. Rather than thinking, *It's stupid of me to be so anxious,* he simply noted the anxious thoughts and feelings when they appeared. These were important first steps.

Acting with awareness. Glenn also learned how to focus on what he's doing while he's doing it. He learned how to be fully engaged. So now, when running a meeting, he looks attentively around the room, listens carefully, and guides the discussion. When thoughts and feelings about how he's doing come to mind, he notices them briefly, labels them as thoughts and feelings, and reengages with running the meeting. This is a big change in the nature of his awareness.

Acceptance and willingness. Glenn learned to accept the presence of anxious thoughts and feelings. This doesn't mean that he likes them, approves of them, or wants them to be there. Rather, he allows them to come and go in their own way and time while still proceeding with what he's doing. He realizes that negative thoughts (*I'm no good at this*) don't have to control his behavior—he now can choose whether to act on them. Even though he feels anxious, he's willing to chair the meeting as best he can, without quitting early, because he values being a helpful employee and wants to advance his career.

Self-compassion. Glenn also realizes that he's not alone—fear of speaking in groups is a common problem. Rather than judging himself harshly, Glenn recognizes that his anxious thoughts and feelings are understandable given his long-standing fear and his lack of previous experience with running meetings. He tries to help himself constructively; for example, he brings water to meetings in case his mouth gets dry, gives himself credit when he does reasonably well, and recognizes where his skills could improve.

Glenn is now much happier and more satisfied with his life. Because he learned mindfulness skills, he is aware of anxiety whenever it appears, but not in a brooding, self-critical, and emotionally reactive way. Instead, he's *mindfully* aware. Mindful awareness doesn't get rid of Glenn's anxiety, but it helps him manage it constructively. As Glenn continues to practice mindfulness, his anxiety about public speaking will become less intense. Eventually, he may enjoy running meetings. But he'll also know that he can handle it even when he's feeling anxious. Knowing that anxiety doesn't have to control his behavior will give him a feeling of inner strength.

If this brief description of Glenn's mindful behavior seems odd, unnatural, or unrealistic to you, that's because learning to be mindful during difficult times is like learning to swim or ride a bicycle: it takes practice, and feels awkward at first. This book is full of tools to make the process easier: worksheets, exercises, and personal stories of people who have benefited from practicing mindfulness. If you work with this book consistently, it can teach you all the skills that Glenn used and help you apply them to your own life.

Why I Wrote This Book

I've been a professor of clinical psychology for over twenty-five years. My colleagues and students and I work with many types of people seeking help for a wide range of problems: depression, anxiety, stress, impulsive behavior, relationship problems, and more. We're strongly committed to a scientific approach. This means that we use the latest methods—methods scientifically proven to be highly beneficial. We're researchers as well as clinicians and teachers: we conduct studies to learn more about what mindfulness is, how it works, and how best to teach it.

During the past few decades, psychologists and other mindfulness experts have developed many programs that teach mindfulness: educational, skills training, and therapy programs. Here are the programs with the best scientific support.

Mindfulness-based stress reduction (MBSR; Kabat-Zinn 1990): MBSR is usually taught as an eight-week class. It was originally developed for people with stress, pain, and medical problems and has many benefits:

reducing stress and worry, increasing positive emotions, and improving quality of life. MBSR is also effective for professionals who face significant stress in their work, such as doctors, nurses, and therapists. MBSR includes short and long meditation exercises (five to forty-five minutes) that involve sitting or lying quietly while observing your breath, thoughts, sensations, and emotions. It also includes mindfulness of daily activities, such as eating and walking.

Mindfulness-based cognitive therapy (MBCT; Segal, Williams, and Teasdale 2002): MBCT is based on MBSR. It was developed for people with depression and is effective in preventing and treating it. MBCT has also been adapted for anxiety, stress, and health problems. It increases positive emotions and helps people gain clarity about important life goals. MBCT is usually taught as an eight-week class and includes meditation exercises and mindfulness during daily activities.

Dialectical behavior therapy (DBT; Linehan 1993a): DBT was originally designed for people with borderline personality disorder, a condition that includes strong negative emotions, impulsive behavior, and stormy relationships. DBT is also effective with eating problems, depression, anxiety, and drug problems and is helpful for anyone wanting to learn how to handle negative emotions. DBT can include individual therapy, group classes, or both. It teaches a wide variety of mindfulness exercises but doesn't require formal meditation.

Acceptance and commitment therapy (ACT; Hayes, Strosahl, and Wilson 1999): ACT is flexible and can be provided as individual therapy, group classes, or workshops. It includes a wide variety of mindfulness exercises, stories, and metaphors. ACT emphasizes identifying your true priorities in life and making your behavior consistent with them. It's helpful for many problems, including depression, anxiety, stress, chronic pain, alcohol and drug abuse, and health problems.

Other Promising Programs

- **Mindfulness-based relapse prevention** (MBRP; Bowen, Chawla, and Marlatt 2011), for substance abuse

- **Acceptance-based behavior therapy** (ABBT; Orsillo and Roemer 2011), for anxiety

- **Mindfulness-based eating awareness training** (MB-EAT; Kristeller, Wolever, and Sheets 2013), for binge eating and obesity

Research consistently shows that these programs are beneficial for a wide variety of problems: depression, anxiety, stress, drug and alcohol abuse, eating problems, health problems (insomnia, pain, the stress of having illnesses such as cancer), and more. They also increase positive emotions and general satisfaction with life.

Each program has its own perspective and teaches mindfulness in its own way, but there's quite a bit of overlap. Having worked with these programs for many years, I'm convinced that each has important wisdom to contribute to people who would like to learn about mindfulness to improve their quality of life. This book combines the wisdom from all of these mindfulness programs and presents it in a self-help format.

How This Book Is Organized

In this book, each chapter builds on previous ones, so it's best to read them in order the first time through. If you find that particular chapters are especially important for you, it may be helpful to return to them. For example, if you're prone to rumination, or if specific mindfulness skills resonate with you, rereading the chapters that cover those topics may be beneficial. The book is divided into four parts.

Part 1: Introduction

The first two chapters introduce mindfulness and invite you to try a few simple exercises. These chapters are designed to provide a taste of mindfulness and whet your appetite for learning more. They won't give you a thorough understanding of mindfulness; that requires reading the rest of the book and practicing the exercises.

Part 2: Psychological Traps

Chapters 3 through 6 explain the psychological traps that Glenn fell into: rumination, avoidance, emotion-driven behavior, and self-criticism. These chapters describe how the traps work, why it's so easy to fall into them, and how mindfulness can get us out. These traps are very common. No matter what form of stress, worry, or unhappiness is troubling you, there's an excellent chance that one or more of these traps—and perhaps all four—are contributing to it. Each chapter in part 2 includes several tools:

- A short questionnaire for examining your own tendency to fall into the trap

- A worksheet to guide you in observing and understanding your patterns of thinking, feeling, and reacting

- Introductory mindfulness exercises that will help you get out of the trap or avoid falling into it

Part 3: Mindfulness Skills

Chapters 7 through 12 provide a more comprehensive understanding of mindfulness skills, how to practice them, and how they help. These chapters include exercises, worksheets, and personal stories of people who have practiced the exercises and benefited from them. Although each chapter focuses on a specific mindfulness skill, it's important to recognize that all the skills work together.

Part 4: Putting It All Together

Part 4 has two chapters. Chapter 13 includes exercises that combine the mindfulness skills. This will provide a clearer understanding of how to bring everything together. Chapter 14 discusses happiness: what it means and how practicing mindfulness will help you find it.

How to Make the Best Use of This Book

While working with this book, keep the following points in mind.

It's impossible to understand mindfulness without practicing it. Reading about mindfulness and talking about it with others is helpful, but practicing mindfulness is a bit like skiing down a mountain, floating in the ocean, singing in a choir, riding a bicycle, or walking the streets of an exotic foreign city. You don't really know what it's like until you do it yourself.

Mindfulness can seem paradoxical and puzzling at first. Feeling puzzled is a normal part of the journey. See if you can adopt an open-minded, curious attitude. The nature of mindfulness, and how it can help you, will become clearer as you work with it, especially if you do the exercises and complete the worksheets.

It takes a while to see the effects of practicing mindfulness. Trying the exercises just once or a few times probably won't be very helpful. Until you've had time to practice the exercises consistently over a period of time, it's best not to draw conclusions about whether mindfulness will help you.

Frequently Asked Questions

Before we go any further, let's consider a few of the most common questions about mindfulness.

"How Much Practice Is Necessary?"

No one really knows, although teachers agree that regular practice is important. In our clinic, we offer mindfulness programs of eight weekly classes. We encourage participants to practice mindfulness nearly every day for the entire eight weeks before deciding whether it's helpful. Most people begin to see benefits within four weeks. A few people see benefits right away.

I recommend daily practice while working with this book over a period of eight to twelve weeks. That may sound like a big commitment, but it doesn't have to be. On the website for this book (http://www .newharbinger.com/29033) you'll find recordings to guide you in practicing some of the exercises. Most of these take five to twenty minutes. The book also includes exercises for being mindful while doing things you were going to do anyway, such as eating, driving, walking, or washing the dishes. Virtually any activity can be a mindfulness exercise if you pay attention to it with a nonjudgmental attitude. That doesn't require any extra time.

"Is Mindfulness a Religious Practice?"

Mindfulness was originally discussed in ancient Buddhist traditions, but it's about paying attention—a human ability that we all share, regardless of our religious background or beliefs. In the modern-world contexts of psychology and mental health, mindfulness is taught as a set of skills and exercises for improving health and well-being. Mindfulness exercises can be practiced in a completely nonreligious way.

Some of the exercises in this book are based on meditation. This means that they invite you to sit quietly and focus your attention on specific things, like the sensations of your breath moving in and out of your body or sounds you can hear in the environment. You can sit cross-legged on the floor if you like, but it isn't necessary. Many people prefer to sit in a chair. Mindfulness meditation is a way of teaching yourself to observe your present-moment experiences with acceptance and friendly curiosity. It is *not* a way to empty your mind, stop your thoughts, or numb your feelings. It helps you develop clarity and insight about your thoughts and feelings so that you can make wiser decisions about what to do in difficult situations.

"Is a Self-Help Book for Me?"

If you're interested in learning about mindfulness and willing to work with a book, then this one has excellent potential. The problems it discusses are part of being human. The mindfulness exercises are explained carefully, and instructions are provided to guide you in practicing them. The book is intended to be useful for people with a wide range of problems and concerns, as well as people seeking personal growth and insight.

If you have a clinically significant psychological disorder (such as severe depression or borderline personality disorder) or a traumatic background that causes you great distress, engage in severe drug or alcohol abuse, or if you're at risk for harming yourself, it would be wise to consider working with a therapist. This book is designed to be useful in conjunction with therapy, although it's important to talk with your therapist about whether it fits with the work you're doing.

"What If I'm Feeling Skeptical About Mindfulness?"

It's perfectly okay to feel skeptical. I felt skeptical myself when I started learning about mindfulness in the 1990s. I had no experience with meditation and learned about mindfulness when I did intensive professional training in dialectical behavior therapy. At that time, I thought mindfulness was for monks in monasteries, not for scientific psychologists. But I needed to learn DBT for my professional work as a clinical psychologist, teacher, and supervisor, so I started practicing the exercises.

To my surprise, the exercises had a big impact on me. I developed a great interest in learning more. I read books by noted mindfulness teachers and went to mindfulness training sessions, conferences, and meditation retreats. I studied the mindfulness-based programs described earlier. I conducted research on mindfulness.

The more I learned, the clearer it became that mindfulness was making a huge difference in my life. I felt more appreciative of the external world and more at ease with my inner workings. Mindfulness improved my self-understanding and insight, clarified my priorities, and made me happier. It didn't get rid of stress and difficulties, but it did help me handle them more effectively. The same was true for the people I was working with: clients, colleagues, and students. Today, I continue to practice regularly using the skills described in this book. Mindfulness permeates how I see the world and live my life.

However, this doesn't mean that I'm mindful every minute. I'm actually a somewhat absentminded professor (as my students will tell you). It also doesn't necessarily mean that mindfulness will change your life. However, research shows that practicing mindfulness helps a great many people. My own research, teaching, clinical work, and personal experience confirm this. I'm confident that if you work your way through this book with open-minded interest and a spirit of exploration, there's an excellent chance it will make a difference to you. And, as with anything else, you will get more out of it if you put more into it. So let's get started.

CHAPTER 2

Welcoming All
Visitors to the Mind

The content and quality of our lives depend on our level of awareness.

—Sharon Salzberg

Imagine that a winter storm has caused trees to fall on power lines all over your city. You and countless others have no electricity. Your house is cold. You can't cook, watch TV, or use your computer. After dark, you rely on candles and flashlights. According to the newscast on your battery-powered radio, the electricity won't be restored for days.

You consider your priorities and options: Do you need more candles, batteries, blankets, or food that doesn't need cooking? Which shops are still open? Should you try to get a kerosene heater? Where will you find kerosene? Could you stay with friends or relatives for a few days? What would be best for your two young children, your dog, your house?

From the library, which still has power, you contact your sister, who lives one hundred miles away and was unaffected by the storm. She invites you to stay with her for as long as necessary. You gratefully accept. Now you have a clear goal: to get your family to your sister's home. You start packing, preparing the car, securing your house, and notifying people that you'll be away.

Problem-Solving Mode

While handling this situation, you're in a state of mind called problem-solving mode: focusing on goals and thinking rationally about how to achieve them (Segal, Williams, and Teasdale 2013; Williams and Penman 2011). When we're in problem-solving mode, we notice *discrepancies*: differences between the way things are (at home with no power, uncomfortable) and the way we want them to be (at a family member's house, more comfortable). To reduce the discrepancies, we analyze the problem, think of potential solutions, put plans into action, keep track of progress, and revise plans when necessary.

Problem-solving mode is extremely useful for managing crises. In fact, it's essential for accomplishing any complex project. Renovating a kitchen, writing a book, growing a vegetable garden—all require planning, working toward goals, checking on progress, and dealing with difficulties. On a larger scale, problem-solving mode is responsible for many of humanity's great achievements, such as computers, air travel, and medicine. All of these were developed by generations of scientists, engineers, inventors, and others working to reduce discrepancies between the status quo and a desired future.

Even an ordinary day requires frequent use of problem-solving mode. Daily life is full of discrepancies between the present situation (haven't showered, dressed, fed the cats, eaten breakfast, or gone to work) and the desired situation (all of that done by 9 a.m.). Some of this behavior is so automatic that we don't think of it as problem solving—it's our normal routine. But the mental process is the same: noticing discrepancies, acting to reduce them, and checking on progress.

Many people enjoy solving problems, large or small, one after another. Some choose a profession based on a love of skillful problem solving. Plumbers, mechanics, and doctors, among others, devote their careers to solving problems for others' benefit; many find the work rewarding and fulfilling.

Problem-solving mode is so helpful that we expect it to work for every problem that arises. Unfortunately, in some circumstances it doesn't work very well. Let's consider two examples.

* Alicia's Story *

Alicia is in training to become a history teacher. She's teaching her first lesson to a class of sixteen-year-olds in a few days. She feels nervous about it and wishes she felt calm. This is a discrepancy and seems to call for problem-solving mode.

At first, problem solving is useful: It helps Alicia think of ways to feel less nervous. She works hard on her lesson plan. She practices the lesson with fellow trainees. She chooses what to wear to feel comfortable in the classroom, which is often too warm.

But she's still terribly nervous. She reminds herself that she's well prepared, that her fellow trainees enjoyed the lesson, and that it doesn't have to be perfect—it's a training exercise and her supervisor will provide feedback afterward. She takes deep breaths and relaxes her face and shoulder muscles. In the evening, she goes for a vigorous bike ride.

These strategies help, but she's not nearly as calm as she'd like to be. Every time she thinks of the lesson, her heart races. *What's wrong with me?* she asks herself. *Why can't I settle down? I'll never succeed if I can't control my nerves.* She tries to stop thinking about the lesson, but it keeps coming back to her mind. Then she ruminates about it. *This is going to be terrible*, she tells herself repeatedly. *The students will have no respect for me.* She imagines the lesson going badly, the students rolling their eyes and refusing to participate, and her supervisor having to step in. *I have no future as a teacher*, she thinks as she gets into bed. These thoughts make it hard for Alicia to fall asleep. She gets up and drinks two glasses of wine. This helps temporarily, but she wakes up at 4 a.m. and can't go back to sleep.

Alicia's attempts to feel less nervous were helpful at first, but now they're making matters worse.

Why is this happening? Unfortunately, it's often difficult to get rid of negative emotions, especially in situations like Alicia's, where it's normal to be nervous. We can take reasonable steps, as Alicia did, but it's unlikely that nervousness will completely disappear. Trying too hard to get rid of nervousness led Alicia into some of the psychological traps discussed in chapter 1: rumination, self-criticism, and emotion-driven behavior.

* *Alan's Story* *

A week ago, Alan asked his girlfriend of two years to marry him. She declined. She's moving away to take a new job, isn't ready for marriage, and doesn't want to continue the relationship. She was clear that she won't change her mind.

Alan is facing a huge discrepancy between the way things are and the way he'd like them to be. He's understandably upset. His mind automatically jumps into problem-solving mode, trying to think of ways to change the situation. He ruminates about what he could have done differently but arrives at no clear answers. Judgmental thoughts circulate through his mind. *I guess I just wasn't good enough for her,* he tells himself. *I can't believe I messed this up. There must be something wrong with me.* These thoughts lower his mood and create tension. He becomes irritable and snaps at people who are trying to be supportive. Then he criticizes himself and avoids his friends. Like Alicia, Alan has fallen into several psychological traps.

How Mindfulness Helps

When we need to do something important but stressful, or when we face painful situations that can't be changed, it's difficult to handle our feelings wisely. Problem-solving mode can cause trouble because it keeps us focused on trying to change things even when change is unrealistic. In these situations, we need skills for accepting unpleasant realities. Practicing mindfulness teaches us how to accept the things we can't change. Paradoxically, this leads to healthier, more meaningful change.

Let's look at what happens with Alicia and Alan after they learn the mindfulness skills taught in this book.

* *Alicia's Story, Continued* *

Alicia recognizes that she's done everything she can to prepare for her history lesson. Ruminating about nervousness and trying to eliminate it aren't helping. She adopts a mindful perspective: observing her racing heart and shaky feelings with a nonjudgmental and self-compassionate attitude. When self-critical and pessimistic thoughts come to mind (*I'll never succeed if I can't stay calm*), she recognizes that they're just thoughts and that she doesn't have to believe them or act on them. She accepts that anxious thoughts and feelings are natural under the circumstances. She reminds herself of her long-standing desire to be a history teacher and reaffirms her willingness to take the necessary steps. *Teaching my first lesson is part of the process,* she tells herself. *To work toward my goal, I'm willing to do things that make me nervous.*

Alicia feels much better, but not because she's gotten rid of her nervousness. Rather, the way she *relates* to her feelings of nervousness has changed. She has shifted from problem-solving mode to mindful acceptance mode, a distinctly different state of mind. She realizes that she can allow the nervous feelings to come and go on their own while she proceeds with what she needs to do. She doesn't have to control the nervous feelings, and they don't have to control her. This understanding gives her a strong sense of well-being.

* Alan's Story, Continued *

Alan also shifts into mindful acceptance mode. He recognizes that the end of a long relationship is painful for most people and that he needs to take care of himself. He observes his feelings of sadness, noticing the sensations of heaviness and hollowness. Other thoughts and feelings appear: anger at his girlfriend and fear of being alone. He accepts them as normal for the situation and allows them to come and go. When he has judgmental and despairing thoughts about himself, his feelings, or his future (*I wasn't good enough; I'll never find anyone else*), he notices them, labels them as thoughts, and doesn't dwell on them.

Instead, he asks himself what he needs: a good meal, a long walk, an amusing movie, an important task, a chat with a friend? He turns his attention to constructive behavior, such as working on a project or making plans to see his family. He accepts that these behaviors don't change the fact that his relationship ended. They don't get rid of his sadness—the sad feelings will pass gradually, in their own time. Even so, he feels better than when he was ruminating and is less likely to lose his temper. He recognizes that he can carry on with his life, gently and kindly, while going through a period of great sadness.

Acceptance Mode

Alicia and Alan's stories illustrate important points about mindful acceptance mode. It's *mindful* because it involves paying attention, not ignoring or denying the realities of the situation. Mindful acceptance is friendly and compassionate, not critical or judgmental. It differs from problem-solving mode because we're not trying to reduce discrepancies or fix anything—we're *allowing* certain realities to be as they are, even if we don't like them (Segal, Williams, and Teasdale 2013; Williams and Penman 2011).

Mindful acceptance does *not* mean saying, "I guess I just have to accept this," and resigning yourself to hopelessness and passivity. It's not weak or spineless, and it doesn't mean you don't care. It won't keep you stuck in misery. On the contrary, mindfulness increases clarity and broadens our perspective. Because we're observing closely, we're more likely to see what's actually happening—in the situation and in our hearts, minds, and bodies. If we've made mistakes, a state of mindful awareness helps us see them clearly, reflect on them, and learn from them. As a result, we're more likely to choose wise actions. We're better able to see opportunities for meaningful change, such as advancing toward an important goal or finding a new path.

Introduction to Practicing Mindfulness

To practice mindfulness means to focus your attention on the present moment in a nonjudgmental and accepting way. In any given moment, we have many choices about what to focus on. We might choose something outside the body, such as sights, sounds, or scents in the environment. Or we might focus internally, on sensations, thoughts, emotions, or images. If we're being mindful, we observe them with openness and acceptance, allowing them to be the way they are. The next three exercises are an excellent introduction to mindfulness practice (inspired by elements from Hayes 2005; Linehan 1993b; Segal, Williams, and Teasdale 2002; and Williams et al. 2007).

EXERCISE: Mindfulness of Sounds

What sounds can you hear right now? As best you can, observe them with interest as they come and go. See if you can bring a nonjudgmental, accepting attitude to all the sounds you can hear, whether they're pleasant, unpleasant, or neutral. For example, you might notice birds singing a lovely song, a lawn mower making an obnoxious noise, or footsteps passing outside the room.

Do you notice a tendency to judge the sounds or to figure out what's making each sound? Are you thinking about how to avoid the unpleasant sounds or hear more of the pleasant ones? If so, see if you can let go of these thoughts. Practice observing the sounds as they occur and accepting them as they are. Adopt a friendly, curious, and open-minded attitude toward the sounds. Notice their qualities, such as pitch, volume, or duration. Notice periods of silence between sounds. Close your eyes or look away from this page and try this for a minute or two.

Your mind is likely to wander off. This is normal. When you notice that your mind is elsewhere, gently bring your attention back to observing sounds.

EXERCISE: Mindfulness of Sensations

Focus your attention on your right hand. What can you feel at this moment? Is your hand warm or cool, sweaty or dry, itchy, tingly, numb, or neutral? Is it touching something? Do you feel the texture or temperature of whatever your hand is touching? Spend a few moments closely observing the sensations in your right hand with an attitude of acceptance and curiosity. Allow the sensations to be exactly as they are, even if they're unpleasant. If you don't feel much of anything in your hand, practice observing the absence of sensation and accepting that as your current experience.

Your mind will wander off. When you notice that it has, gently bring it back. As best you can, refrain from criticizing yourself about the wandering mind. Everyone's mind wanders.

EXERCISE: Practicing Mindfulness on a Walk

Going for a walk provides good opportunities to observe the external world *and* notice what your mind and body are doing (Hayes 2005; Williams and Penman 2011). Before trying this practice, consider the following examples of walking in a park in different mental modes.

Melinda: Walking in Problem-Solving Mode

Melinda has an important meeting a few blocks from her office. The quickest way to get there is to walk through a park. Melinda sets out with no time to spare, keeping to the stone path to avoid the damp ground and thinking of what she'll say during the meeting. Suddenly, she comes upon a work crew. They've dug up a large section of the stone path, creating a muddy mess.

Oh no, she thinks. *Why didn't they put up a sign? I don't have time to turn back. I'll just have to go around.* Melinda feels frustrated and annoyed but focuses on her goal of getting to the meeting—on time and looking professional. She detours quickly around the mud, trying to keep her feet dry. She arrives with just enough time to stop in the restroom and wipe the worst of the dirt and grass from her shoes.

Valerie: Walking in Mindful Acceptance Mode

Valerie is walking in the park during her lunch break. She's not in a hurry and has no particular destination. Her only goal is to be back in her office in half an hour. She feels the air on her skin, smells the fresh scents, watches the trees swaying in the breeze, and appreciates the sounds of the birds. Thoughts and daydreams pass through her mind, but she doesn't dwell on them; instead, she returns her attention to the environment around her.

When she comes to the dug-up portion of the path, she observes the mud, looks around, decides to go back the way she came, and walks in another section of the park.

Rob: Walking in Shifting Mental Modes

Rob begins his walk in mindful acceptance mode, feeling the warm sun, seeing flowers in bloom, and hearing children playing. He senses the ground under his feet and feels his arms gently swinging. Someone starts up a lawn mower. For a moment he observes the sound mindfully, noticing its pitch, volume, and texture. He smells the mower's fumes and the scent of cut grass.

Then a thought comes to Rob's mind about the state of his own lawn. Another thought follows, about the neighborhood teenager who hasn't mowed it lately despite promising to do it every week. A feeling of frustration arises. Rob's body becomes tense. Soon his mind is caught up in a stream of thoughts about his lawn. He pictures it looking shaggy and unkempt and his neighbors talking about it. He imagines storming over to the teenager's house and demanding that he do his job.

Suddenly, Rob realizes that he's been carried away by his thoughts. His body is still walking in the park, but his mind has been elsewhere, working (not very constructively) on the problem of the lawn. He notices that he is scowling, his fists are clenched, and his heart is beating faster. Gently, he brings his attention back to the present environment, feeling the breeze, smelling the air, seeing the grass and trees, hearing the lawn mower. He decides that after his walk he'll make a rational plan for dealing with his lawn. For now, when thoughts about the lawn come to mind, he notices them in the same way he notices other things. *Hey, there's a thought*, he says to himself. *Oh, there's a butterfly.*

Instructions for Mindful Walking

Walk anywhere you like: in a park, your neighborhood, or even an indoor shopping mall. Choose a time when you don't have conflicting demands. Start by walking mindfully as best you can. Choose something specific to focus on. For the first few minutes, you might observe sounds. As before, notice them with an attitude of friendly curiosity, even if you find some of them unpleasant. See if you can let go of analyzing the sounds;

instead, focus on simply hearing them. If you like, play with variations: Focus on just one specific sound for a while, then switch to a different one. Then expand your awareness to include all the sounds at once. Listen for sounds ahead of you or behind you, or to your left or your right. Refrain from judgments about how well you're doing. If you're hearing sounds, you're doing fine.

Then switch to seeing. Notice colors, shapes, or movements in your environment. Do you notice a tendency to label or analyze what you see? As best you can, let go of thinking about what you see and focus on just observing it. For example, instead of saying, *That's a rosebush*, notice shapes and colors, patterns of light and shadow, and the textures of the leaves or petals.

Then switch to observing the scents in the air, the sensations of your feet moving along, the sun on your skin, or anything else. Practice noticing without judgment, allowing whatever you observe to be just as it is, even if it's unpleasant.

Before long, your mind will wander off. This is completely normal. Minds naturally wander, so refrain from criticizing yourself as best you can. See if you can recognize where your mind went. Were you thinking about a problem, like how to get your lawn mowed or what to say in a meeting? Were you concentrating on a goal? Did your mind travel into the future or the past? Perhaps you were daydreaming about a variety of things. It doesn't matter. When you notice that your mind has wandered, gently bring it back to observing the present moment and accepting it as it is. The more you practice this, the stronger your mindfulness skills will become.

Why It's Helpful to Practice Mindfulness

Think about what happens when you pursue the goals that are most important to you. Is it always easy and pleasant? For most people, a meaningful and satisfying life includes stressful, challenging, even painful experiences (Hayes, Strosahl, and Wilson 2012). They seem to be inescapable.

For example, parenting includes many joys and satisfactions, but good parents also have to cope with stressful events and circumstances: health problems, accidents, academic issues, behavioral or emotional difficulties, peer-group problems, and the ever-changing balance between closeness and independence. Likewise, a career can be rewarding and fulfilling but entails significant costs: difficult professional training, long hours, competition with highly qualified peers, and evaluation by critical supervisors.

Pessimistic thoughts, such as *I'll never succeed at this* and *This is too much for me*, inevitably come up as we pursue our most important goals. Negative emotions arise, such as anxiety, sadness, disappointment, boredom, and anger. We feel urges, perhaps to give up, lash out, or distract ourselves in unhealthy ways. We might prefer to avoid these unpleasant thoughts, feelings, and urges, but they're a normal part of an active, engaged, satisfying life. The alternative—an inactive, disengaged, unsatisfying life—causes its own type of unhappiness.

Practicing mindfulness teaches us that we don't have to fight with painful thoughts and emotions. Instead, we can choose a mental mode. When the problem-solving mode would be useful, we can analyze the situation and work toward changing it. When problem-solving mode isn't useful, we can observe our thoughts and feelings with openness and acceptance rather than struggling to suppress, escape, or change them. Mindfulness teaches us a valuable lesson about ourselves: we are more than our thoughts and feelings. Thoughts and feelings are like visitors; they come and go. We enjoy some of them and dislike others. Either way, we can learn from them. Most importantly, we don't have to be controlled by them.

The mindful approach to thoughts and feelings may seem unnatural or confusing to you. Or you may think it makes sense but feel uncertain of how to apply it to your own life. These reactions are common and normal. Your understanding will increase as you work through the rest of this book.

For now, it may be helpful to consider the following poem, "The Guest House," by the Persian poet Rumi (reprinted with permission from Barks 2004). It was written in the thirteenth century and is popular today among mindfulness teachers. It uses a powerful metaphor to portray mindful acceptance of thoughts and emotions, especially unpleasant ones. It invites us to contemplate the idea that treating our thoughts and feelings as honored guests can make our lives richer and more satisfying. Read it slowly and let it sink in.

✳ **The Guest House** ✳

This being human is a guest house.
Every day a new arrival.

A joy, a depression, a meanness,
some momentary awareness comes
as an unexpected visitor.

Welcome and entertain them all!
Even if they're a crowd of sorrows,
who violently sweep your house
empty of its furniture,

still, treat each guest honorably.
He may be clearing you out
for some new delight.

The dark thought, the shame, the malice,
meet them at the door laughing,
and invite them in.

Be grateful for whoever comes,
because each has been sent
as a guide from beyond.

In Western culture, this is an unorthodox way of relating to negative thoughts and emotions. Meet them at the door, welcome them, and invite them in. Don't try to chase them off, ruminate about them, or criticize yourself for having them. This can be very difficult without the necessary skills. We will see in the following chapters how attempting to bar the door or run away from thoughts and feelings causes us to get stuck in psychological traps, and how practicing mindfulness skills can set us free.

PART 2

Psychological Traps

CHAPTER 3

Rumination

You'll never plow a field by turning it over in your mind.

—Irish proverb

At 8 a.m., Keith discovers that his car won't start. He thinks, *Oh no, I have a meeting at 8:30! I'm going to be late. This is such a pain. What am I going to do?*

Keith thinks about who might give him a ride. First he pictures his coworkers one by one, trying to remember where they live. Then he considers his neighbors, wondering if any are still at home and where they work. He thinks of several friends. For a moment, he imagines himself on a bicycle. He considers taking the bus.

None of these ideas seem very promising. He only knows a few of his coworkers well enough to ask for such a favor, and they don't live nearby. He hardly knows his neighbors at all. Most of his friends start work at 8:00 and have probably already arrived at their jobs. He doesn't own a bicycle. The bus service in his town isn't very good; he's never used it and has no knowledge of the routes, the schedules, or even where the nearest stop is.

I could call a taxi, he thinks. *But it will take time to arrive and I'll be late for the meeting.*

Then he thinks about the meeting: *How bad would it be if I missed it?* he asks himself. *People sometimes miss this meeting and nothing terrible happens.* But then he remembers something on the agenda that he wants to discuss. *This is so inconvenient!* he thinks. *What else could I do? Would my boss agree to postpone the meeting?*

Postponing the meeting seems unlikely. Then Keith remembers a recent meeting in which someone who was out of town participated by speakerphone. *Speakerphone!* he thinks. *I'll call the office and tell them I'm having car trouble. I'll ask the assistant to set up the speakerphone. Then I can participate in the meeting, call the mechanic about the car, and get to work later.*

***

Frank has the same problem: At 8 a.m., he discovers that his car won't start. But instead of considering ways to handle the situation, Frank gets caught up in a different kind of thinking.

Why does this sort of thing always happen to me? he wonders. *What's wrong with me that I can't do something as simple as get to work on time? This is completely my fault. I thought the car sounded a little funny yesterday, and I didn't do anything about it. Why didn't I take it to the mechanic immediately? That was really stupid. I should have known something was wrong.*

Frank remembers other occasions when he's missed work because of unexpected problems: *I've done this too many times,* he tells himself. *Just last winter when the pipes froze and I had water all over the house, that was a disaster! I missed two days before I got that sorted out. That was my fault too. I forgot to leave the faucet dripping to keep the pipes from freezing.*

Then he makes pessimistic predictions: *People are going to think this is typical of me, always so unreliable. I can imagine what they'll be saying when I walk in late. I bet my boss is wondering if I should really have this job.*

Frank's thinking becomes repetitive. He keeps telling himself he's an idiot, irresponsible, and undeserving; chastising himself for not taking care of the car; and asking himself why he can't handle things better.

Helpful and Unhelpful Ways of Thinking About Problems

Keith and Frank thought about the same problem, but in different ways and with different results. Within a few minutes, Keith decided on a reasonable course of action and felt better, whereas Frank made no progress and his mood spiraled down. Keith was engaged in constructive problem solving. Frank was ruminating.

Constructive Problem Solving

Keith's way of thinking included several steps shown in many studies to be useful for solving problems (Nezu, Nezu, and McMurran 2008).

Step 1. Focusing on a Clearly Defined Problem

Keith stayed focused on the specific problem: how to get to work on time, or how to handle the situation if arriving on time wasn't possible.

Step 2. Brainstorming

Keith thought of several ways to get to work: getting a ride from someone, riding a bicycle, taking the bus, calling a taxi. Then he thought of ways to cope with not arriving on time. Some of his ideas weren't workable (he doesn't have a bicycle), but that didn't matter. At the brainstorming stage, the point is to think of many potential solutions. This increases the chances of coming up with something useful.

Step 3. Making a Decision to Try Something

Keith decided to try the speakerphone option. It seemed promising. He knew there was a speakerphone in the office, that the assistant could set it up, and that it had been used recently and worked well.

Unconstructive Rumination *Neg*

In ordinary language, the word "rumination" sometimes means "pondering" or "reflection," both of which can be normal and healthy ways of considering something carefully. Psychologists, however, use the term "rumination" to refer to the type of thinking that Frank was doing: negative, repetitive, prolonged, unhelpful thinking (Watkins 2008). Frank didn't focus on the specific problem, think of potential solutions, or make a decision to try something. Instead, he remembered previous difficulties (frozen pipes) and imagined future misfortunes (people thinking badly of him, losing his job). He criticized himself for perceived failings and asked himself vague questions (*What's wrong with me?*) that didn't help with the immediate situation.

This unconstructive form of rumination—also known as brooding, stewing, obsessing, worrying, overthinking, dwelling on things, or turning something over and over in the mind—was of no help to Frank. The thoughts went round and round in his head, didn't solve anything, and made him feel worse.

Common Topics of Rumination

We can ruminate about many things: negative emotions, current problems, stressful events from the past, future disasters, and more. Psychologists recognize several types of rumination. The topics are different, but the style of thinking is the same for each: negative, repetitive, prolonged, and unhelpful. Below is a summary of common types of rumination.

- Ruminating about sadness and depression includes (Conway et al. 2000; Treynor, Gonzalez, and Nolen-Hoeksema 2003):

  - Repetitive, unconstructive thinking about feeling sad, blue, and dejected

  - Brooding about how exhausted or unmotivated you feel and why you feel so bad

  - Stewing about how terrible your situation will be if you continue to feel this bad

  - Obsessing over questions with no clear answers, such as *What have I done to deserve this?* or *What's wrong with me?*

- Ruminating about anger includes (Sukhodolsky, Golub, and Cromwell 2001):

  - Dwelling on how angry you feel and the event or situation that caused the anger

  - Replaying the incident in your mind over and over

  - Obsessing about how unfair the situation was or how badly others behaved

  - Fantasizing about revenge

  - Having repeated mental arguments with people

- Ruminating about future disasters includes (Borkovec, Ray, and Stober 1998; Meyer et al. 1990):

  - Worrying about misfortunes that might afflict you or your loved ones—illnesses, accidents, losing a job, failure in school, financial or relationship problems, or anything else

  - Asking *What if…?* and then imagining disastrous scenarios (*What if I get fired?*)

- Ruminating about ongoing problems or past events includes (Robinson and Alloy 2003):

  - Telling yourself repeatedly that the problem or stressful event was completely your fault, even if it wasn't

  - Dwelling on the idea that things like this always happen to you, that it's going to ruin things for you, or that you can't cope

- Ruminating about social interactions includes (Brozovich and Heimberg 2008):

  - Worrying or obsessing about your behavior with others: whether you said the wrong thing, looked foolish, offended someone, and so on

  - Replaying conversations or interactions in your mind

  - Repeatedly imagining what you wish you'd said

  - Stewing over what others think of you now

* Bill's Story *

Bill has had chronic back pain since a car accident two years ago. Every morning, he gets out of bed, feels the pain in his back, and starts thinking: *Why does this pain never get better? It's ruining everything. I can't function with this pain. I can't believe my doctors haven't found a way to control this. I'm going to be completely useless if this goes on. What if the rest of my life is wasted? What have I done to deserve this?*

Bill's thoughts continue along these well-worn tracks for long periods of time. His doctor encourages him to walk more, do gentle exercises, see his friends, and resume activities he used to enjoy. Bill constantly tells himself that he should try harder, but he hasn't summoned the energy to follow his doctor's advice. He ruminates about that too. *Why can't I get going?* he asks himself repeatedly. *I'm always so tired. I rest all the time; I should have more energy. What's wrong with me?* Rumination is causing Bill to feel depressed and hopeless. He spends most of his time lying in a recliner and watching TV, becoming more and more isolated.

Bill is ruminating in several of the ways described above. He obsesses about his current symptoms: pain, depression, fatigue, and lack of motivation. He stews about his future. He dwells angrily on his doctor's failure to get rid of his pain.

Chronic back pain is a serious problem. If Bill stops ruminating, he'll still have back pain. But his doctor has given him good recommendations for managing it. Rumination keeps Bill focused on the most negative aspects of his situation. It lowers his mood, saps his motivation, and prevents him from focusing on constructive problem solving. If he didn't spend so much time ruminating, he'd have more energy and motivation to walk, stretch, and see friends, even if he still had pain. His quality of life would begin to improve.

SELF-TEST: Rumination

Everyone ruminates now and then. If it doesn't happen often or persist for long periods, it probably won't do much harm. This self-test (loosely based on Trapnell and Campbell 1999 and the research on topics of rumination described earlier) will help you examine your tendency to ruminate. Using the rating scale provided, in each blank space write the number that indicates how true each statement is for you.

1	2	3	4
Rarely true	Sometimes true	Often true	Very often true

_2_ When I'm sad or blue, I keep thinking about how bad I feel.

_4_ When something angers or upsets me, it replays in my mind for a long time.

_4_ I worry about bad things that might happen in the future.

_3_ I dwell on my problems for long periods of time.

_1_ In my mind, I go over my embarrassing or awkward moments again and again.

Add up your ratings. If you scored between 11 and 14, you may have a moderate tendency to engage in unhelpful rumination. If you scored between 15 and 20, this could be significant cause for concern.

14

Consequences of Rumination

Research shows that rumination has many serious consequences (Nolen-Hoeksema, Wisco, and Lyubomirsky 2008; Watkins 2008):

- It intensifies negative moods. Ruminating about sadness makes depression worse. Ruminating about anger strengthens angry feelings.

- 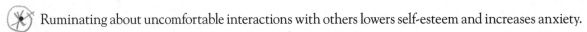 Rumination interferes with motivation, concentration, memory, and problem solving.

- People who ruminate when they're sad or discouraged are more susceptible to serious depression, binge eating, and alcohol abuse. They're also more likely to develop post-traumatic stress disorder if something extremely stressful happens to them.

- Angry rumination increases heart rate, blood pressure, and muscle tension and keeps the body from returning to a resting state.

- Rumination harms relationships. People who ruminate when they're angry are more aggressive— they criticize others harshly, lose their temper, and retaliate when they feel wronged. In addition, constant obsessing about anything tends to annoy others, even if they want to be loving and supportive.

- Ruminating about uncomfortable interactions with others lowers self-esteem and increases anxiety.

Rumination Is a Psychological Trap

If rumination is so harmful, why do we do it? There are several important reasons.

We mistakenly believe that rumination should help. Sometimes rumination feels like constructive problem solving. We think we're analyzing our problems, situations, or personality to gain an understanding of why we're unhappy or stressed. It seems logical that this type of thinking would lead to deeper insight and better moods. Unfortunately, this belief is mistaken. Rumination worsens negative moods and interferes with problem solving (Nolen-Hoeksema, Wisco, and Lyubomirsky 2008; Watkins 2008).

Rumination provides temporary protection from painful emotions. Imagine that someone has done something that hurt your feelings. Ruminating about how badly this person behaved makes you feel angry. The anger may be unpleasant, but it distracts you from the pain of your hurt feelings. Anger is often preferable to hurt feelings because it makes us feel justified or energized. We sometimes enjoy dwelling on others' misdeeds when we're upset with them. Like a prosecuting attorney, we mentally build the case against the accused, feeling stronger and more confident as we amass the evidence. This keeps us from feeling vulnerable or thinking about painful realities, such as the role we might have played in the situation or serious problems in the relationship that need to be resolved.

Angry — can be productive
doesn't allows us to focus on other things

Rumination distracts us from constructive but difficult behavior. Suppose you are partly responsible for the episode in which your feelings got hurt. Perhaps the other party isn't entirely to blame. To repair the relationship, it might be necessary to bring up the subject for discussion, to apologize, or to change your behavior. This may feel awkward and painful. As long as you stay absorbed in rumination, you don't have to confront the need to do something difficult.

Rumination is a psychological trap. We get caught in the trap because of the short-term benefits and the illusion that it should help. But the price is high. In the long run, rumination worsens negative moods, saps our motivation to behave constructively, makes us more likely to do things we regret later, and keeps the body in an unhealthy state of tension.

EXERCISE: Understanding Your Patterns of Rumination

The following worksheet will help you observe and understand your tendency to ruminate. In order to benefit from this exercise, it's important to pay attention to your thinking processes. Try to notice when you're dwelling on repetitive thoughts about an unpleasant situation, a problem, or a negative mood.

As you become more aware of your thinking, you may find that you're criticizing yourself for ruminating. As best you can, let go of the criticism. Instead, adopt the perspective of an explorer who takes a keen and open-minded interest in whatever is discovered. See if you can explore your mental patterns with an attitude of friendly curiosity.

Below, you'll find three versions of the rumination worksheet. The first contains instructions. It's followed by an example worksheet from Ellen, a woman in her forties who often feels socially awkward and worries that people don't like her. She's been attending a monthly book club as a way to make new friends. She's also been ruminating about a recent minor car accident.

After the example, you'll find a blank worksheet for your own use. Once you've read through the instructions and example, complete the worksheet for one of your episodes of rumination using the blank version. Make extra copies of the worksheet first, as the exercise is especially useful if you complete it several times. After you've done it once, be alert to future episodes of rumination and fill out the worksheet again. This will help you identify negative thinking patterns over time.

Each time you complete the worksheet, choose one specific occasion to write about: an episode of rumination that occurred on a particular day at a specific time. The most recent episode might be the easiest to remember, but choose one that stands out in your mind.

Don't worry about trying to keep a perfect record. The purpose of the exercise is not to criticize yourself but to gather information, in a nonjudgmental way, about your thought processes. Using the rumination worksheet is one way of developing mindfulness skills that will help you deal more effectively with unhealthy thinking patterns.

WORKSHEET: Understanding an Episode of Rumination

Remember to maintain an attitude of friendly curiosity.

Day and time	Triggering event	Ruminative thoughts	Emotions	Aftereffects and consequences	
When did this episode of rumination occur? Writing this down helps you be specific about which episode you're working with, isolating it from other things going on in your life.	What started the episode? Where were you? What was going on? Were other people involved? The trigger might be an event in the external world, such as being criticized at work. Or it could be an emotional state that came over you for no clear reason; maybe you woke up feeling depressed or anxious and started ruminating.	What thoughts were going round and round in your head? As best you can, write down your thoughts exactly as they appeared in your mind. If you had images or pictures in your mind, describe them.	What emotions were you feeling while you were ruminating? You may have felt one or more negative emotions, such as sadness, anger, anxiety, guilt, or shame. Note them here. If you felt any positive emotions, note them also.	How did you feel after the episode? What happened next? Include body sensations, thoughts, emotions, and urges. Also include any effects on your behavior or interactions with others.	

WORKSHEET: Understanding an Episode of Rumination

Your name: *Ellen*

Remember to maintain an attitude of friendly curiosity.

Day and time	Triggering event	Ruminative thoughts	Emotions	Aftereffects and consequences
Wednesday around 3 p.m.	I was at my book group meeting. I was sharing my thoughts about the book when a group member checked her cell phone for messages.	I talk too much. People are noticing that it takes me too long to make my point. They get bored with what I'm saying. They're not taking me seriously. No one wants me here. Why can't they listen to me? They shouldn't be so judgmental. I listen when they talk. They should pay attention when I talk.	First I felt shame and fear, then I was angry.	I was quieter than usual during the rest of the meeting. Afterward I didn't chat with anyone or make a coffee date like I usually do. I went straight to my car.

When I got home I felt lonely and had no energy. I overate. When my daughter called wanting to talk about her divorce, I was more impatient with her than usual. I felt hopeless about relating normally to other people. |
| Monday, 4 p.m. | I was driving and started thinking about my accident last week, when I hit another car in a parking lot. | I'm a terrible driver; I should have been more careful. What's wrong with me? Why wasn't I paying attention? | I felt guilty and depressed. | I realized I was feeling worse and I wasn't paying attention to driving because I was so absorbed in my thoughts. |

WORKSHEET: Understanding an Episode of Rumination

Your name: _____

Remember to maintain an attitude of friendly curiosity.

Day and time	Triggering event	Ruminative thoughts	Emotions	Aftereffects and consequences

After you've completed this worksheet several times, reflect on any patterns that may have emerged:

- Do you tend to ruminate about particular topics, such as how sad you feel, how badly you or others behaved, or potential future disasters?

- Do you tend to ruminate in specific situations?

- What are the usual consequences of your rumination?

Mindfulness
• No Judgement
• Staying in present moment

How Mindfulness Helps with Rumination

What should we do in place of rumination? As discussed earlier, constructive problem solving is much more helpful: identifying a specific problem, thinking of possible solutions, and trying something that might help.

But what if there isn't a specific problem to be solved?

After one of her book club meetings, Ellen went shopping. She put her purchases in the car, backed out of her parking space, and hit another car in the passenger-side door, making a large dent. No one was hurt, but Ellen felt terrible. She apologized, provided all of her contact and insurance information, and made sure that the other driver's costs would be covered. She resolved to be more careful in the future.

There's nothing else that Ellen can do about the situation, but she ruminates about it. She constantly asks herself how she could have been so careless, tells herself she's a terrible driver, and replays the incident in her mind.

Why is this happening? Ellen is feeling guilt and regret about the accident. This is normal. In fact, these feelings may help her remember to drive more carefully. But Ellen's mind doesn't want to let go of the incident. It sees a discrepancy between the way things are (*I caused an accident*) and the way she wants things to be (*I wish I hadn't*). Her mind is stuck in problem-solving mode, trying to think its way out of this discrepancy.

In this situation, problem-solving mode isn't very useful. It may help Ellen think of one or two more things she could do—for example, choosing parking spaces that she can exit by driving forward (when possible) or buying a newer car with a rearview camera (when she can afford one). But she can't change the past. Every driver has moments of inattention that might cause an accident. Brooding about her mistake won't improve Ellen's driving. In fact, rumination will have unintended effects: she'll feel worse and be more preoccupied, *increasing* the chances of another accident.

In situations like this, mindfulness is a healthy alternative to rumination.

Using Mindfulness to Reduce Rumination

If you've been using the rumination worksheet, you've already started applying mindfulness skills to rumination: You've been observing your thinking patterns with a friendly, curious, nonjudgmental attitude. To begin building on these skills, let's revisit the poem from the previous chapter: "The Guest House," by Rumi. (If you don't remember it very clearly, turn back to the end of chapter 2 and reread it.)

According to the poem, unwanted thoughts and feelings are our guests. Let's look at how this mindful perspective applies to rumination. What does it mean to treat each guest honorably, as the poem suggests, even if we'd rather be rid of some of them?

Imagine that you operate a bed-and-breakfast. Some of your guests like to linger in your cozy breakfast room, getting to know each other and discussing all manner of things: the weather, the local attractions, the news of the day. A few of your guests have strong opinions about the state of the world. Some are angry about it; others are sad or anxious. These guests talk endlessly about the difficulties of the times, why things are going so badly, why we can't solve our problems, what's wrong with society, what our leaders should do about it, why these constructive steps will never be taken, and on and on. These guests are ruminating, and you find it unpleasant.

As the host, what can you do? Can you tell your guests to go out and enjoy the sights and leave you in peace? Perhaps you could, but it would be inhospitable, and it might not work. Some guests would rather stay indoors all day and continue the conversation. Can you persuade the guests to discuss more pleasant topics? Probably not, and they wouldn't like it if you tried. People immersed in troubling concerns often resist being steered to other topics. And a guest house that discourages conversation among the guests might lose customers. This bed-and-breakfast is your livelihood, and you love its welcoming feeling.

And so, as a gracious host, you're polite and cheerful to all of your guests. Every morning, you serve a nice breakfast. You ask your guests if they slept well. You help them with their plans for the day. Then you're free to go about your work. You don't have to participate in the unpleasant conversation. You don't have to agree with everything that's said. You can turn your attention to more pleasant guests or to tasks that need doing in the house. You can still hear the louder guests, but their voices fade into the background as you attend to your duties in the kitchen, the guest rooms, and the garden.

Now let's apply this image to your own experience: You are the guest house. Your thoughts and feelings are the guests. You probably have some unpleasant guests (everyone does). Some of them are loud, critical, and unreasonable. You wish they would leave or be quiet, but it's impossible to control them. Instead, you recognize that you have many guests. Arguing with the unpleasant ones doesn't seem to help, so you turn your attention to the other guests. You continue with your activities. You look around. You can still enjoy the world and do good work even with unpleasant guests droning on in the background.

It's important to recognize that this is difficult. Rather than in your house, ruminative thoughts are in your *head*. They feel very close. Moreover, ruminative thoughts are often about you. They're saying that you're an idiot, that you've messed things up again, that you can't cope, that things will never go your way, that other people don't treat you well, and so on. Thoughts about ourselves often feel compelling and important.

With practice, however, it's possible to see these thoughts as unpleasant guests in your internal bed-and-breakfast, to be treated with respect (briefly) and then allowed to be themselves while you turn your attention elsewhere. This can be a huge relief. Trying to make ruminating guests go away or talk about something else is exhausting. Practicing mindfulness teaches us that the internal guest house is more spacious than we realized: there's room for many guests. We learn to welcome them all, regardless of whether we like what they have to say. We learn that we don't have to fight with them or try to control them. We can allow them to come and go in their own time while directing our attention as we choose, pursuing activities that we value, and appreciating the breadth and depth of the present moment.

What does this mean for Ellen? When she sees ruminative thoughts (*How could I have been so careless? I'm a terrible driver*), she recognizes them. *Ah*, she says, *There are the ruminating guests again*. She realizes

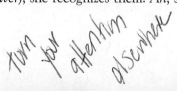
turn your attention elsewhere

that it's natural to feel regret after a car accident, that making mistakes is part of being human. She accepts the feeling of regret as an unpleasant guest, but one with a useful purpose: it reminds her to be attentive when driving. For a moment, she might ask herself if there's anything else she can do about the accident. *No*, she decides. *Other than paying attention while I'm driving—and I'm doing my best—I've done everything I can.* She sees that dwelling on judgmental ruminative thoughts won't help and gently turns her attention to whatever she's doing in the moment.

Steps to Follow When You Catch Yourself Ruminating

When you notice that ruminative thoughts have come to visit, try the following steps.

Step 1. Labeling

As soon as you recognize that you've fallen into the trap of rumination, label it by saying to yourself, *This is rumination*, *Ruminative thoughts have come to my mind*, or *The ruminating guests are here again.* If you notice judgmental thoughts, such as *I'm such an idiot* or *This is really stupid*, notice that these are judgments. As best you can, practice labeling the rumination in a gentle, matter-of-fact tone and letting go of the judgments.

Step 2. Redirecting Your Attention

Rumination often arises when we're doing something without paying attention, such as walking, driving, or washing the dishes. If this happens, continue with what you're doing, but see if you can focus your attention on the activity more mindfully. If you're driving, feel the steering wheel in your hands and see the road in front of you. If you're washing the dishes, feel the sensations of your hands in the water, see the suds and the light glinting off the dishes, hear the sounds as you work, and smell the dish soap. If you're walking the dog, notice the movements of the dog's legs or tail, hear the panting, feel the pull on the leash and your feet on the ground, and observe the smells in the air and the colors of your surroundings.

Step 3. Choosing a New Activity (If Possible)

If you were doing something unconstructive when the rumination arose, like moping in bed, choose something else to do (Addis and Martell 2004). If you're ruminating about a specific problem and you could do something constructive about it, take steps in that direction. Otherwise, choose something enjoyable, such as reading an engaging book, calling a friend, or watching something funny on TV. Or do something that will give you a feeling of accomplishment, such as paying bills, working in the garden, or cooking an interesting dish. It might be helpful to make a list of activities to keep on hand. If you don't feel like doing anything when rumination crosses your threshold, gently coax yourself to do something anyway, just as you might with a reluctant child. If one activity isn't helpful, try another one. As best you can, focus your attention on what you're doing.

When ruminative thoughts come up again, politely say hello to them and carry on with your activity, as if the thoughts were guests passing by in the corridor of your bed-and-breakfast. You might continue to hear them, but you don't have to participate in their conversation. Keep shifting your attention back to what you're doing—gently and without giving yourself a hard time.

Keeping an Open Mind

If the Guest House metaphor feels unnatural, unrealistic, or too difficult at this point, that's understandable. It's a new way of thinking that may seem quite foreign. See if you can keep an open mind about it, with a spirit of exploration and friendly curiosity. And also remember that your journey with mindfulness has just begun. As you continue, you'll learn many more skills that will help with rumination.

Even as your mindfulness skills improve, you'll occasionally have thoughts and feelings that are so threatening or unpleasant that you'll want to get rid of them. Trying to suppress or avoid particular thoughts and feelings is another trap. In the next chapter, we'll explore the avoidance trap and how mindfulness skills can be helpful in staying out of it.

Chapter Summary

- Rumination, or brooding about or dwelling on things, is an unhelpful form of negative repetitive thinking. When we're ruminating, negative thoughts cycle through our minds, intensifying negative moods without solving anything.

- Rumination has many unhealthy consequences. It reduces motivation and interferes with concentration and memory. It increases the risk of depression, anxiety, alcohol abuse, binge eating, and post-traumatic stress.

- Observing our thinking processes can help us learn to recognize rumination and distinguish it from constructive problem solving.

- The Guest House metaphor is a helpful way to cultivate a mindful attitude toward unpleasant thoughts and feelings. Allowing difficult thoughts and feelings to come and go, as if they were guests in a bed-and-breakfast, and turning our attention to other aspects of the present moment can help us get out of the rumination trap.

CHAPTER 4

Avoidance *makes things worse*

> Try to pose for yourself this task: not to think of a polar bear, and
> you will see that the cursed thing will come to mind every minute.
>
> —Fyodor Dostoyevsky

Since the 1980s, psychologists have been studying an interesting paradox: the more we try *not* to think about something, the more we think about it. In the first of several famous experiments, university students were asked to sit alone in a room for five minutes, with no books or electronic devices. Half of them were instructed to try not to think of a white bear (Wegner et al. 1987). If thoughts of white bears came to mind despite their efforts, they rang a bell. On average, they rang the bell six times, or just more than once per minute. Before the experiment started, they probably weren't thinking of white bears so often. They only started thinking of them every minute when asked *not* to think about them.

The experiment continued for another five minutes, in which the students were asked to think about white bears. They had many thoughts of white bears. In fact, they had significantly *more* thoughts about white bears than the other group of students in the study, who were asked to think about white bears from the beginning but were never told not to think about them. This pattern was labeled the rebound effect. Suppressing thoughts of white bears for five minutes caused the thoughts to bounce back at a higher rate than if they were never suppressed.

Thought suppression, or deliberately trying not to think about something, is a common psychological trap. On the surface, it looks like a sensible way of dealing with unwanted thoughts. But it often backfires and makes the thoughts more frequent. The same thing happens with unwanted emotions and urges. The more we try to avoid or suppress them, the stronger they become. In this chapter we'll consider how this trap works, why we fall into it, and how mindfulness skills can lead us out.

Suppressing Unwanted Thoughts and Feelings

Most of us have thoughts we'd like to avoid (Najmi and Wegner 2008). We have painful memories of moments we'd prefer to forget. We worry about upcoming stressors, like giving a speech, even when we'd rather not think about them. People trying to cut back on smoking, drinking, or overeating are often troubled by persistent, unwanted thoughts about cigarettes, alcohol, or food. People suffering from post-traumatic stress, depression, and anxiety often have intrusive, negative thoughts that are very upsetting. Nearly everyone has the occasional unwanted thought that seems bizarre or even shameful (Baer 2001)—thoughts of jumping off a tall building, shouting something nasty during a gathering, or attacking someone.

Thought suppression seems like an obvious way to help ourselves feel better when we're preoccupied with something troubling. Conventional wisdom suggests that we should put such things out of our minds. However, since the original white bear experiments, many studies have confirmed that trying to suppress upsetting thoughts has paradoxical effects: the thoughts come to mind more often, and emotional distress gets worse.

In one experiment, smokers trying to quit were asked to sit alone in a room for five minutes. Half were told to avoid all thoughts of smoking. The others were told that they could think about anything that came to mind, including smoking. Those told not to think about smoking reported more smoking-related thoughts (Salkovskis and Reynolds 1994). Other studies show similar patterns in heavy drinkers trying not to think about alcohol (Palfai et al. 1997) and in people trying to suppress memories of stressful or traumatic events (Shipherd and Beck 2005). The pattern is clear: for people with troubling thoughts, trying to get rid of the thoughts can make matters worse.

* Theo's Story *

A year ago, Theo lost a high-paying job. After eight months of searching, he found a position at one-third his former salary. He and his wife sold their heavily mortgaged house and rented an apartment. He traded his expensive car for an economical one. Instead of flying to the Caribbean for a vacation, they walked to a nearby park every day with their three-year-old son.

Theo tells himself how lucky he is. He knows it's hard to get a new job and sell a house in the current economy. He knows people who have been unemployed for longer than he was. And yet he finds it hard to stop longing for the life he used to have: the big home with the landscaped yard, eating out on a whim, the expensive private school where he and his wife had planned to send their son. *How did I lose all that?* he keeps asking himself. Feelings of guilt and regret wash over him.

Don't think about it, he tells himself repeatedly. *Don't dwell on the past.* But daily life is full of reminders. Every time he sees an expensive car, he remembers that he used to drive one. Walking into his small apartment triggers thoughts of being a poor provider.

I have no right to feel bad, he tells himself. *Many people are worse off. I should appreciate what I have.* But the more Theo criticizes himself for his inability to control his thoughts and emotions, the worse he feels.

Theo is caught in the suppression trap. He has set an unrealistic goal for himself: to keep certain thoughts, images, and emotions out of his mind. This won't work. Troubling thoughts and feelings come to mind whether we want them to or not. Trying to suppress them makes them worse.

Mindfulness skills will help Theo with this problem. Later in this chapter, we'll see how. First, let's consider other types of unhealthy avoidance.

Other Forms of Avoidance

Your emotions will be heard they get louder

Sometimes we try to avoid uncomfortable thoughts and feelings by staying away from the people, places, and activities that bring them up. This has appealing short-term benefits: we feel better if we don't put ourselves in awkward or stressful situations. In the long run, however, problems get worse and life becomes less satisfying and meaningful. The following stories illustrate the short-term benefits and long-term costs of avoiding situations and activities.

*   Andrew's Story   *

Andrew suffers from severe social anxiety. He'd like to have friends and social connections, but he avoids situations where he might feel shy and uncomfortable about not knowing what to say. He comes to work very early in the morning so he won't have to chat with coworkers on the way in from the parking lot. He brings his lunch and eats at his desk instead of joining his coworkers in the cafeteria. He works late and waits until the hallway is quiet before leaving.

Andrew enjoys bicycling and goes for long rides alone on the weekends. He hasn't joined the local cycling club because of fears that the other members won't like or accept him. As a teenager, he enjoyed the youth group at his church. He tried going to church where he currently lives, but couldn't summon the courage to talk to anyone and left feeling disappointed in himself and resentful of the church members for not being friendlier.

Andrew hopes that someday he'll meet someone who understands him and with whom he feels at ease. He'd like to have a family, but he avoids situations and activities that could lead him toward these goals. The short-term payoff for avoidance is that he doesn't have to feel unpleasant sensations, such as a pounding heart, sweaty palms, or a dry mouth. He doesn't have to experience the flood of negative thoughts that arise in social situations, such as *I never know what to say* or *People must think I'm a loser*. On the other hand, his loneliness is getting worse, and he isn't making any progress toward his long-term goal of having a family.

*   Roger's Story   *

Roger doesn't like helping his children with their homework. As a child, Roger was unmotivated in school and got below-average grades, despite above-average intelligence. Later, he earned a certificate in electrical technology and now makes a good living as an electrician. But he still feels incompetent with academic tasks.

Every evening after dinner, Roger does the dishes and thoroughly cleans the kitchen. Then he pays bills, does laundry, and makes household repairs while his kids do their homework. As soon as they've finished, he plays games or watches TV with them before bedtime.

Roger is a single parent. No one else is available to help the kids with their homework. Roger tells himself that he's encouraging his children's academic independence while taking good care of the house. But his children need more supervision with their homework. They're getting lazy about it and not learning as much as they could. Nevertheless, Roger avoids helping them with their homework because he's afraid of looking foolish if he doesn't understand their assignments.

*   *Kate's Story*   *

Kate would like to be promoted at work, but she's afraid of criticism and disapproval. She works hard on every assignment and rarely makes mistakes. Her presentations and reports are highly polished. On the other hand, she spends much longer on these tasks than most of her coworkers. She barely meets her deadlines, completes only the tasks assigned to her, and never volunteers for anything else because she doesn't have time.

Kate's boss hasn't offered her a promotion because she perceives Kate as competent but slow. Kate's boss would prefer less perfectionism and more initiative. Kate tells herself that her primary goal is to do excellent work. However, her overpreparation is driven by avoidance. She's avoiding the sinking feeling and thoughts of inadequacy that come up when she makes even the smallest mistake. As a result, her career has stalled.

Why It's Difficult to Recognize Avoidance Behavior

These stories illustrate several important points about avoidance:

*   It's easy to fool ourselves into thinking that avoidance behavior is helpful. We tell ourselves something that sounds convincing: *I need to stay away from social activities until I get control of my anxiety, My children need to be independent about doing their homework,* or *My reports need to be as good as I can possibly make them.* If we act in accordance with these thoughts, we feel better in the short term. In the long run, problems get worse.

*   The same behavior can be constructive or avoidant, depending on the motivation. Doing the laundry so the children have clean clothes is constructive. Doing the laundry to avoid helping the children with their homework is problematic. Taking the stairs to get more exercise strengthens your body. Taking the stairs to avoid coworkers in the elevator contributes to loneliness.

*   The same behavior might be constructive and avoidant at the same time. For example, you might go to a friend's birthday party to make your friend happy *and* to avoid an assignment for work or school. If this is true, then a nonavoidant approach might require a compromise, such as going to the party for an hour and then working on your assignment.

SELF-TEST: Two Types of Avoidance

Everyone engages in avoidance now and then. We try to suppress our thoughts and feelings, or we stay away from uncomfortable situations or activities. If it doesn't happen often or persist for long periods, it probably won't do much harm. This self-test (inspired by Gámez et al. 2011) will help you examine your tendency toward avoidance. In each blank space, write the number that indicates how true each statement is for you, using the rating scale provided below.

1	2	3	4
Rarely true	Sometimes true	Often true	Very often true

Suppression of Thoughts and Feelings

___3___ *When something upsetting comes to mind, I try very hard to stop thinking about it.*

___2___ *When negative thoughts come up, I try to put them out of my mind.*

___2___ *I try to distract myself when I feel something uncomfortable.*

___3___ *I work hard to get rid of upsetting feelings.*

12 ___2___ *When distressing memories come up, I try to push them out of my mind.*

Avoidance of Situations, Behaviors, or Activities

___3___ *I won't do something if I think it will make me uncomfortable.*

___3+1___ *I tend to put off unpleasant things that I need to do.*

___2___ *I go out of my way to avoid stressful situations.*

___2___ *I'm quick to leave any situation that makes me feel uneasy.*

14 ___4___ *I avoid doing things that might bring up uncomfortable thoughts and feelings.*

Add up your ratings for each section. If you scored between 11 and 14 on either section, you may have a moderate tendency to engage in unhelpful suppression or avoidance. If you scored between 15 and 20 on either section (or between 30 and 40 in total), your suppression and avoidance may be more seriously problematic. You may be struggling fruitlessly to keep unpleasant thoughts, memories, or feelings out of your mind. Or you may be procrastinating on important tasks, or avoiding situations or activities that would help you reach valued goals.

Why We Fall into the Avoidance Trap

If avoidance is so harmful, why do we do it? There are several good reasons (Hayes 2005).

Avoidance is useful in many situations. Avoiding dark streets in dangerous parts of town reduces the chance of being robbed. Avoiding a colleague who comes to work with the flu reduces the likelihood of getting sick. Vicious dogs, tornadoes, hot stoves—many things should be avoided. It's part of human nature to feel fear, anxiety, nervousness, or reluctance in situations that might be dangerous. These feelings motivate us to stay away from harm.

Short-term distraction is sometimes helpful. How do you feel about dental work? If you have an appointment coming up in a few days, would you rather not think about it? Computer games, books, TV, and other absorbing activities may keep your mind occupied temporarily. In this case, avoidance has short-term benefits (less anxiety about the dental work) but probably no significant long-term harm. What about when you're watching a scary movie or having blood drawn—do you cover your eyes or look away? If so, you're avoiding short-term discomfort. In the long run, you won't adapt to these experiences, but this may not be a problem. Your quality of life probably won't suffer.

We think we should be able to get rid of unpleasant thoughts and feelings. As children, we may have been told not to worry, not to cry, or not to be sad, angry, or nervous, even when these were normal reactions to situations. Such directives from adults are often well-intentioned, but they lead children to believe that mature people have their thoughts and feelings under complete and voluntary control. This assumption may persist into adulthood. It's an illusion. Many people who look calm and happy on the outside are struggling on the inside. Even the happiest, most well-adjusted people can't completely control their thoughts and feelings.

We're susceptible to short-term effects of our own behavior. It's part of human nature to be strongly influenced by the immediate effects of our behavior. When avoidance reduces distress and makes us more comfortable, we're encouraged to keep using it, even when it's inconsistent with important long-term goals, stops us from solving our problems, or makes us feel worse over time.

EXERCISE: Understanding Your Patterns of Suppression and Avoidance

We all have our own ways of suppressing and avoiding. The following worksheet will help you observe and understand your patterns. Remember that avoidance behavior is a natural reaction to unpleasant thoughts, feelings, and situations. Sometimes it's automatic and unplanned. Occasionally it looks like constructive behavior. It can be difficult to discern whether a specific behavior is a form of avoidance. Looking closely at the short-term and long-term effects helps us clarify what's happening. This worksheet will help you learn to recognize various forms of avoidance and respond to them in skillful ways.

As you become more familiar with your avoidance patterns, you may find that you're criticizing yourself for avoiding. Remember that mindfulness of your mental processes means observing them with friendly curiosity rather than judgment. The purpose of filling out this avoidance worksheet is not to criticize yourself, but to develop self-awareness and insight that will make it easier to deal with stress in the future.

As before, there are three versions of the worksheet. The first contains instructions. The second is an example from Andrew, the lonely man from earlier in the chapter who avoids his coworkers. He used to believe that staying away from stressful situations would help him feel better, and that after he felt better he could start working toward his goals. By completing this worksheet, Andrew began to understand that trying to avoid his thoughts and feelings backfires: the more he tries to avoid feeling anxious, the more he feels lonely and unfulfilled.

After the example, you'll find a blank worksheet for your own use. Again, make multiple copies of it. You'll be better able to see patterns in your behavior if you fill it out for several situations.

WORKSHEET: Understanding Your Patterns of Avoidance

Remember to maintain an attitude of friendly curiosity.

Day and time	Event or situation	Avoidance behavior	What were you avoiding?	Short-term benefits of avoidance	Long-term harm of avoidance
When did this avoidance behavior occur? Writing down the day and time helps you be specific and reveals patterns.	What triggered your avoidance behavior? Where were you? What was going on? Were other people involved? Common situations for avoidance: Relationships Work, school Household tasks Money, finances Self-care	Describe your behavior in the situation. Be specific about what you did that helped you avoid something. Examples: Suppressed thoughts or feelings Distracted yourself with activities (TV, eating, shopping) Did something useful (exercise, work, chores) to avoid something else Turned down an opportunity in order to avoid stress or discomfort	Did you try to suppress thoughts, memories, images, emotions, sensations, urges, or temptations? Did you stay away from particular people, situations, or activities?	What was the short-term reward or payoff for avoiding? The short-term effects are often positive or desirable. Perhaps you didn't have to put yourself in a difficult situation, or do or think about something unpleasant; or you didn't feel unwanted sensations, emotions, or urges.	What was the long-term harm of avoiding? The long-term effects are often harmful. Perhaps you feel worse, or a problem gets worse in the long run; or avoiding prevents you from making progress toward an important goal.

WORKSHEET: Understanding Your Patterns of Avoidance

Your name: Andrew

Remember to maintain an attitude of friendly curiosity.

Day and time	Event or situation	Avoidance behavior	What were you avoiding?	Short-term benefits of avoidance	Long-term harm of avoidance
Saturday 9 a.m.	Riding my bike, saw two cyclists at side of road, repairing flat tire.	Could have stopped to see if they needed help, but I just gave a little wave and rode on.	Awkwardness of talking to people I don't know.	Didn't have to face up to feeling awkward talking to new people.	Felt guilty about not checking to see if they needed help. Missed opportunity to meet other cyclists.
Tuesday lunchtime	Coworker stopped by my office, asked me to go to lunch in cafeteria.	I said no, too much work to do.	Feeling awkward and embarrassed if I can't keep conversation going through lunch.	Got a little work done over lunch. Didn't have to talk to coworker, which could have been awkward.	I feel lonely at work. People will ignore me if I'm never sociable.
Wednesday 3 p.m.	Good-bye party at work for someone who's moving away.	Came late, sat off to one side, only talked to one person, left early.	Having to make small talk. Feeling awkward and nervous.	Didn't have to worry about what to say or keeping conversations going.	Felt like a loser. I barely know my coworkers.

WORKSHEET: Understanding Your Patterns of Avoidance

Your name: _____

Remember to maintain an attitude of friendly curiosity.

Day and time	Event or situation	Avoidance behavior	What were you avoiding?	Short-term benefits of avoidance	Long-term harm of avoidance

How Mindfulness Helps with Avoidance

Avoidance of unpleasant thoughts and feelings often backfires. But as you learned in chapter 2, ruminating about them also backfires. If we shouldn't avoid them and shouldn't dwell on them, what can we do?

Mindfulness of thoughts and feelings is the healthy path between avoidance and rumination.

*   Theo's Story, Continued   *

Theo is at the playground with his little boy. A passing car, just like the one he used to drive, catches his eye. He feels a sharp pang of envy and regret. Images of his former life flash through his mind. *I can't believe I lost all that,* he thinks. Then he feels guilty for dwelling on the past.

But now he knows the mindfulness skills taught in this book. *Okay,* he says to himself. *Those are thoughts and feelings about the past. They're visitors who come along now and then. They can come and go as they please. I can't really control them. Let me focus on what I'm doing right now.* He digs his bare feet into the sandbox where his son is playing, feeling the gritty texture, noticing that the sand is warm near the surface and cooler below. He takes a deep breath and feels the air flowing through his nose. He looks at his son, seeing the sun glint off his hair, watching his body move and the concentration on his face as he digs in the sand. "What are you building now?" Theo asks. "Can I help?"

Theo is using the Guest House metaphor, discussed in chapter 3. He's allowing his thoughts and feelings to come and go at their own pace as if they were guests in his bed-and-breakfast, while turning his attention to what he's doing in the present: playing with his son. This isn't a form of avoidance. He's not suppressing his painful thoughts and feelings; he's completely aware of them. But he's also not ruminating about them. He's accepting them as visitors to his mind while continuing with an activity he values and finding contentment in the present moment.

Another Metaphor: Passengers on the Bus

The Passengers on the Bus metaphor (Hayes, Strosahl, and Wilson 1999) is an alternative to the Guest House metaphor. It provides another way of understanding the mindful approach to thoughts and feelings.

Imagine that you're a shy, lonely person and your goal is to have more friends and a satisfying social life. To work toward this goal, you're trying to be more sociable: initiating conversations, going to parties, and inviting people to lunch and the movies.

It's difficult because of the thoughts and feelings that come up. Socializing makes you feel sweaty, tense, and anxious. Your thoughts are like intimidating people in your head. "You're an awkward misfit," they say. "You're the type who never fits in. This won't work. People don't want to spend time with you."

Now picture yourself driving a bus. Your destination is A Better Social Life, and you're steering in this direction. Imagine that your thoughts and feelings are the passengers on the bus. They sit in the back, shouting at you. "Turn around," they say. "There's no point in going this way. You'll never have friends." They're loud and persistent.

You have a sinking feeling that the passengers might be right, but you're determined to try. *I have to do something about these nasty passengers*, you say to yourself. *I'll never get anywhere with them interfering like this. They're dragging me down.*

So you stop the bus and walk to the back. "You have to be quiet," you say to the passengers. "This is important to me. To have any hope of improving my social life, I need to stay calm. I can't have you shouting at me." But the passengers are stubborn and won't be quiet or change their minds.

"Well if that's your attitude, you can't ride on my bus," you say. "Out you go." But they won't leave, and they're too heavy to push out the door.

You realize that your bus isn't going anywhere.

"Okay," you say in frustration. "What will you do to me if I keep driving toward my goal?"

"We'll tell you where you should go," they reply.

"But what if I don't?" you ask. They stare at you blankly.

You realize an important fact about the passengers. They have loud, ugly voices and discouraging things to say, but they can't literally hurt you. You don't have to believe them or follow their orders. With this new insight in mind, you return to the driver's seat and resume driving the bus in your chosen direction.

The passengers continue to talk. They tell you why you'll never succeed and shouldn't try. It's unpleasant and you wish you could be rid of them. With practice, however, you become more skillful at driving in the direction you want to go, despite what the passengers say. Their voices begin to fade. You find them less upsetting. You begin to understand: your passengers are the voices of previous experiences that can't be changed. You develop nonjudgmental acceptance of your passengers and allow them to be who they are.

And you don't let them drive the bus.

✳ ✳ ✳

Notice what you're *not* doing when you take this mindful attitude toward your unpleasant thoughts and feelings:

- You're not suppressing or avoiding them. You're allowing them to ride on your bus.

- You're not ruminating about them. You can hear them, but most of your attention is devoted to driving in your chosen direction.

- You're not trying to change them. You're accepting them for what they are.

- You're not allowing them to control your behavior. You're deciding for yourself where to drive.

✳ *Andrew's Use of Mindfulness Skills* ✳

When Andrew filled out his avoidance worksheet, he wrote that he avoided going to lunch with a coworker because he felt awkward and shy. But he wants to have more friends at work. Let's picture the same situation after Andrew works his way through this book.

Andrew Is More Aware of What's Happening in Each Moment

When a coworker asks him to lunch, Andrew observes that he's tempted to decline because he feels anxious—his heart is beating faster and he's afraid of not having enough to talk about. But he remembers that he'd like to have more friends at work. Being mindful of the moment gives him a chance to choose thoughtfully, rather than automatically declining the invitation and then criticizing himself.

Andrew Finds Thoughts and Feelings Less Scary

Andrew still has occasional negative thoughts (for example, *I'm boring, This will be awkward, What if I don't have enough to talk about?*) and unpleasant feelings (pounding heart, sweaty hands, and so on), but now he thinks of them as passengers on his bus and allows them to come and go. He realizes several important facts about the passengers:

- They're unpleasant but not harmful.

- He has little control over which passengers get on, where they get off, or what they say.

- No matter what they say, the passengers don't have to control his behavior.

Andrew Pursues Important Goals Even When Having Unpleasant Thoughts and Feelings

When his coworker asks him to lunch, Andrew accepts the invitation, despite his trepidation. Of course, there's no guarantee that lunch will go well. But there's a good chance it will be fine, and that he'll be pleased he took a step that's consistent with his goals.

In time, as he takes these steps regularly, Andrew's anxiety will diminish as his social life improves. Even if anxiety is still present on some occasions, Andrew now understands that he can pursue a satisfying social life whether he feels anxious or not. He's much happier—not because his anxiety has completely disappeared, but because he's relating to it differently. He's able to make room for it without being controlled by it. He understands that avoiding social situations makes things worse.

Working with Your Avoidance Patterns

Here's an outline of steps to follow in working with your patterns of avoidance:

1. Use the avoidance worksheet to become more familiar with your patterns.

2. When you catch yourself trying to avoid your thoughts and feelings, remind yourself that they're passengers on your bus.

3. See if you can find a way to drive your bus in the direction you'd like to go: toward something that's consistent with your important long-term goals. This may require that you allow the passengers to be themselves, rather than fighting with them.

4. Be kind to yourself about the unpleasant passengers on your bus. Everyone has them. They're part of being alive.

5. Continue working with this book. Later chapters will provide more mindfulness exercises that can help decrease suppression and avoidance.

Even skillful drivers find that strong emotions occasionally take control and send the bus off course. This is emotion-driven behavior. It's another trap; and, in the next chapter, we'll look at how mindfulness skills can lead us out of it.

Chapter Summary

- Avoidance of unpleasant thoughts and feelings often backfires. If we try to suppress them or get rid of them, there's a good chance they'll get stronger.

- Avoidance of difficult situations or activities reduces anxiety temporarily, but in the long run it interferes with progress toward important goals.

- Mindful observation of our avoidance patterns helps us stay out of this trap. We learn to recognize when we're tempted to avoid something and can instead make a wise decision about how to proceed.

- When pursuing important goals requires that we do something uncomfortable, like socialize when feeling shy and nervous, mindfulness reminds us that our thoughts and feelings don't have to control our behavior. Like passengers on a bus, they might be unpleasant and unkind, but we don't have to obey them. We can allow them to come and go while continuing with behavior that's consistent with our goals.

CHAPTER 5

Emotion-Driven Behavior

Cherish your own emotions and never undervalue them.

—Robert Henri

Mari had a stressful day at work. During a staff meeting, her boss criticized a report she'd written. Then he assigned her two more projects with impossible deadlines. After work, Mari played tennis with a friend. Although she normally enjoys tennis, Mari was preoccupied with work and couldn't concentrate. After missing several shots, she felt so frustrated that she shouted an obscenity and slammed her racket on the ground. Her friend didn't say anything, but she looked disgusted and turned down Mari's invitation to go for a drink afterward.

On the way home, Mari got irritated at a slow driver. She honked several times and then passed the other car so fast that a police officer pulled her over and warned her to be more careful. Once home, Mari didn't feel like making dinner. She drank several beers while watching TV and fell asleep on the couch. She woke up at 3 a.m. and went to bed, but she couldn't sleep. She tortured herself with recriminations about her lack of self-control. Embarrassing images of slamming her racket on the ground in front of her friend and speeding past the slow driver replayed in her mind. She got up at 6:30 a.m. and went to work feeling exhausted and angry with herself.

Losing Control Under Stress

When we're upset or under stress, we often do things that we later regret. Psychologists call this *emotion-driven behavior* (Allen, McHugh, and Barlow 2008). We usually know that we're behaving unwisely, but we lose control and follow our urges anyway because it relieves the intensity of our feelings. Unfortunately, the relief is temporary and the behavior is usually inconsistent with our long-term goals. When Mari slammed her tennis racket on the ground, it reduced her frustration for a moment, but she doesn't like herself when she behaves this way, and she fears that her friend now thinks less of her. Speeding past the slow driver was exhilarating and relieved her impatience, but she knows she deserved a ticket and was lucky to get off with a warning. Drinking beer all evening dulled her negative emotions, but it impaired her ability to work the next day. Mari admires people who keep their cool under stress. She'd like to be one of them.

SELF-TEST: Emotion-Driven Behavior

Everyone gives in to unhelpful emotion-driven behavior now and then. If it doesn't happen often, it probably won't do much harm. This self-test (based loosely on Whiteside and Lynam 2001) will help you determine whether you're susceptible to unconstructive emotion-driven behavior. In each blank space, write the number that indicates how true each statement is for you, using the rating scale provided below.

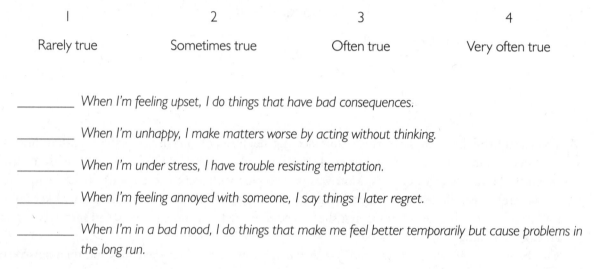

1	2	3	4
Rarely true	Sometimes true	Often true	Very often true

_____ *When I'm feeling upset, I do things that have bad consequences.*

_____ *When I'm unhappy, I make matters worse by acting without thinking.*

_____ *When I'm under stress, I have trouble resisting temptation.*

_____ *When I'm feeling annoyed with someone, I say things I later regret.*

_____ *When I'm in a bad mood, I do things that make me feel better temporarily but cause problems in the long run.*

Add up your ratings. If you scored between 11 and 14, you may have a moderate tendency to engage in unhelpful emotion-driven behavior when you're upset. If you scored between 15 and 20, your emotion-driven behavior may be causing you more serious problems. You're probably aware of the consequences but find it difficult to maintain your self-control under stress. In the rest of this chapter, we'll explore why this happens and how mindfulness skills can help.

What Is an Emotion?

In order to understand emotion-driven behavior, we need to understand emotions. We often experience emotions as subjective, internal feelings that are hard to describe. In order to communicate about emotions, we learn to label them: sadness, anger, fear, embarrassment, envy, happiness, disappointment, boredom, and so on. The English language includes more than five hundred such words (Averill 1975). Although some have similar meanings (such as fury, rage, and wrath), the existence of so many different terms shows that we're capable of a huge variety of emotional experiences. Each has its own subtle qualities of feeling, tone, and intensity. Here are some emotion terms, grouped into general categories of emotion (for similar lists, see Goleman 1995 and Linehan 1993b):

- **Sadness:** anguished, dejected, depressed, disappointed, dismayed, gloomy, glum, hopeless, hurt, melancholy, sorrowful

- **Fear:** afraid, anxious, apprehensive, edgy, frightened, jumpy, nervous, panicked, tense, terrified, uneasy, worried

- **Anger:** aggravated, annoyed, bitter, furious, grouchy, hostile, irritated, outraged, resentful, spiteful, vengeful

- **Shame and guilt:** ashamed, chagrined, contrite, embarrassed, guilty, humiliated, mortified, regretful, remorseful, repentant

- **Happiness:** blissful, cheerful, content, delighted, elated, enthusiastic, excited, glad, gleeful, joyful, satisfied, thrilled

- **Love:** adoring, affectionate, caring, compassionate, friendly, infatuated, passionate, sympathetic, tender, warm

- **Surprise:** amazed, astonished, shocked

- **Disgust:** contemptuous, disdainful, revolted, scornful

- **Other:** bashful, bored, calm, interested, proud, reluctant, skeptical, suspicious

Most emotions come and go like waves in the ocean. When allowed to run their natural course, emotions usually last only a few seconds or minutes. Repeated or ongoing events and circumstances, such as the loss of a loved one, can prolong them. So can ruminating, as discussed in chapter 2. Longer-lasting emotions are called moods. Moods are usually less intense than emotions. A grumpy mood may last all day, but the full heat of rage is of shorter duration.

Everyone has their own emotional style. Some people have very intense emotions, both positive and negative. Others have mostly mild or moderate emotions. Some people have strong positive emotions and mild negative ones; others have the opposite pattern. Many people tend to feel one dominant emotion in a variety of situations. For example, if you often feel anxious, you may think of yourself as a nervous person or a worrywart. If you're usually cheerful, others may think of you as a happy person, even though you have your share of negative emotions.

The Three Components of an Emotion

Whatever your emotional style, you may have noticed that when you're feeling an emotion, several things are happening in your body and mind. Single words, such as "happy" or "sad," may not fully capture the complexity of an emotional experience. We can understand our emotions more easily if we break them down into three components: sensations in the body, thoughts in the mind, and urges to act in certain ways (Barlow et al. 2011).

Sensations in the Body

If you're fearful or anxious, you may feel your heart racing, your palms sweating, and your muscles tensing. If you're angry, your face may feel hot and your fists tight. Sadness often brings sensations of heaviness or slowness, while happiness can make us feel energetic and light. Some sensations are common to more than one emotion. For example, a flushed face could reflect anger, embarrassment, or excitement. Feeling energized could reflect anger or elation—two quite different emotions.

Thoughts in the Mind

Thoughts often take the form of phrases or sentences. If you're anxious or fearful, you may have thoughts such as *I need to get out of here*, *This is going to be a disaster*, or *What if something terrible happens?* If you're feeling regretful, you might think, *I wish I had* (or *hadn't*)… or *If only….* If you're disappointed, you may be thinking, *Things never work out for me*. Anger usually includes thoughts like *This isn't fair*, *I hate this*, or *How could she…?*

Many people have images in their minds while they feel an emotion. As you joyfully anticipate your wedding day, you might envision exchanging rings with your loved one, with your friends and family gathered around. If you're anxious about a presentation, you might picture the audience looking inattentive and bored.

Urges to Act

Urges, also known as action tendencies, are desires or impulses to behave in particular ways. Sometimes we act on these urges—that's emotion-driven behavior. Other times we restrain ourselves. Most emotions include urges to do specific things. If you're feeling depressed, you may have an urge to stay in bed all day. If you're angry, you might have impulses to yell, curse, throw things, or slam doors. If you're feeling anxious, you'll probably have an urge to get away from the situation. For example, if you're afraid of crowds but a friend persuades you to go to a movie, you might feel an impulse to leave when you see that the theater is nearly full. Positive emotions also include urges—for example, to clap your hands when you're happy or to hug someone you love.

The table below shows the three components of Mari's emotions after that stressful day at work.

Emotion and situation	Body sensations	Thoughts	Urges
Frustration while playing tennis	Heart pounding Hands tight	*What's wrong with me?* *Why can't I hit the ball?* *I'm such an idiot.*	Curse Slam her racket on ground
Irritation at a slow driver	Heat in face Tension in hands Clenched jaw	*What's wrong with you?* *Don't you know how to drive?*	Pound the steering wheel Honk Accelerate rapidly
Dejection after getting home	Fatigue Hollowness in abdomen Eyes near tears	*I don't feel like doing anything.* *Nothing's going right for me.*	Lie around Drink beer Watch TV

Why Do We Have Emotions?

Research shows that basic emotions, including happiness, sadness, anger, fear, disgust, and surprise, are expressed with distinct facial expressions that are similar all over the world (Ekman 1973). Even people who have been blind since birth smile when they're happy, frown when they're sad, and clench their teeth when they're angry, despite having never seen these expressions on other people's faces. Scientists believe that these emotions are universal aspects of human nature that evolved as they did because they're necessary for survival. Although emotions can be difficult and painful, we have them because they're helpful to us. Emotions serve several purposes (Linehan 1993b; Barlow et al. 2011).

Telling Us Important Information

Fear is a signal that something in the environment may pose a threat. Sadness alerts us to a significant loss or personal setback. Anger is a message that we've been wronged. Guilt suggests that we've wronged someone else. These messages help us respond wisely.

Motivating and Preparing Us to Take Constructive Actions

Some emotion-driven behavior is helpful. If a car speeds toward you while you're crossing the street, fear provides the energy to jump out of the way. If you have an important presentation coming up, anxiety can motivate you to research your topic thoroughly, practice your presentation, and anticipate likely questions from the audience. When you've suffered a major loss, sadness reduces your energy level and encourages you to withdraw from normal activities; this is helpful for a while because it gives you time to accept the loss and adapt to your new circumstances.

Anger provides energy to make changes in unfair situations. It can motivate you to stand up for your rights or the rights of others. Guilt pushes you to apologize and make amends if you've wronged someone. Love motivates caring for others. Passion provides the energy for creative achievements. In general, if we handle our emotions constructively, they can protect us from harm, energize us to accomplish important goals, and help us maintain our relationships.

Communicating to Others

Facial expression, behavior, tone of voice, and body language communicate to others how we're feeling. This allows them to help if they can. Sadness lets others know we need support. Anger tells them that we're feeling mistreated. Fear communicates a need for protection. The nonverbal communication of emotion is especially useful for children too young to speak or comprehend language. Imagine a young child who's reaching for a sharp knife that has fallen to the floor. A frightened gasp and horrified look from the nearest adult communicates effectively that the knife is dangerous. And, of course, if hunger, pain, and unfamiliar situations didn't cause noticeable distress in babies, adults would be less likely to attend to their needs, and fewer babies would survive.

Emotion-Driven Behavior Can Be a Trap

Emotions evolved to be useful, yet they often cause trouble. How does this happen? Emotions are often triggered quickly. Bodily reactions and impulses arise before we have time to think. Sometimes these instantaneous responses are necessary for survival. If a wild animal is attacking, it's safer to fight or flee immediately than to consider the pros and cons of doing either.

Unfortunately, our spontaneous reactions aren't always well suited to modern life. When fear arises, blood flows to the legs to make it easier to run away. Hormones are released into the bloodstream to prepare the body for physical action. This is great if you're being chased by an assailant. It's less useful if you're about to give a speech, interview for a job, or ask someone for a date. The body perceives a threat and it prepares to fight or flee, even when you wish it would stay calm.

Anger presents similar problems. The body is flooded with hormones that create energy. The face may take on a threatening expression. Urges arise to speak loudly and behave aggressively. This is helpful if you need to fight an attacker but less useful when you're angered by a coworker during a staff meeting or a driver on a crowded highway.

Given these difficulties, it's understandable that some of our emotion-driven behavior is unconstructive or even harmful. We get trapped in several ways:

- We're trapped by our genetic heritage to feel emotions that evolved for conditions that predate modern times. To behave according to contemporary social norms, sometimes we have to suppress or override our emotions. This is difficult and creates tension.

- We're also trapped by the short-term effects of emotion-driven behavior, which often feels satisfying in the moment but causes trouble in the long run.

- We're trapped by a uniquely human characteristic: the ability to feel emotions about our own emotions. These are called secondary emotions.

Secondary Emotions

A secondary emotion occurs in response to another emotion (Linehan 1993a). Consider Mari, who felt angry when her boss criticized her work. Then she told herself she shouldn't be so sensitive and felt ashamed of being angry. Anger was the primary emotion—a natural response to being criticized. Shame was the secondary emotion—a reaction to the anger. When thinking about secondary emotions, it's important to remember several points:

- Secondary emotions are common. We can feel angry about feeling anxious, embarrassed about feeling sad, anxious about feeling depressed, and many other combinations. We can also feel guilty about being happy, embarrassed about how much we love something, or worried about when contentment will end.

- Secondary emotions are learned from experience. If a child is consistently shamed for expressing anger, the child may learn that anger is bad or wrong. Feeling shame whenever anger arises can then become a lifelong pattern.

- Secondary emotions are brought on by negative judgments about primary emotions. If you tell yourself that you're overreacting or that your primary emotion is wrong, bad, silly, crazy, weak, stupid, or immature, you'll get upset with yourself for having the primary emotion. This is unfortunate, because primary emotions are natural responses to events or situations. Criticizing ourselves for having them makes matters worse, as emotions get stronger and more complicated and last longer.

- Once secondary emotions have complicated the situation, unhealthy emotion-driven behavior becomes more likely. The following table shows some examples of primary emotions, judgments about them, secondary emotions, and the unhealthy emotion-driven behaviors that may result.

Primary emotion	Judgment about the primary emotion	Secondary emotion	Unhealthy emotion-driven behavior
Sadness about the death of a pet	*It's silly to feel sad about this.*	Embarrassment about feeling sad	Avoiding supportive friends who would understand your sadness and help you feel better.
Anger at a friend who canceled a date	*I shouldn't feel angry. I'm overreacting.*	Shame or disappointment in yourself for feeling angry	Drinking or eating too much to stifle anger and shame. Avoiding your friend.
Anxiety about giving a talk	*Feeling anxious is a sign of weakness and shows I'm incompetent.*	Anger at yourself for feeling anxious	Losing your temper with others. Avoiding preparing for the talk.

"But What If I Really Am Overreacting?"

When strong emotions arise, we often tell ourselves that we're overreacting. Remember that *I'm overreacting* is a judgmental thought about an emotion you're feeling. This thought is likely to come to mind if your emotional reaction has certain qualities:

- It's more intense than the average person would experience in this situation.

- It's stronger than your usual emotions.

- It's more intense than someone else thinks it should be.

- It's puzzling or confusing. You don't understand why you're feeling this way.

When you tell yourself that you're overreacting, you're implying that the intensity of your emotion doesn't make sense or isn't justified. In reality, intense emotions occur for several reasons:

- The tendency to have strong emotions can be inherited. Some people naturally have intense emotions because of their brain and body chemistry, whereas others have calmer temperaments.

- Strong emotional reactions to seemingly minor events may be related to previous experiences. For example, you may feel deeply sad about a TV show if it reminds you of a sad experience in your past. Others may wonder why the show has affected you so strongly.

- Normal conditioning processes can cause apparently neutral aspects of the environment to trigger emotions for reasons that we don't always recognize. For example, an unfamiliar parking lot can make you feel nostalgic if it resembles one where you found a stray kitten that brought you years of companionship. You may not realize why the parking lot has triggered this feeling, but it makes sense in its own way.

- Temporary conditions in your mind and body can influence your emotions. If you're tired, hungry, sick, or stressed, minor events can trigger surprisingly intense feelings. This is normal.

If you're telling yourself that you're overreacting because your emotion is intense or unexpected, remember that emotions happen for reasons. Even if you don't see how they make sense, they do. They may seem odd or stronger than you'd like, but if you criticize yourself for feeling what you feel, there's a good chance you'll feel worse. This will increase the risk of unhelpful emotion-driven behavior. You'll be less able to make wise decisions about what to do.

EXERCISE: Understanding Your Emotional Experiences

To handle our emotions skillfully, we have to understand them. The following worksheet (inspired by McKay, Wood, and Brantley 2007) will help you observe your emotional experiences and respond to them with wisdom and insight. If you're not accustomed to paying attention to your emotions, it may feel awkward at first, but it gets easier with practice. As you become more aware of your emotions, you may find that you're criticizing yourself for having particular feelings or for the intensity of your feelings. See if you can let go of the criticism. Remember that being mindful of your emotions means observing them with friendly curiosity, not judging yourself for having them.

As before, there are three versions of the worksheet. The first contains instructions. The second is an example from Jim, who just got a new job after being fired a few months ago. He's worried about getting fired again.

After the example, you'll find a blank worksheet for your own use, to help you practice being mindful of your emotional experiences. Again, make copies so that you can do this exercise more than once. The more you practice, the more skillful you'll become. Consider doing this exercise three times over the next week, or even daily if you have strong emotions more frequently. Each time you complete the worksheet, choose one specific occasion to write about: an emotional experience that occurred on a particular day at a specific time. Remember that a perfect record isn't your goal. The purpose of the exercise is to practice being observant, curious, open-minded, and nonjudgmental about your emotions. In time, you'll become less susceptible to unhealthy emotion-driven behavior.

WORKSHEET: Understanding an Emotional Experience

Remember to maintain an attitude of friendly curiosity.

Day and time When did this emotional experience happen?	Writing down the day and time helps you be specific about which emotional experience you're working with and also helps you see patterns over time.
Triggering event Describe the situation that triggered your emotion.	This might be an event that happened in the external world, such as learning that a friend was in a car accident. It could be an internal experience, such as remembering that a friend is having surgery tomorrow. If you're unsure of the trigger, leave this blank for now. Over time, you'll become more skillful at identifying the triggering event.
What emotions did you feel? Underline the strongest emotion.	If you need help with emotion names, look back at the list earlier in this chapter. If you felt more than one emotion, write them all down. Underline the strongest emotion and use it for the rest of the worksheet. If you like, you can fill out other worksheets for the other emotions that you felt.
Intensity of the strongest emotion (1–10)	Rate the intensity of the emotions using a scale of 1 to 10, where 1 is the mildest emotion possible, and 10 is the most intense.
What thoughts or images were going through your mind?	Your thoughts might include interpretations or assumptions about the situation or predictions about what will happen. If you had images in your mind, describe them.
What sensations did you notice in your body?	Did you notice a change in your heart rate or breathing, or any muscle tension or trembling? Did you feel hot, cold, or sweaty? Did you feel heavy or light? Did you experience sensations in your chest, stomach, face, eyes, head, or hands, or anywhere else?
What did you feel like saying or doing? (urges)	Did you feel like escaping or avoiding a person or situation? Shouting or throwing things? Staying in bed? Eating or drinking too much? Talking to someone?
What did you say or do? (behavior)	If you acted on your urges, describe what you did. If you restrained yourself in any way, write that down too.
Secondary emotions	Did this emotion trigger other emotions? For example, did you get angry with yourself for feeling sad? Did you feel ashamed of yourself for getting angry?

WORKSHEET: Understanding an Emotional Experience

Your name: Jim

Remember to maintain an attitude of friendly curiosity.

Day and time When did this emotional experience happen?	Thursday morning around 10:15 a.m.
Triggering event Describe the situation that triggered your emotion.	I was sitting at my desk at work. My boss walked by and gave me an angry look.
What emotions did you feel? Underline the strongest emotion.	nervousness, <u>fear</u>
Intensity of the strongest emotion (1–10)	7
What thoughts or images were going through your mind?	He's going to fire me. He's not happy with my work. I knew this job would never last. I'm going to be unemployed again. I'll never get another job as good as this one.
What sensations did you notice in your body?	My heart was beating fast, and my breathing was shallow. I had a sinking feeling in my chest.
What did you feel like saying or doing? (urges)	I had an urge to just give up and go home. I also wanted to go into my boss's office and make him tell me what I've been doing wrong and give me another chance.
What did you say or do? (behavior)	I made myself stay at my desk and keep working, even though I couldn't concentrate. Later I told a coworker about it. He told me not to worry—that the boss was in a bad mood all day because his daughter wrecked his car.
Secondary emotions	I got mad at myself and told myself I was an idiot for jumping to conclusions and getting scared for no good reason. I felt embarrassed about it.

WORKSHEET: Understanding an Emotional Experience

Your name: _____

Remember to maintain an attitude of friendly curiosity.

Day and time When did this emotional experience happen?	
Triggering event Describe the situation that triggered your emotion.	
What emotions did you feel? Underline the strongest emotion.	
Intensity of the strongest emotion (1–10)	
What thoughts or images were going through your mind?	
What sensations did you notice in your body?	
What did you feel like saying or doing? (urges)	
What did you say or do? (behavior)	
Secondary emotions	

How Mindfulness Helps with Emotion-Driven Behavior

If you have strong emotions, you may already be very much aware of them (Orsillo and Roemer 2011). Increasing your emotional awareness by practicing mindfulness may seem like an unhelpful thing to do. The key is to remember the difference between problem-solving mode and mindful acceptance. In problem-solving mode, we may be acutely aware of negative emotions, but we think of them as problems that need solving. We have negative judgments about them and try to escape them or get rid of them. We forget that unpleasant emotions are normal in many situations and may be sending important messages.

The alternative is to observe our emotions mindfully, accepting them as visitors to the guest house or passengers on the bus. See if you can watch them unfold moment by moment and observe the sensations with interest and curiosity. Notice the associated thoughts. Recognize that thoughts like *It's stupid to feel this way* and *I'm overreacting* are judgments, rather than truth or reality. Acknowledge the urges to behave in particular ways without necessarily acting on them. Over time, emotions will become less scary and easier to understand, even when they're complex.

For some people, the most troubling aspect of negative emotions is emotion-driven behavior: overeating when they're sad, yelling and throwing things when they're angry, and so on. Practicing mindfulness skills is an excellent way to address this problem. Over time, observing our emotions without judgment creates a space between the emotion and the corresponding behavior. This gap provides an opportunity to choose what to do.

For example, by practicing mindfulness, Mari will learn to observe when she's feeling an urge to slam her tennis racket on the ground. She'll recognize the feelings of frustration, the self-critical thoughts, and the tension in her body, and she'll have a moment to choose: she could either slam her racket down or refrain from doing so. This doesn't mean she's suppressing her feelings. Instead, she's learning to make room for them without letting them drive her behavior.

Introductory Exercises for Practicing Mindfulness of Urges

The following exercises will help you develop a mindful approach to mild, commonplace urges, which are easier to work with than the urges caused by intense negative emotions. Practicing these introductory exercises is a good way to get started on reducing emotion-driven behavior that causes problems in your life. Try doing one of these exercises three times over the next week, and continue practicing whenever urges arise. Later in the book, chapters 11 and 13 will provide detailed descriptions of exercises that help with more intense urges triggered by strong emotions.

If you have self-critical thoughts while practicing mindfulness of urges (*I shouldn't feel this way*, *This urge is bad*, and the like), notice that these are thoughts. Practice exploring your urges with an attitude of openness and interest.

EXERCISE: Observing Naturally Occurring Urges in Daily Life

Observing urges that arise naturally through the course of your day is a good place to begin. You can practice with any urges. Here are a few suggestions to help you get started:

- When you brush your teeth, observe the process carefully. Notice when you feel the urge to spit. Observe the urge without spitting. Notice the nature of the urge and how you feel while having the urge. You will have to spit eventually, so make a deliberate decision about when to spit. Practice not being controlled by the urge.

- The next time your nose itches, observe the urge to rub it. Notice what the urge feels like without acting on it. Keep observing and see if the urge gets stronger or subsides. Decide for yourself if and when to rub your nose. If you rub your nose, do so mindfully. Observe the movements and sensations.

- If you get itchy insect bites, try this exercise with urges to scratch.

- As you go through your day, practice with other urges that arise.

EXERCISE: Observing Self-Induced Urges

You can also practice by setting up situations that will trigger behavioral urges:

- Set a piece of a food you like in front of you. Notice if you have an urge to eat it. Observe the urge. Keep observing and see if the urge gets stronger or subsides. Either way, make a deliberate decision about whether to eat the food.

- Eat something slowly and notice when you have the urge to swallow. For a few moments, observe the urge without swallowing. Decide when to swallow.

- Hold a book or another object at arm's length in front of you or to one side. Notice the sensations in your arm. Before long, you'll have an urge to set the object down. For a short time, observe the urge without acting on it. Make a mindful decision about when to set the object down. Be sure not to overstrain your arm.

Remembering the Attitude of Friendly Curiosity

As you experiment with these exercises and start paying more attention to your urges in daily life, you may find it difficult to let go of judging and criticizing yourself for having particular urges or for acting on them. Unfortunately, self-criticism usually makes matters worse. It's another psychological trap. In the next chapter, we'll take a more detailed look at self-criticism and how mindfulness skills can help us avoid it.

Chapter Summary

- Emotions are complex experiences. They include bodily sensations, thoughts, and urges to act in particular ways.

- Although emotions can be painful, we have them because they serve useful purposes. They give us important information, help us communicate to others, and can motivate us to behave constructively if we handle them in healthy ways.

- Unfortunately, when we're feeling negative emotions, we often do things we regret. Unconstructive emotion-driven behavior is a trap. We do it because it temporarily relieves unpleasant feelings, but it causes problems and makes us feel worse in the long run.

- Mindful observation of emotional experiences helps us recognize their components, including bodily sensations, thoughts, and urges. We learn to observe them without judgment and without acting on them in impulsive ways. With practice, mindfulness of urges gives us time to decide wisely how to respond.

CHAPTER 6

Self-Criticism

If we treat ourselves harshly, this is the way we are likely to treat other people.

—Karen Armstrong

It's late in the afternoon and you've had a long day at work. You stop in the restroom before heading home and notice a shred of lettuce stuck in your front teeth. It must have been there since lunch. You've seen several people this afternoon, including two new customers, and no one said anything. Which set of thoughts goes through your mind?

A: *I'm such an idiot. Why didn't I check the mirror after lunch? People must have been laughing at me all afternoon.*

B: *Oh dear, how embarrassing. Well, this sort of thing happens to everyone now and then.*

Here's another scenario: You applied for a job that you really wanted. Out of more than fifty applicants, you and two others were invited for interviews. Your interview went very well and you felt optimistic. But this afternoon you learned that you didn't get the job. You're extremely disappointed. All evening you've been sitting on the couch, eating cookies and watching silly TV shows. Now it's time to go to bed. Which set of thoughts goes through your mind?

A: *It's disgusting how many cookies I ate. I have no self-control. No wonder I didn't get that job. I really didn't deserve it.*

B: *I've had a big disappointment. I was really qualified for that job, and it's a shame I didn't get it. Cookies and TV are okay for a little while, but I need to take care of myself. Tomorrow I'll ask my friend to go for a walk with me.*

Your thoughts might fall somewhere in between, but if they're closer to option A than to option B, you may be falling prey to self-criticism. It's quite common. Most of us criticize ourselves frequently, often harshly (McKay and Fanning 1992). Self-criticism feels like an inner voice. Depending on the situation, it says things like *I'm an idiot, I'm a loser, I'm not good enough, I made a total mess of that, I'll never amount to anything, I'm disgusting (stupid, lazy, ugly, useless, crazy...)*, and so on. Sometimes it calls you by name, as if you were a separate person: *Ruth, you're hopeless. You can't do anything right.* The inner critic can be brutal.

Criticism from Others

When we want to develop our skills or learn new ones, constructive criticism is valuable, even essential. It's part of good teaching and provides the information we need to do better. Criticism from others is most helpful when it has the following characteristics (Bergner 1995; Ossorio 1990):

- It provides specific information about what went wrong and what to do differently.

- It's offered with a considerate, respectful tone.

- It judges the work rather than the person.

- It points out strengths as well as weaknesses.

The following table provides examples of constructive and unconstructive criticism provided by two cooking teachers.

Teacher A: Constructive criticism	Teacher B: Unconstructive criticism
Specific *The oven wasn't hot enough when you put the chicken in to roast. That's why it didn't turn brown and crispy on the outside.*	Vague *This chicken looks awful.*
Considerate *That's a common mistake.*	Inconsiderate *How could you be so careless?*
Directed at the work *These muffins are a little dense and tough and didn't rise very well. That shows the batter was mixed too much.*	Directed at the person *You did a terrible job with these muffins.*
Balanced *The fish is nice and tender, but the vegetables were simmered for too long.*	Unbalanced *You overcooked the vegetables. The meal is ruined.*

To learn about cooking in a helpful and supportive atmosphere, most people would prefer to join teacher A's class. Notice that constructive criticism is clear about mistakes and weaknesses—it doesn't say that everything is excellent when it isn't.

Research confirms the benefits of constructive criticism (Baron 1988). When university students received constructive criticism (rather than vague, insulting, personal, or one-sided criticism), they felt less angry and tense. They were more willing to collaborate with the person providing the criticism. They set higher goals and felt more confidence in their ability to reach them. A study with employees of a large company found that criticism from supervisors that embarrassed or blamed the recipients without helping them improve was a major cause of conflict in their workplace.

Self-Criticism

The same principles apply to self-criticism. If we're going to criticize ourselves, we should do so in the style of teacher A from the cooking class. But much of the time, we behave like teacher B. We don't think specifically about what went wrong, how we might improve, or how to get help if we need it. Instead, we're vague (*I did a terrible job*), inconsiderate (*My ideas are really stupid*), judgmental of ourselves rather than our behavior or our work (*I'm incompetent*), and unbalanced (*I can't do anything right*). Sometimes we threaten ourselves with future misfortunes (*If I go on like this, I'll never accomplish anything*).

Facing our mistakes and weaknesses in a helpful way is already difficult enough. Insulting ourselves with harsh self-criticism makes us feel worse. It interferes with the ability to improve when improvement is needed. It also keeps us from accepting aspects of ourselves that can't be changed or that are fine the way they are.

SELF-TEST: Self-Criticism

Everyone is self-critical at times. This self-test (based loosely on Blatt, D'Afflitti, and Quinlan 1976; Gilbert et al. 2004; and Neff 2003) will help you determine whether harsh, unconstructive self-criticism is a problem for you. Using the rating scale provided, in each blank space write the number that indicates how true each statement is for you.

1	2	3	4
Rarely true	Sometimes true	Often true	Very often true

_____ *I criticize myself harshly for things I've said or done.*

_____ *I put myself down or call myself names when something goes wrong.*

_____ *I blame myself for my failures without taking credit for my successes.*

_____ *I'm intolerant of my own flaws and weaknesses.*

_____ *I tell myself I'm an idiot or not good enough.*

Add up your ratings. If your score is greater than 10, you may be criticizing yourself excessively. If you scored between 15 and 20, your self-criticism may be causing you significant problems, especially if you're attacking and condemning yourself, rather than taking a constructive, balanced view of your strengths and weaknesses.

* *Isabel's Story* *

Isabel is an intelligent and hardworking student who was raised in a critical family. Her parents, who hadn't gone beyond high school, were determined that their only child would go further. They closely supervised Isabel's schoolwork and criticized any grades that were less than outstanding. Isabel did well in school and was admitted to a large university, where she found the work much more difficult. She worried that she had only come this far because of her parents' relentless pressure and that she wasn't bright enough for university work. She coped by adopting a highly self-critical style, constantly telling herself that she wasn't very competent and could avoid failure only by working extremely hard.

For two years, Isabel earned good grades despite her shaky confidence. In her third year, she was invited to work with a faculty advisor on a research project. Although she doubted her ability to succeed, her parents were thrilled and Isabel felt she couldn't say no.

After several meetings to discuss the topic for her project, Isabel's advisor, Dr. Haley, gave her a deadline for writing a rough draft of the first section of the paper. For the first time in her life, Isabel found that she couldn't complete her assigned work. She didn't understand how to organize her ideas or what the first section should include. Every time she tried to work on it, she was overwhelmed with self-critical thoughts: *This isn't good enough. I'm incapable of doing this. I'm going to fail.* She sent an e-mail to Dr. Haley requesting a one-week extension, which he granted. Isabel criticized herself further. *It's stupid of me to need an extension. Dr. Haley will think I'm an idiot. I'm obviously hopeless at this.*

Filled with uncertainty about how to continue, Isabel began to procrastinate. Then she criticized herself for not working. *What's wrong with me?* she wondered, as her anxiety intensified. *Why can't I just do it? I have no discipline at all. I'm not cut out for this.* Ashamed of her lack of progress, Isabel didn't mention the problem to anyone.

The week's extension passed. Dr. Haley sent e-mails expressing concern. Isabel didn't reply. She avoided the building where Dr. Haley's office was located. After two weeks of constant rumination about her uncompleted assignment, Isabel unexpectedly saw Dr. Haley in a coffee shop. "Hi, Isabel," said Dr. Haley. "Nice to see you!"

"Hi," said Isabel, hoping he wouldn't mention the paper.

"What's going on with your paper?" Dr. Haley asked. Isabel burst into tears and said she was giving up the research project.

Dr. Haley insisted on meeting with her the next day. He reminded Isabel that the advisor's job is to provide guidance, that the purpose of the first draft is to get constructive feedback, and that the student's job is to bring up questions and concerns during regular meetings. He helped her outline the first section. Isabel promised to meet weekly and to bring a draft, no matter how rough, to their next session.

The Consequences of Harsh Self-Criticism

Isabel's story illustrates an interesting paradox about unconstructive self-criticism: most of us do it for the purpose of self-discipline or self-correction, yet many studies show that harsh self-criticism actually interferes with progress toward our goals.

In one study, 180 overweight adults signed up for a weight-loss program (Powers et al. 2011). Before the program started, they completed a questionnaire measuring unconstructive self-criticism. Then they were weighed. After six months of working on diet and exercise, they were weighed again. Those who were more harshly self-critical at the beginning of the program had lost less weight six months later.

University athletes in swimming or track and field showed a similar pattern (Powers et al. 2009). At the beginning of the athletic season, they completed a self-criticism questionnaire and identified their most important goal for the season, such as improving their time in the 100-meter backstroke or learning to do a triple jump. At the end of the season, the more self-critical athletes had made less progress toward their goals.

Why do highly self-critical people make less progress than those who don't judge themselves so harshly? Instead of motivating and energizing us to pursue our goals, self-criticism triggers feelings of shame, guilt, sadness, anger, frustration, embarrassment, disappointment, and hopelessness (Powers, Koestner, and Zuroff 2007). It saps our energy, morale, motivation, and confidence, making it hard to keep going in the face of difficulties. We're likely to procrastinate and avoid, as Isabel found. We're less likely to seek help when we need it. Progress slows, which leads to more self-criticism, creating a vicious cycle.

Unconstructive self-criticism has many other negative effects. People who criticize themselves severely are more likely to become depressed, anxious, and lonely. They're more likely to have trouble in their romantic relationships, perhaps because they expect their partners to judge them as harshly as they judge themselves and are therefore less open (Lassri and Shahar 2012). Self-critical people are more likely to binge eat, especially if they grew up in critical or emotionally abusive families (Dunkley, Masheb, and Grilo 2010). People who have experienced an extremely stressful event, like a serious accident or an assault, are more likely to develop symptoms of post-traumatic stress if they're highly self-critical (Harman and Lee 2010).

Why Do We Criticize Ourselves So Harshly?

When asked why they criticize themselves, most people say that it's for their own good. Many of us believe that self-criticism prevents laziness, complacency, and self-indulgence. We think it helps us meet responsibilities, maintain self-discipline, and prevent mistakes. We probably learned this in childhood, perhaps from parents or teachers who didn't understand the difference between constructive and unconstructive criticism. When children are harshly criticized but rarely praised, encouraged, or given constructive feedback, they may learn that criticism is the only way to motivate good behavior (Gilbert 2005).

Shame and Fear of Rejection

Self-criticism is closely connected with shame, an intensely unpleasant emotion that includes feelings of inferiority and a desire to hide or conceal oneself. As discussed in chapter 5, emotions evolved because they help us survive. For example, fear helps us escape danger, and anger helps us defend ourselves. Experts believe that shame may have a similar purpose (Gilbert et al. 2004).

Most people feel a strong need to belong to a group: a family, a circle of friends, or a larger community. Most groups have rules of behavior. When a group member violates these rules, the group or its leaders may try to shame the wrongdoer as a way of controlling the person's behavior. The wrongdoer who expresses shame may be treated more leniently and allowed to stay in the group. If the wrongdoer expresses no shame, the group may inflict severe punishment, such as rejection and isolation. Shame, therefore, appears to exist for a reason: It can help us avoid conflict and ostracism.

Unfortunately, most of us are so sensitive to rejection that we've learned to internalize this process, and we inflict it on ourselves. If we've done something that we fear others won't like, we use harsh self-criticism to punish ourselves. Then we submit to our own self-criticism by feeling ashamed. This may be useful if it helps us avoid getting thrown out of our family, school, or workplace or keeps us out of prison. But if the self-criticism is excessive, vague, demeaning, and unbalanced, it interferes with our ability to improve. It also interferes with our mental health.

Is Shame the Same as Guilt?

Shame and guilt are similar but not exactly the same. Shame is focused on the whole person and creates feelings of overall worthlessness (*I am a bad person*) and the desire to hide or disappear. Shame is so painful that we often try to escape it by shifting blame to others, lashing out in anger, or denying responsibility for misdeeds. Guilt is also painful, but it's focused on specific behaviors and creates the desire to confess, apologize, and make amends (Tangney and Dearing 2002).

Imagine spilling a bowl of spaghetti sauce on a friend's new carpet. If you're telling yourself you're an awful person and wishing you could disappear, that's shame. If you're focused on your friend's feelings, regretting the distress you've caused, apologizing, trying to clean up the mess, and offering to pay for professional carpet cleaning, that's guilt. You might be feeling both emotions at once. Excessive, harmful self-criticism is more likely to stem from shame, and to intensify shame, in a vicious cycle that makes it harder to handle the situation as you'd like to.

Harsh Self-Criticism Is a Psychological Trap

We get caught in the trap of unconstructive self-criticism for several reasons. We learn it in childhood, and we believe it should keep us on track—and sometimes it does, at least for a while. But many of us are so sensitive to failure and rejection that we use it too harshly, forgetting that constructive suggestions usually work better when improvement is required, and that kindness is more helpful than cruelty whether improvement is needed or not.

This point may be clearer if you imagine giving harsh criticism to someone you care about. If a good friend tells you that he had lettuce in his teeth all afternoon and is feeling a little foolish, what would you say?

A: "You're such an idiot. Why didn't you check the mirror after lunch? People must have been laughing at you all afternoon."

B: "Oh dear, how embarrassing. Well, this sort of thing happens to everyone now and then. I once gave a presentation with mustard on my shirt. And I know a lawyer who walked out of the restroom and into the courtroom with the back of her skirt caught in her underwear."

Now imagine that a friend says that she didn't get a job she really wanted and watched stupid TV shows all evening while eating a whole bag of cookies. What would you say?

A: "I can't believe how many cookies you ate. That's disgusting. You have no self-control. No wonder you didn't get that job. You really didn't deserve it."

B: "You've had a big disappointment. You were really qualified for that job, and it's a shame you didn't get it. Cookies and TV are okay for a little while, but it's good to take care of yourself at times like this. Let's go for a walk tomorrow."

If option A makes you cringe, that's probably because you would never be so unkind to someone you care about. Most of us can easily imagine saying such things to ourselves but not to loved ones. Why is this? We know that we wouldn't reject a friend for such minor things. We understand that it won't help; in fact, it will hurt the friend and damage the friendship. Yet we're so sensitive to rejection and failure that when we make mistakes or fall short of our usual standards, we fear the worst. We think we're deteriorating into hopeless messes and that we'll be laughed at or even shunned. We get caught in the self-criticism trap. It's bad for our mental health to treat ourselves this way.

EXERCISE: Understanding Your Patterns of Self-Criticism

If you've been criticizing yourself for a long time, it may have become a habit. You may be doing it automatically, without realizing what's happening. To change this habit, it's important to observe and understand your patterns of self-criticism. The following worksheet will help. It may be painful to take a close look at your self-critical thoughts, but it has important advantages. Putting your thoughts on paper makes them seem less like the absolute truth. Seeing them written down will help you take a more balanced perspective on them. You'll realize when they're unfair, unreasonable, unconstructive, and even cruel.

See if you can bring the same attitude of friendly curiosity and interest to this task that you've practiced with the other psychological traps. Remember that self-criticism is very common in Western society. Most of us have been trained to be self-critical. It's important not to chastise yourself for it.

As before, there are three versions of the worksheet. The first contains instructions. The second is an example from Isabel. After the example, you'll find a blank worksheet for your own use, to help you practice being mindful of any tendency toward harsh self-criticism. As with most of the other worksheets in this book, this one is more helpful if you use it repeatedly, so make several copies. Keep blank worksheets handy and fill one out as soon as possible after each episode of harsh self-criticism. The longer you wait, the harder it is to remember the thoughts that went through your mind. After filling out several, see if you observe any patterns. What do you criticize yourself about? Could you talk to yourself more constructively?

WORKSHEET: Understanding Self-Criticism

Remember to maintain an attitude of friendly curiosity.

Day and time	Triggering event	What self-critical thoughts were in your mind?	Aftereffects and consequences	What would you say to a friend in this situation?
When did this episode of self-criticism occur?	What situation or circumstance started the self-critical thoughts? Where were you? What was going on? Were other people involved? Also describe what you were criticizing yourself for. Was it your behavior, thoughts, feelings, or urges?	What were you saying to yourself? Write down the self-critical thoughts exactly as they appeared in your mind. If you had mental images, describe them.	What did you notice after criticizing yourself? Describe any thoughts, emotions, physical sensations, or urges, and note any effects on your behavior. Did you do anything self-defeating, like avoid people or situations?	Imagine that someone you care about experienced the same triggering event. What would you say to this person?

WORKSHEET: Understanding Self-Criticism

Your name: *Isabel*

Remember to maintain an attitude of friendly curiosity.

Day and time	Triggering event	What self-critical thoughts were in your mind?	Aftereffects and consequences	What would you say to a friend in this situation?
Thursday evening around 8 p.m.	*I was working on my research paper. I got stuck and didn't know how to continue.*	*I'm incompetent. I shouldn't be doing this project. I'm not smart enough.*	*I felt anger and disappointment at myself and discouraged about my lack of progress.* *I gave up on the paper and watched TV. Then I couldn't sleep, and the next day I felt hopeless and unmotivated.*	*Of course this is difficult. You've never done a research paper before. You wouldn't have been invited to do this if you weren't capable of succeeding. Don't beat yourself up. Make a list of your questions and go see your advisor tomorrow.*
Tuesday around 3 p.m.	*I e-mailed my math professor to make an appointment for help with some homework I don't understand.*	*I should be able to do this on my own. Most students don't need extra help. I'm being a nuisance.*	*I felt dejected and annoyed with myself for needing extra help.*	*It's part of the professor's job to provide help when students need it. You're doing the right thing by asking for help.*

Self-Criticism

75

WORKSHEET: Understanding Self-Criticism

Your name: _____

Remember to maintain an attitude of friendly curiosity.

Day and time	Triggering event	What self-critical thoughts were in your mind?	Aftereffects and consequences	What would you say to a friend in this situation?

How Mindfulness Helps with Self-Criticism

Most self-criticism is a form of thinking. *I'm a loser, I'm weak, I'm immature, I'm silly, I'm ugly, I'm stupid*, and so on are all thoughts. When thoughts like this appear, we often believe they're completely true. Psychologists call this fusion (Hayes, Strosahl, and Wilson 1999). When we're fused with our thoughts, we take them seriously because we assume that they're facts—that they reflect important realities. So when you have a thought like *I'm a complete idiot and I'll never amount to anything*, it probably feels like you've realized something significant about the way things truly are. Fusion with thoughts leads to negative emotions, such as disappointment, anger, and sadness, along with unhelpful behavior.

Practicing mindfulness teaches us to understand thoughts in a different way. We learn that we're constantly thinking, that thoughts appear and disappear, and that they aren't necessarily realistic, important, or meaningful. We don't have to believe them or act on them. Instead, we can allow them to come and go in their own time while continuing to behave in ways that are consistent with our goals. We can choose to act on our thoughts when it's helpful to do so, but we don't have to be ruled by them. This attitude toward thoughts is called defusion.

Suppose you make a mistake at work and the thought *I'm so incompetent* pops into your head. If you're fused with this thought, you believe it unquestioningly. It feels like the truth—like an important fact. The thought triggers emotions: you feel embarrassed, ashamed, disappointed, and angry at yourself. The emotions trigger urges: perhaps to curse, throw something, quit your job, or get drunk.

If you're being mindful, you recognize that *I'm so incompetent* is just a thought. Moreover, it's a judgmental, unbalanced, unkind thought. You observe the emotions that it triggers and the urges that follow. *Okay*, you say to yourself. *I made a mistake, and now I'm feeling embarrassed and frustrated and I'm tempted to give up and go home.*

Now you're in a position to choose what to do. You might curse, throw your coffee mug at the wall, and storm out, or you might take a short break to allow yourself time to settle down. Then you might think constructively about how to remedy the situation, remembering to treat yourself with respect while you do so, as you would a friend who had made the same mistake.

Mindfulness of thoughts doesn't mean making thoughts go away. As discussed in chapter 4, trying to suppress our thoughts often backfires. The same is true of self-critical thoughts. Mindfulness involves simply observing thoughts without judging yourself for having them, and without necessarily believing them, taking them seriously, or doing what they tell you to do (Segal, Williams, and Teasdale 2013). This is a difficult skill to learn, but it isn't impossible.

Exercises for Defusing from Self-Critical Thoughts

The following exercises (inspired by Hayes 2005 and Segal, Williams, and Teasdale 2013) will help you develop a mindful approach to self-critical thoughts, rather than trying to get rid of them or being controlled by them.

EXERCISE: Labeling Your Thoughts as Thoughts

When you notice a self-critical thought, like *I'm an idiot*, say it again to yourself with one of the following phrases in front of it: "I'm having the thought that…" or "I'm noticing the thought that…." If you're having numerous self-critical thoughts at once, label them as a group. If you notice a repeating pattern of thoughts, label them as a tape that plays in your mind. Here are some examples:

Thought	Labeled thought
I can't do anything right.	*I'm having the thought that I can't do anything right.*
I'm an idiot.	*I'm noticing the thought that I'm an idiot.*
I'm stupid, useless, and ugly.	*I'm noticing a lot of self-critical thoughts right now.*
No one likes me.	*The "No one likes me" tape is playing again.*

EXERCISE: Greeting Your Thoughts Like People Passing By

Imagine that the self-critical thoughts are guests in your guest house, passengers on your bus, or people passing by on the street. When they criticize you, greet them politely without getting into a discussion about what they're saying. Then continue on your way. Here are a couple of examples.

Thought	Greeting
You'll never amount to anything.	*Good morning, Mrs. Criticism. Have a nice day!*
You're hopeless.	*Hello, Mr. Judgment. Lovely weather we're having!*

EXERCISE: Noticing the Radio in Your Mind

When you notice unconstructive self-critical thoughts, imagine they're coming from a radio in your mind that's stuck on a station that features criticism of you. For example, imagine the announcer saying, "Our latest bulletin: New research confirms that Ruth is a lazy good-for-nothing! Experts report they've suspected it all along—details at 11!" or "News flash! Ruth is acting like an idiot again. You won't believe what she did this time. Stay tuned for this developing story!"

When you hear these things, remind yourself that it's the radio in your mind. You can't turn it off, but you don't have to get caught up in it or believe everything it broadcasts.

EXERCISE: A Two-Day Experiment

Are you still concerned that if you don't take your harsh self-criticism seriously you'll get lazy? If so, try this two-day experiment (inspired by Orsillo and Roemer 2011): On the first day, criticize yourself in your usual way. Notice all your mistakes, faults, and weaknesses and scold yourself for them. On the second day, practice the three preceding exercises and give yourself only constructive criticism.

Throughout each day, carefully observe how you feel: How does it compare to a typical day? How motivated are you to pursue your goals? Also notice your behavior: Are you achieving more or less than usual? Is your behavior constructive and consistent with your goals?

Carefully observe the differences between the two days. There's a good chance you'll discover that you're happier and more effective when you're kind and constructive with yourself.

Final Thoughts about Psychological Traps

In part 2 of this book, we've explored several important psychological traps: rumination, avoidance, emotion-driven behavior, and self-criticism. Although each trap had its own chapter, you may have realized by now that they're not completely separate. We can easily fall into several traps in quick succession. Unpleasant thoughts and feelings arise and we try to avoid or suppress them. This works temporarily, but in time the thoughts and feelings get worse. Then we ruminate about our problems, hoping to find a more effective way of getting rid of them, but rumination intensifies the difficulties. We get so upset that we lash out, or we overindulge in food, alcohol, shopping, or other distractions. Then we criticize ourselves for our behavior, calling ourselves weak, immature, stupid, and worse. This makes us feel even more stressed, anxious, and unhappy. We try to suppress or avoid these feelings or the situations that bring them on, and the vicious cycle repeats.

Why Are These Traps So Difficult to Avoid?

There are several reasons why it's very difficult to stay out of these traps.

Each Trap Is an Unhelpful Version of a Useful Strategy

When they're constructive, persistent thinking, avoidance of difficulties, emotion-driven behavior, and self-criticism help us learn, solve problems, and survive. Unfortunately, each has an unhelpful version that isn't constructive, but a trap. Unless we're paying very close attention to our behavior and its consequences, it can be hard to tell the difference between the helpful and unhelpful versions of these strategies. A summary is provided in the following table.

Useful strategy	Unhelpful version of strategy
Persistent thinking	**Rumination**
Problem solving	Depressive rumination
Planning	Angry rumination
Reflection	Worrying
Avoiding true dangers in the external world	**Avoiding or suppressing internal experiences**
Harmful objects	Thoughts, memories, and images
Dangerous situations	Emotions and sensations
Risky activities	Temptations and urges
Constructive emotion-driven behavior	**Harmful emotion-driven behavior**
Protection of self or others (fear)	Temper outbursts or lashing out at others
Correction of injustices (anger)	Overeating
Creative achievements (passion)	Misuse of alcohol or drugs
Care for others (love)	Excessive shopping or other distractions
Constructive self-criticism	**Harmful self-criticism**
Specific	Vague
Considerate	Demeaning
Balanced	Unbalanced

The Behaviors That Lead Us into the Traps Seem Reasonable on the Surface

In the short term, when we use the unhealthy versions of avoidance or emotion-driven behavior, we feel better. Likewise, rumination can make it seem that we're doing something useful, like working on a problem, and harsh self-criticism may seem to offer the hope of preventing laziness. As a result, we feel encouraged to continue using these strategies.

These Behaviors Create Vicious Cycles in the Long Term

Over time, these traps intensify the problems we're trying to solve. This makes us think we need to try harder. But using the same strategies with increased effort gets us even more stuck in the traps. It's difficult to see this pattern unless we're mindfully observing our experiences.

Looking Ahead

Having read this far, you've learned a huge amount about how psychological traps work in general. If you've completed the self-tests and worksheets, you have important new insights about how the four traps discussed here are affecting you. If you've practiced the exercises, you've made an excellent start on learning the mindfulness skills that will help you out of these traps.

Getting this far in the book is like climbing a mountain up to base camp. Take a moment to rest and congratulate yourself on your progress. If you're not entirely confident that you've adapted to the altitude, go back and reread previous chapters, use the worksheets, and practice the exercises a few more times before moving on.

When you're ready to forge ahead, the rest of this book provides detailed descriptions of numerous additional exercises, with instructions on how to practice them and apply them to your life. First, however, let's recall the Passengers on the Bus metaphor from chapter 4. The bus is your life, and you're trying to drive it in the direction you want to go. Falling into psychological traps makes you steer your bus off course. Struggling with stress, anxiety, and unhappiness causes you to lose sight of your chosen directions. Do you know where you want to drive your bus? The next chapter will help you clarify your thoughts on this important question.

Chapter Summary

- Unconstructive self-criticism is vague, inconsiderate, judgmental, and unbalanced.

- We often criticize ourselves harshly because we think doing so is necessary to prevent mistakes and laziness and to maintain our self-discipline. In reality, unconstructive self-criticism triggers negative emotions, reduces motivation and energy, and encourages procrastination and avoidance. It can lead to depression, anxiety, stress, and unhealthy behavior.

- Mindfulness of our self-critical thoughts helps us see these patterns. It teaches us to recognize harshly self-critical thoughts and allow them to pass through the mind without getting caught up in them or believing everything they say.

- If we've made mistakes or our behavior needs improvement, mindfulness helps us respond wisely to the situation.

PART 3

Mindfulness Skills

CHAPTER 7

Values and Goals

Our souls are hungry for meaning, for the sense that we have
figured out how to live so that our lives matter.

—Harold Kushner

Ryan is a high school science teacher. His parents work in the medical field and wanted him to become a doctor. As a teenager and young adult, Ryan was unsure of what he wanted from life. At his parents' urging, he pursued premedical studies in college. He liked the science classes, worked hard, and earned excellent grades. In his free time, he volunteered as a tutor for a high school in a low-income neighborhood. He enjoyed helping the students with their homework and supporting them in the struggles of adolescence. He decided that as a doctor, he would specialize in adolescent medicine.

In his senior year, Ryan was accepted into medical school. At this point, to his surprise, he began to feel depressed. The prospect of years of medical training was exhausting. Ryan saw a psychologist at the student health center, who encouraged him to join a mindfulness group, where he learned to observe his thoughts, feelings, and emotional reactions in a nonjudgmental and open-minded way. In time, he realized that his motivation to succeed in premedical studies was based on a desire for approval from his parents and praise and respect from his classmates and teachers. He doubted whether these rewards could sustain him through the rigors of medical school. He loved teenagers and wanted to make a career of working with them. He also loved science. But he was much more interested in education than in medicine.

Ryan met with an advisor to discuss becoming a high school science teacher. He told his parents that he had decided not to go to medical school and was pursuing a teaching degree. They were disappointed and puzzled. Why would he give up a prestigious and lucrative career? Ryan acknowledged that he would earn less money, but he felt lighter and happier than he had in a long time. He had found a purpose that was truly his own.

Building a Meaningful Life

Where do you want to drive your bus? What do you really care about, deep down? What would you like to be remembered for? What path are you on? Practicing mindfulness can help you answer these questions and build a life that feels meaningful, satisfying, and rich.

Happiness

Many people say that happiness is their primary goal in life. But what do we mean by "happiness"? One definition equates happiness with pleasure or feeling good (Waterman 1993). According to this view, a happy person experiences mostly positive emotions and relatively little pain. Another definition emphasizes the satisfaction that comes from being true to oneself, finding one's inner strengths, and using them in ways that give meaning and direction to life, even when doing so is difficult and stressful (Peterson, Park, and Seligman 2005).

Research shows that both ways of defining happiness are useful (Ryan and Deci 2001). People who have more positive emotions report higher levels of overall satisfaction with life. In fact, studies show that positive emotions are more than merely enjoyable; they also motivate and energize us for healthy behavior (Fredrickson 2001). Just as fear creates the urge to escape and anger the urge to attack, feelings like love, joy, contentment, interest, and pride create urges to explore the environment, take in new information, savor the present moment, share feelings with others, play, be creative, and plan future achievements. These behaviors help us build social bonds, cultivate new skills, and develop long-term goals and purposes. All of this contributes to happiness and well-being.

Does this mean you should simply pursue whatever feels best in the moment? Probably not. Pursuit of positive feelings for their own sake can become a trap. For example, some drugs create intensely positive feelings, but regular use can ruin careers and relationships. TV, computer games, and surfing the Web can be quite enjoyable, even almost addictive, without contributing to quality of life in a meaningful way. There's nothing wrong with TV and computer games in moderation. But if you're thinking seriously about where to drive your bus, you'll find more satisfaction by identifying your most important values and goals and using them to guide your behavior.

Values and Goals

The word "values" has many meanings. In the context of mindfulness and mental health, your values are your personal choices about what matters most to you in life. They're the important principles that guide your actions (Hayes 2005). Here are some examples of values:

- Being a kind and caring friend.

- Being a loving and supportive parent.

- Being competent, productive, helpful, or creative in your work.

- Contributing to your community or other worthy causes.

- Taking good care of your health.

Values are like compass points: they provide a direction but not a final destination. Values-consistent behavior is a journey that never ends. Being a supportive friend, for example, is a lifelong process.

To live in a values-consistent way, it's helpful to set specific, realistic goals. Goals are like milestones along the journey. If you value being competent and helpful in your work, you might set goals for learning a new software program, adopting it for your daily tasks, and teaching your coworkers to use it. Each goal can be completed and crossed off your to-do list, but the underlying values of competence and helpfulness continue. New goals will arise that reflect them.

Values help us choose goals that feel worthwhile. They also make it easier to persist when the pursuit of long-term goals isn't going well. If you're writing a book, running a business, raising a child, or learning to swim, you'll experience frustration, disappointment, pain, and anxiety along the way. Your underlying values (such as creativity, contributing to the community, caring for others, or challenging yourself) provide the energy to persevere and the wisdom to choose a new goal if a previous one becomes unattainable.

* *Don's Story* *

Don is an avid runner who values physical fitness, his relationship with his father, and contributing to worthy causes. When his father was diagnosed with leukemia, Don signed up with an organization that raises money for cancer research by training amateur athletes to run marathons. Don requested donations from his friends, colleagues, and acquaintances; attended frequent coaching sessions; and gradually increased his running speed and distance. After a few months of training, he injured an ankle and had to withdraw from the marathon. Although terribly disappointed, he took comfort in having already raised several hundred dollars for cancer research. He continued to serve the organization by helping coordinate its annual one-mile walk—another fundraising event.

Don's situation illustrates several important points. His goals—to run the marathon and raise money for cancer research in honor of his father—were consistent with his values and realistic, though ambitious. Training for a marathon and asking people for money can be uncomfortable. Don persevered because of the importance of the values these behaviors served. When the marathon became impossible, his values helped him find a new goal that was satisfying in a different way.

Traps We Fall into When Pursuing Values and Goals

Many studies have confirmed that people who consistently work toward valued goals feel happier, more fulfilled, and more satisfied with their lives. But it's important to choose our values and goals carefully, because we can fall into traps while pursuing them.

Trap 1: Adopting Other Peoples' Values and Goals

Research shows that autonomy is a basic psychological need and contributes to happiness and well-being (Ryan and Deci 2000). Autonomy is the ability to make your own decisions about how to think and behave, rather than relying excessively on others' opinions or approval. Autonomous people resist social pressures that are inconsistent with their inner standards or preferences. People who pursue freely chosen goals that they genuinely value make better progress and feel happier than people whose goals are based on others' wishes and the avoidance of disapproval (Sheldon and Elliott 1999).

The desire to avoid disapproval is completely understandable. Disapproval makes us feel anxious, resentful, and insecure. However, avoiding such feelings is often a trap that makes matters worse in the long run. Before realizing that he wanted to be a science teacher, Ryan had fallen into this trap. He was motivated primarily by the approval of others. To find his own values and goals, he had to recognize his inner strengths and interests: teaching, science, and working with teenagers. Then he had to pursue these interests despite others' opinions.

Trap 2: Focusing on What We'd Like to Avoid

Sometimes people state their values in terms of what they'd like to avoid, rather than what they want to pursue. For example, they might say their primary goal is to never be depressed again; to never have another panic attack; to never get drunk, overeat, or say the wrong thing; or to never again be as badly hurt, disappointed, or embarrassed as they have been. Unfortunately, it's impossible to live a rewarding life without risking emotional and physical pain. When people try to avoid anything that might hurt, their lives become severely constricted (Harris 2008). Their happiness and vitality dry up. This causes its own type of pain: dissatisfaction, boredom, and regret about lost opportunities.

When thinking about what you really want from life, ask yourself, *Is this value or goal focused on avoiding something?* If the answer is yes, try stating your value or goal in a different way. Instead of "My goal is to never feel depressed again," consider, "I value caring for my mind and body so that I can face life's challenges more effectively." Think about what you'd do if you were less susceptible to depression. Spend more time with your family? Work on your career? Develop new skills? Volunteer for a worthy cause? Enjoy your leisure time? State these as your values, and set goals that are consistent with them.

Trap 3: Expecting the Road to Always Be Clear, Straight, and Enjoyable

It's easy to assume that once you've found your true path, you'll always enjoy traveling along it. This is a fallacy. While often deeply rewarding, values-consistent behavior can be scary, painful, annoying, confusing, or dull (Hayes 2005). We encounter obstacles, take wrong turns, and even crash occasionally. Ryan found some of his education classes exciting and inspiring, but others were frustrating and tedious. He failed a required foreign language class on his first attempt and barely passed the second time. He had to remind himself repeatedly that these classes were necessary to realize his long-term plans.

Ryan has now taught science in a poverty-stricken, inner-city high school for several years. He's warm, accepting, and generous with his time, providing extra help with academic and personal problems. He's made a huge difference in the lives of many of his students and finds this deeply satisfying. Despite his best efforts, a few of his students have dropped out of school and are now unemployed, abusing drugs and alcohol, or committing crimes. Ryan feels a great sense of failure and regret about these students. Occasionally, he's tempted to find a job with less stress and disappointment. Most of the time, however, he realizes that he genuinely values working with disadvantaged teenagers, even if he's unsuccessful in some cases. He finds meaning and purpose in doing the best he can.

Identifying Your Values and Goals

If identifying your values feels daunting, it may help to consider the types of values that provide meaning and satisfaction to others, even if you don't share all of them. The following domains of life are commonly considered by people who are thinking seriously about what matters most to them (Wilson and DuFrene 2008).

Relationships

Most people feel a strong need for personal connections and wouldn't be happy or satisfied without trusting and supportive relationships (Ryan, Huta, and Deci 2008). The specific nature of the desired relationships varies considerably. For many people, a marital or long-term relationship with a partner is very important; others enjoy the single life. Many people wish to raise children; others prefer to remain childless. Extroverted people enjoy a large circle of friends and an active social life; introverts prefer a small number of friends seen less often. Some people like to work closely with colleagues or coworkers; others prefer to work more independently.

To identify your values in the domain of relationships, think beyond the relationships you'd like to have. Getting married and having children are goals, rather than values. The underlying question is how you'd like to *be* in these relationships. Loving, attentive, and kind? Open, honest, and communicative? Assertive, independent, and strong?

Work

Work is a broad domain that includes education and household management, in addition to a job or career. Most people are happier if they have knowledge, skills, and competencies and can use them to solve problems and accomplish worthwhile tasks (Ryff and Keyes 1995). Work, school, and household management provide rich opportunities for skillful, competent behavior. Whether your work is complex or straightforward, interesting or dull, pleasant or unpleasant, it can also provide a sense of purpose—a way to contribute to something that matters to you.

To identify your values in this domain, think beyond the jobs you'd like to have. Getting a job is a goal. The underlying question is what matters to you about doing the work. What types of contributions would you like to make? What sort of employee, student, or household manager would you like to be? Productive, competent, or dependable? A good problem solver? A supportive colleague? A helpful service provider? An innovator?

Community Involvement

The domain of community involvement includes contributing to causes or organizations that are consistent with your ideals. Depending on what you value, you might volunteer with an animal welfare group, an environmental organization, a political campaign, a homeless shelter, or a literacy program. The list of possibilities is virtually endless. What kinds of contributions would you like to make?

Self-Care, Personal Growth, Recreation, and Leisure Activity

Many people value their physical and mental health, both for their own sake and because good health makes it easier to participate in other domains of life. Exercise, sleep, and a healthful diet nurture our bodies and minds. Leisure activities reduce stress and reenergize us for important work. Some people value religion or spirituality as a way of caring for themselves and others or expanding their understanding of life. Some find value in appreciating beauty through nature and the arts and choose to spend time outdoors, play an instrument or sing, or attend concerts, plays, or art exhibits.

Viewing Valued Domains Flexibly

Many valued activities fall into more than one category. Parenting is a relationship, but it also requires numerous skills and competencies, like changing diapers, helping with homework, and communicating with teenagers. Volunteering with community organizations may be a way of developing friendships and building skills as well as contributing to worthy causes. Church involvement can be a form of self-care or personal growth, a way to make friends, and a way to help others.

What About Wealth and Fame?

When asked what they most want from life, some people think of being rich, famous, or attractive. Psychologists call these extrinsic goals because they depend on the judgments, attitudes, or behavior of other people (Kasser and Ryan 2001). Wealth depends on others paying you a salary, leaving you an inheritance, or buying something that you sell. Fame and attractiveness depend on the recognition and admiration of others.

There's nothing wrong with aspiring to be rich, famous, or attractive, or with enjoying these attributes if you have them. However, research shows that people who emphasize these goals are less happy and satisfied with their lives than people who focus on intrinsic values, such as relationships, health, meaningful work, and community involvement. If extrinsic goals are important to you, look for underlying values by asking what they make possible. For example, wealth may allow you to provide financial security for yourself and your family or contribute to causes you believe in. In this case, acquiring wealth is a goal, whereas caring for yourself, your family, and your community are values.

* *Samantha's Story* *

Samantha is a freelance writer in her midthirties. She's interested in the environment and writes articles for newspapers and magazines about climate change, wildlife conservation, and ecotourism. She has a happy and stable relationship with her boyfriend, but she's unsure whether she wants to get married and is confident that she doesn't want children. She loves animals, has two dogs, and volunteers with her local humane society. She lives in a small, economical house so that she can afford to travel. She visits other countries once or twice a year to learn about environmental issues and volunteer for conservation projects and at wildlife sanctuaries. She writes about her experiences in her articles.

Samantha has an uneasy relationship with her parents. They wish she would marry her boyfriend, start a family before it's too late, and join their business—a successful paint and wallpaper shop. They'd like her to take over the shop when they retire in five years. Samantha isn't interested in doing so, but she hasn't discussed this with her parents and helps in the shop whenever an employee is ill or away. She would prefer to limit her time there to focus on her writing and travel, but she hasn't found a way to say no to her parents' frequent requests. She's their only child, and she fears disappointing them.

EXERCISE: Clarifying Your Values

The following worksheet (inspired by Hayes 2005) will help you think about your most important values. First you'll find an example filled out by Samantha. It's followed by a blank version for your own use. Make several copies so you can continue to clarify your values over time. As you complete the worksheet, remember these points:

- If you're thinking of something that can be completed, obtained, or checked off a list (such as getting a master's degree), that's a goal, not a value. Write down the value that the goal will serve, such as "developing my professional skills."

- If you're thinking of a way you'd like to feel (for example, confident), remember that feelings aren't completely under your control and that values-consistent behavior sometimes feels unpleasant. What would you be doing if you felt more confident? Inviting people over for dinner? Sharing your poetry with others? If so, your values might be "cultivating relationships" or "sharing the fruits of my creativity."

- If you're uncertain of your values in some domains, leave them blank for now. Start paying attention to how you feel in various situations within those domains, and your values may become clearer.

Some domains may be unimportant to you. Not everyone values everything. But consider whether you're fooling yourself because you find certain areas painful and would rather not think about them. Do you really value spending your weekends alone, or are you avoiding the discomfort of finding ways to socialize?

- Values can appear to conflict with each other, usually because of the time required to pursue them. If you value working hard at your job and spending time with your children, you may find it difficult to do both to your satisfaction. Often there's no easy solution to this problem and you have to find a compromise.

- Reflecting on values can be painful. You may realize that your behavior hasn't been consistent with your true priorities. Feelings of disappointment, resentment, and sadness may arise, along with self-critical, pessimistic, and hopeless thoughts (*I'll only be disappointed, I'll never achieve my goals*, and so on). These thoughts and feelings are natural. They're passengers on your bus. You don't have to let them control your behavior. Keep in mind that values-consistent behavior can start anytime, regardless of what you've been doing and despite any difficult thoughts and feelings that may be present.

- There are no right or wrong answers.

WORKSHEET: Describing Your Values

Your name: *Samantha*

In this domain…	I value…
Spouse or partner	*Being open and honest with my boyfriend.*
Parenting	*Not applicable. I don't plan to have children.*
Other family	*Being assertive with my parents and standing up for myself. Also being loving, caring, and respectful.*
Friends	*Feeling connected. Sharing about myself in addition to listening to others.*
Work	*Spending my time on meaningful projects, being productive, and enjoying my work.*
Education and training	*Attending occasional writing workshops and seminars about the environment and climate change. Learning while traveling.*
Household management	*Being clean and organized enough to be productive and comfortable. Avoiding perfectionism about appearance and neatness.*
Community involvement	*Volunteering with the humane society (helping stray cats and dogs), teaching an occasional writing class, and volunteering while traveling.*
Self-care	*Eating, sleeping, and exercising to be healthy and strong.*
Personal growth	*Traveling to other countries to work on environmental projects.*
Recreation and leisure	*Taking the dogs on walks, going to movies with my boyfriend, seeing friends.*
Spirituality	*I'm not very religious, but travel helps me feel in touch with the larger world and connected with others in different cultures.*
Appreciation of beauty	*Traveling (mostly for scenery and wildlife), doing photography and painting, and walking the dogs in the arboretum.*
Other	*Staying in touch with people I meet on my travels. Taking care of my dogs.*

WORKSHEET: Describing Your Values

Your name: _____

In this domain...	I value...
Spouse or partner	
Parenting	
Other family	
Friends	
Work	
Education and training	
Household management	
Community involvement	
Self-care	
Personal growth	
Recreation and leisure	
Spirituality	
Appreciation of beauty	
Other	

EXERCISE: Assessing How Values Consistent Your Behavior Is

The next worksheet (inspired by Wilson and DuFrene 2008) provides a way to examine whether your behavior is consistent with what matters most to you. For each domain, use a scale from 1 to 10 to rate the following three aspects of your values and behavior.

Importance: How important are your values in this domain at this point in your life?

1	2	3	4	5	6	7	8	9	10

Not at all important   Moderately important   Extremely important

Action: How active have you been within this domain in the last few weeks?

1	2	3	4	5	6	7	8	9	10

Not at all active   Moderately active   Extremely active

Satisfaction with action: How satisfied are you with your recent action in this area?

1	2	3	4	5	6	7	8	9	10

Not at all satisfied   Moderately satisfied   Extremely satisfied

Confronting discrepancies between your values and your behavior can be uncomfortable, but it illuminates priorities and helps you set goals for being true to them. First you'll find an example filled out by Samantha, then a blank worksheet for your own use. Again, make copies of the worksheet so you can continue to assess how well your behavior aligns with your values over the weeks and months to come.

WORKSHEET: Rating Your Values and Behavior

Your name: *Samantha*

Domain	Importance (1–10)	Action (1–10)	Satisfaction with action (1–10)	Notes
Spouse or partner	9	7	5	*Arguing with my boyfriend about the time I spend in my parents' shop.*
Parenting	1	1	10	*Not an issue.*
Other family	8	4	4	*My parents ask me to work in the shop a lot. I give in too much.*
Friends	9	8	8	*Doing well here. (My friends also think I should assert myself with my parents.)*
Work	9	5	2	*Too little time writing, too much in my parents' shop.*
Education and training	5	4	9	*Writing workshop coming up this summer.*

Household management	5	3	9	No major concerns here.
Community involvement	7	6	9	Volunteering with the humane society and teaching at the writing center.
Self-care	6	6	8	No major concerns here.
Personal growth	8	5	2	Agreed to work in the shop during an employee's maternity leave and had to cancel a wildlife trip.
Recreation and leisure	7	5	6	Doing okay here.
Spirituality	5	5	4	Wildlife trips are spiritual for me, but I canceled one to help in the shop.
Appreciation of beauty	7	5	5	Enjoying walking the dogs, but I regret missing the wildlife trip.
Other: dogs, contact with distant friends	9	8	8	Doing well here.

WORKSHEET: Rating Your Values and Behavior

Your name: _____

Domain	Importance (1–10)	Action (1–10)	Satisfaction with action (1–10)	Notes
Spouse or partner				
Parenting				
Other family				
Friends				
Work				
Education and training				

Household management	Community involvement	Self-care	Personal growth	Recreation and leisure	Spirituality	Appreciation of beauty	Other:

* Samantha's Story Continued *

Samantha's worksheet shows that her behavior is consistent with her values in many domains. However, she's dissatisfied with her response to her parents' requests for help in the shop and their repeated suggestions that she take over the shop when they retire. She regrets having agreed to work full-time for three months while an employee is on maternity leave and wishes she'd been more assertive about saying no. This issue is affecting her relationship with her boyfriend, who urges her to talk more openly with her parents about it. While working in the shop full-time, she's finding it difficult to complete writing assignments and had to cancel a weeklong stay at a wildlife sanctuary in Costa Rica.

Discrepancies between values and behavior indicate that it's important to set goals for change. Samantha realized that she needed to have a serious talk with her parents about her goals for the future and her involvement in their shop. Although nervous about it, she explained herself as lovingly and respectfully as she could. She offered to help them find a new employee and explore options for selling their business when they're ready to retire. They were sad and disappointed but not surprised. They said they supported Samantha in pursuing her values and goals and agreed not to ask her to work in the shop as often.

How Mindfulness Helps with Values and Goals

Practicing mindfulness helps with values and goals in several important ways. It enables us to recognize our values and persist in values-consistent behavior when it's difficult and stressful to do so. It also helps us find a balance between working for the future and living in the present.

Recognizing Your Values

If you've been suffering from anxiety, depression, anger, guilt, or other difficulties, you may think that nothing really matters to you except feeling better. This is completely understandable. Stress and unhappiness often demand most of our attention. However, we all have values that go beyond feeling better, even if we're not fully aware of them. If you're not sure what you truly care about, practicing mindfulness will help you recognize your values. If you pay attention to your daily experiences in an open-minded, friendly, and curious way, you'll begin to notice things. Small moments of meaning and satisfaction will arise, perhaps when you're talking with someone, working on a particular problem or task, or reading about something. These moments are important indicators of what matters most to you.

Practicing mindfulness will also help you observe when you're acting in accordance with other people's standards and values rather than your own. You may begin to notice feelings of discomfort about it. It's important to be open to these moments without judging yourself harshly. Think about what you'd like to be doing instead, and set goals for small changes in your behavior that will lead you in that direction. Over time, your self-understanding and autonomy will increase.

Persisting with Values-Consistent Behavior

Even when we know what we'd like to do and why it's important to do it, unpleasant emotions and thoughts such as *I'll never succeed*, *This is a waste of time*, or *People will disapprove* can undermine our motivation. Instead of taking constructive action, we fall into the traps discussed in part 2 of this book. We try to avoid the unpleasant thoughts and feelings or the situations that bring them up. We ruminate about our problems, which makes it harder to solve them. We behave impulsively in ways we later regret. We criticize ourselves, which creates more negative emotions and reduces our motivation to act.

Research shows that mindfulness helps us persist with difficult or stressful tasks. In one study, students completed a mindfulness questionnaire and then were asked to solve some difficult scrambled word puzzles. Those who were generally more mindful (according to the questionnaire) persisted longer in trying to solve the puzzles (Evans, Baer, and Segerstrom 2009). In another study, people with emotional problems who were in an angry mood were asked either to ruminate about their mood or to practice mindfulness for a few minutes. Then they worked on a stressful computerized math task. Those who practiced mindfulness felt less angry afterward and persisted much longer in working on the stressful task (Sauer and Baer 2012).

Studies like these are a little artificial—for most people, solving arithmetic problems and word puzzles isn't an important value in life. Even so, these studies suggest that mindfulness increases goal-directed behavior.

Appreciating the Journey

Imagine that you have a young child. One day, to your surprise, a wizard appears at your door. "I can grant you one wish," he says. "What is your deepest desire for the future?"

"I want my child to become a happy, healthy, and independent adult," you reply.

"Done!" says the wizard, waving his wand. Your child is instantly transformed into a cheerful thirty-year-old with a lovely family, a rewarding career, and a nice house a few miles away.

Is this what you wanted? Probably not. It has deprived you of the chance to live in the present with your child and watch him or her grow into adulthood. Most people who value caring for a child want to take this journey, even if it's scary and painful at times and doesn't turn out exactly as they'd imagined. They want the shared experiences, the memories, and the intimate knowledge of how their child developed over the years. They want the sense of accomplishment that long-term engagement brings.

Your goals for the future guide your behavior in the present, but the real goal is to participate in the journey. Practicing mindfulness helps you appreciate the countless moments that make up the journey. When it's joyful, fascinating, peaceful, or exciting, you fully feel it. When it's scary, painful, infuriating, or dull, you feel that too. At difficult moments you may wish for the wizard to fast-forward you to your goal. This is entirely understandable. If no wizard appears, mindful observation of the present moment helps you understand what's happening and choose values-consistent behavior. It reminds you of the enduring sense of well-being that comes from doing the best you can with something you care about, even when this is stressful.

Mindfulness keeps you from missing large chunks of your life. In the following chapters, we'll explore in detail the nature of mindfulness and how to cultivate it by practicing various skills and exercises. At the heart of mindfulness is observation: seeing what's happening in the present moment. In the next chapter, we'll consider how to develop mindful observation skills.

Chapter Summary

- Most people are happier and find life more satisfying if they recognize what matters most to them and behave consistently with their values and goals.

- Although pursuing our deepest values and goals can be very rewarding, it's also stressful and uncomfortable at times. Difficult thoughts and feelings may arise when we're engaged in important pursuits.

- Mindfulness helps us identify our values and goals, persist when pursuing them is unpleasant or even painful, and appreciate the journey.

CHAPTER 8

Mindful Observation

Mindfulness means paying attention in a particular way: on
purpose, in the present moment, and nonjudgmentally.

—Jon Kabat-Zinn

At any moment in time, we have many choices about where to focus our attention. The outer world is full of sights and sounds. The inner world is full of thoughts and feelings. When we're mindful, we notice more of them.

Mindful observation has several key characteristics:

- **We can choose what to pay attention to.** Imagine that you're in a classroom listening to a lecture. You hear a bird singing through an open window. For a moment, your attention is drawn to the bird. If you're being mindful, you'll notice that your attention has shifted. If you choose, you can redirect it to the lecture.

- **Mindful observation focuses on the present.** Imagine that you're confused by the lecture. You feel discouraged and frustrated. Then you start thinking, *I'm such an idiot. I'll never understand this. I'll fail this course, and then I won't be able to get the kind of job I want. That will be terrible.* If you're being mindful, you'll realize that you've become absorbed in an imagined future. If you choose, you can come back to the present.

- **Mindful observation is nonjudgmental.** If you're being mindful while sitting in the classroom, you'll recognize that *I'm an idiot* and *That will be terrible* are judgmental thoughts. You'll remind yourself to let go of judging and simply observe.

Mindful observation helps you see what's actually happening in the moment. If your present situation is difficult and stressful, observing it mindfully will help you make wiser decisions about what to do. If your situation is pleasant and enjoyable, you'll appreciate it more. Mindful observation is the key to escaping the psychological traps described in part 2 of the book: rumination, avoidance, emotion-driven behavior, and self-criticism. People who are mindful of the present moment, whether it's pleasant, unpleasant, or neutral, are less susceptible to depression, anxiety, stress, anger, overeating, alcohol abuse, and many other problems (Keng, Smoski, and Robins 2011). They're also happier, more satisfied with life, better able to meet daily demands, and more autonomous and purposeful (Baer et al. 2008; Brown and Ryan 2003).

Notice that being mindful doesn't mean you never get distracted, never get absorbed in the future or the past, or never have judgmental thoughts. These experiences are common and normal, even for people who have practiced mindfulness for many years. Mindful observation means that when these things occur, you notice them without judging yourself. Then you can return your attention to what's happening in the present if you choose.

In this chapter, we'll focus on exercises that cultivate mindful observation skills. First, let's consider an example of nonmindful observation.

* Jill's Story *

Jill is twenty-two years old. She works in a clothing store and also sells her pottery at craft fairs. She's been frightened of thunderstorms since she was five, when a storm came up suddenly while she was in a park with her parents. As they ran to their car, an old tree was struck by lightning and fell onto the playground, knocking over the swings where Jill had been playing moments before.

Ever since, Jill has been anxious about stormy weather. Even gentle rain scares her because she fears that a storm might develop. If she's at home, she stays in her basement when it rains. If she's anywhere else when the rain begins, she races home as quickly as possible, driving dangerously fast and disregarding traffic lights and stop signs. When storms are predicted, she cancels appointments and social activities. She's especially concerned about her attendance at craft fairs. If the weather looks threatening, she leaves early or doesn't show up at all.

Much of the time, Jill is extremely observant of the weather. She notices the shapes and sizes of the clouds, the colors of the sky, the temperature and humidity of the air, and the speed and direction of the wind. But this isn't mindful observation. It's unmindful in several ways:

- **Jill's attention is controlled by the weather.** When she's worried about storms, Jill has trouble thinking of anything else. At work, she gets little done because she's constantly looking out the window, checking the forecast on the computer in the back office, and thinking of excuses to leave early. At craft fairs, she finds it hard to converse with customers because she's preoccupied with getting home.

- **She tries to escape rather than staying present.** Jill has intense reactions to threatening weather. Her heart pounds. She feels sweaty, breathless, and shaky. Rather than mindfully observing storms and her reactions to them, Jill gets absorbed in thoughts about getting home as fast as possible. Her desire to escape is understandable, because intense anxiety is very unpleasant. But her behavior is making matters worse.

- **She's judgmental.** Jill judges the weather as good or bad based solely on how it makes her feel. She judges her reactions as good (staying calm) or bad (feeling anxious). She judges herself as stupid, crazy, and weak for getting upset about conditions that are usually harmless. This makes her more upset and less able to think clearly.

Jill has fallen into all of the psychological traps described in earlier chapters. She ruminates about the weather and how she'll cope with it. She avoids activities and responsibilities when the weather seems threatening. Her frantic driving during storms is emotion-driven behavior. She criticizes herself harshly for her feelings, thoughts, and actions.

However, Jill is working on the mindful observation skills described in this chapter. With practice, she'll learn to observe the weather in a mindful way. She'll begin to appreciate the interesting sights, sounds, scents, and sensations it creates. When necessary, she'll take reasonable precautions during rainy weather, such as closing windows and bringing her cat indoors. She'll learn to stay present with her emotional reactions, noticing them as they happen without taking drastic steps to escape them. She'll see that the sensations of anxiety are unpleasant but not dangerous, that they pass in time, and that she can behave constructively even while feeling anxious. In time, the intensity of her fear will decrease. Even when she's scared, she'll be able to control her behavior.

Mindful Observation: Introductory Exercises

Mindful observation is easier when the present moment is pleasant or neutral than when it's scary, painful, and stressful. The following exercises (inspired by practices described in Linehan 1993b and Segal, Williams, and Teasdale 2013) will help you practice mindful observation of ordinary, nonthreatening experiences. Some of these exercises were introduced in chapter 2. Here you'll have a chance to refine your skills. Later in this chapter, we'll consider how to apply these skills to more difficult situations.

EXERCISE: Hand on a Surface

Put one of your hands on a nearby surface, such as a table, a desk, or the arm of a chair. Observe the sensations in your hand as it rests on this surface. Take a few moments to notice each of your fingers, your thumb, the back of your hand, and your palm. Notice the feel of the air on your skin and the points of contact with the surface. Continue for about a minute. Experiment with keeping your eyes open or closed—either way is fine.

Your mind will wander at some point. When you realize that you're thinking of something else, gently bring your attention back to the sensations in your hand. If you criticize yourself for letting your mind wander, remember that it's normal; everyone's mind wanders. See if you can let go of the criticism and return to observing the sensations in your hand with an attitude of interest and curiosity.

EXERCISE: Hand on Your Head

Put one hand on top of your head. Observe the sensations for a minute or so. See if you can observe the sensations in both your hand and your head. Notice texture, temperature, points of contact, and so on. Then shift your attention to your arm as it works to keep your hand on your head. Notice what you feel in your arm. If you start thinking, analyzing, or judging—for example, *My hair is so thin*, *This is silly*, or *Why does my shoulder ache?*—notice that these are thoughts. As best you can, and without criticizing, return your attention to observing the sensations in your hand, head, or arm.

EXERCISE: Mindful Observation of Sounds

Turn your attention to any sounds you can hear. Listen closely for a minute or two. Be open to sounds, whatever their source. Observe the qualities of the sounds. How long do they last? Are they loud or soft? Is the pitch high or low? Also notice periods of silence between sounds. If you notice a tendency to think about or analyze the sounds—for example, *That's a bird*, *That's the fridge humming*, or *What could be making that sound?*—gently redirect your attention to hearing the sounds.

Do you feel an urge to do something, such as investigate what's making the sound? If so, notice the urge and decide mindfully whether to act on it. Then return your attention to observing the sounds. When your mind wanders off, gently bring it back to sounds.

EXERCISE: Mindful Observation of Sights

Turn your attention to whatever you see around you. Observe the colors, shapes, textures, or movements of what you see. Notice any tendency to label it—for example, *That's a light switch*, *That's a clock*, or *I see a tree through the window*. If possible, allow the labeling to fade away and focus on the experience of seeing. Look closely. Notice if you judge what you see as good or bad, pretty or ugly, desirable or undesirable. If possible, let go of the judgments and focus on seeing what's actually there.

If you have thoughts—for example, *It's getting late*, *I should make dinner*, or *That window really needs washing*—notice that these are thoughts and return your attention to seeing. If you feel an emotion, such as delight when seeing a bird or disgust when seeing an insect, observe that for a moment, allow the emotion to be as it is, and then return your attention to seeing.

Mindful Observation of Daily Activities

Mindful observation can be practiced with many things that we experience in daily life. Janet, a new mother, practiced mindful observation of feeding her baby and wrote a short description of what she noticed:

> My husband and I are both full-time students, and we're always worrying about getting our work done and having enough money. We have a three-month-old daughter, Abby. Whenever I'm away from Abby, I worry about whether she's okay and feel guilty about the time I spend apart from her. But then when I'm with her, I worry about all the work I have to do.
>
> This week I decided to practice mindful observation while feeding Abby. At first I couldn't stop obsessing about how far behind I am in my studies and the money we had to spend when our roof was leaking last week. But one day I was able to gradually bring my attention to the feeding experience, and

I started noticing some amazing things: the feeling of the gentle soft touch of Abby's tiny hand on my stomach, the way her long eyelashes curve up at the very tips, the narrow blue vein that runs from her ear to the back of her skull, the way her breathing changed and her body relaxed as she drifted off to sleep. All of these things might have escaped my attention had I been thinking of other things.

I found that my anxiety about being away from her most of the day was quickly replaced by a calm, happy, peaceful feeling. I sat with her for quite a while after she fell asleep, enjoying the experience of mindfully observing her. When thoughts about work and money came up, I was able to let them pass and just observe Abby.

For Janet, mindful observation while feeding Abby made her more aware of a pleasant activity. Although it was difficult at first to disengage from rumination and worry, once she had turned her attention to Abby, she enjoyed observing her.

Mindful observation is less enjoyable, although very useful, if the present moment is unpleasant and stressful. Wendy, another new mother, also practiced mindful observation with her baby, but her experience was quite different.

My baby Kevin is very emotional. He has crying spells all the time. He seems so desperate, he won't take a bottle, and nothing soothes him. I try so hard to comfort him, but nothing really works except waiting it out. Normally, I struggle really hard to stay calm. I tell myself over and over that if I get upset it only makes things worse. When Kevin finally calms down, I feel drained and exhausted.

One day this week I tried mindful observation. I tried to have a nonjudgmental attitude. I observed Kevin's arms and legs flailing and his little red scowling face. I listened to his cries. I noticed the feeling of his body as I tried holding him different ways and setting him on the bed. I also observed my own thoughts and feelings. The whole experience was really hard. I felt frustrated, worried, sad, and resentful about having such a fussy baby. But I didn't fight with the feelings. I just noticed them and kept observing Kevin. I tried to let things take their natural course and stay present without criticizing.

After Kevin calmed down, I was much less exhausted than usual—I think because I wasn't trying to stifle my feelings. I felt more accepting of having a fussy baby and compassion for both of us having to get through this difficult phase.

For Wendy, mindful observation of Kevin's crying spell was difficult, but it was less stressful than her usual approach of trying to suppress her thoughts and feelings. Mindful observation didn't transform Kevin into an easy baby, but it helped Wendy manage his crying spell and feel compassion for both of them.

Mindful Observation of Breathing

Mindful breathing is an excellent tool for bringing our attention into the present, especially when the moment is difficult and stressful. For centuries, ancient meditation traditions have used mindful breathing to cultivate awareness, insight, and wisdom. There are several key reasons for this:

- Breathing is continuous. You don't have to think back to the last time you breathed or look ahead to future breaths. You're breathing now. If you focus on it, you're in the present. With practice, you can learn to attend to your breathing at any moment you choose.

- Breathing creates sensations and movements: feelings in the nose and throat as the air passes through, and rising and falling or expansion and contraction in the chest or abdomen. Something observable is always happening.

- We don't have to control our breathing; the body breathes on its own. We can use mindful breathing to practice observing something while allowing it to be how it is, rather than trying to change it. Of course, you can change your breathing to some extent if you choose. Singers, actors, swimmers, and players of wind instruments learn to control their breathing in particular ways. But most of the time, breathing is automatic.

- Breathing is sensitive to thoughts, emotions, and physical states. When we feel angry, anxious, tired, interested, or excited, our breathing changes. Depending on the situation, is becomes slower or faster, deeper or shallower, or more regular or uneven. If we consistently observe our breathing, we learn about our internal patterns of thinking, feeling, and reacting. Our self-understanding and insight improve.

Mindful Breathing as a Meditation Exercise

Mindful breathing can be practiced in two ways: as a meditation exercise and in ordinary daily life. It's helpful to practice the meditation exercise first. Sitting in a quiet place with few distractions makes it easier to focus your attention on your breathing. Once you're familiar with awareness of breathing, you can use this skill in daily life. Here are some pointers on mindful breathing meditation before you begin to practice.

How to Sit for Mindful Breathing Meditation

Find a posture that's comfortable, relaxed, and alert. If you choose to sit in a chair, rest your feet comfortably on the floor about hip-width apart. Don't cross your legs. Sit up straight without slouching or slumping, but remember that the spine is naturally curved. Don't try to straighten it completely, as that would create stiffness and tension. If possible, sit a bit forward, without leaning against the back of the chair. Align your head and neck with your spine. Rest your hands on your thighs.

If you prefer to sit cross-legged on the floor, use a meditation cushion or a pillow so that your hips are a little higher than your knees. Gently rest your hands on your thighs or bring them together in your lap, whichever is more comfortable.

Notice Where You Feel the Breath

Next, explore where you can most easily feel the breath going in and out of your body. Some people focus their attention on the nostrils. Often the air feels cooler going into the nostrils and warmer coming out. Others prefer to focus on the chest or abdomen, feeling the sensations of rising and falling, expansion and contraction, or stretching and deflating. Choose one spot to focus on for your first practice; you can try different spots at other times.

How Much to Practice

Start with five minutes, and set a timer so that you don't have to keep track. For the next week, see if you can practice for five minutes every day. Twice a day is even better. If you're willing, increase the time to ten minutes. Eventually, experiment with twenty minutes or even longer.

EXERCISE: Mindful Breathing Meditation

Mindful breathing meditation is taught in many mindfulness programs. Though the details may vary, the basic practice remains the same. (The version here is inspired by Segal, Williams, and Teasdale 2013). Read the following instructions carefully, then put the book aside, set a timer for five minutes, and begin. If you prefer, you can practice with the recording on the website for this book available for download at http://www.newharbin ger.com/29033).

✳ ✳ ✳

To begin, settle into your sitting posture. Gently close your eyes or gaze downward at the floor in front of you.

Focus your attention on the spot you've chosen for observing the breath (nostrils, chest, or abdomen). Observe the sensations and movements as the breath goes in and out of your body. As best you can, follow the breath all the way in and all the way out, letting it go at its own pace and rhythm without trying to change it.

Your mind will wander off. When this happens, notice briefly where it went. You might say to yourself, "Ah, thinking," and then gently return your attention to the breath, observing whether it's going in or out when you come back to it.

Don't try to clear your mind. This isn't the goal. Instead, notice when your mind wanders to thoughts, images, memories, fantasies, plans, or anything else. Then gently turn your attention back to your breath without giving yourself a hard time.

Your mind will continue to drift away. This is normal and is likely to happen repeatedly. Notice if you criticize yourself and see if you can let go of the criticism. Instead, congratulate yourself for coming back to the breath. Practice patience and kindness with yourself. Continue to bring your attention back to the breath, gently and kindly, every time the mind wanders.

When the timer sounds, notice where your mind is. If it's not on the breath, return to the breath for a moment before stopping the exercise.

✳ ✳ ✳

What did you notice? Everyone's experience is different. Some people find this exercise relaxing and enjoyable, others find it difficult and unpleasant, and experiences can vary from day to day. Here are some typical concerns about this practice.

Concerns about how you were breathing. You may have wondered if your breathing was too slow or fast, too shallow or deep, or too uneven. Perhaps you noticed a tendency to control or change your breathing pattern. These are common reactions. However, there's no right or wrong way to breathe while doing this exercise. The goal is only to observe whatever the breath is doing. The next time you practice, see if you can focus on the sensations of the breath without trying to change its pace, depth, or rhythm. Practice friendly interest rather than criticism.

Concerns about how you felt. If you're not accustomed to observing your breath, you may have felt awkward or uncomfortable. Perhaps you felt nervous, impatient, bored, restless, or sleepy. The time might have passed in a flash, or five minutes may have felt like an eternity and urges to check the timer may have come up. Did you criticize yourself for having such feelings? They're all normal and common. They don't mean you're doing the practice wrong or the exercise isn't working. The next time you practice, see if you can let go of the criticism. The goal is only to notice whatever is happening.

Concerns about your mind wandering. Many people assume that if they do the exercise correctly, their minds will become clear and won't wander. This is a common misunderstanding. It's normal for minds to wander. The goal of practicing mindfulness isn't to shut off your mind but to notice when it wanders and where it goes, and then to gently return to observing your breath. The more often you come back, the more you're strengthening your mindfulness skills.

Thoughts about the exercise. Many people have thoughts such as *This is silly*, *I don't see the point of this*, *It isn't working*, or *This won't help me*. It's perfectly okay to have such thoughts. As best you can, notice the thoughts as they go through your mind, and continue with the exercise. Remind yourself that they're only thoughts. As in previous chapters, imagine your thoughts as people passing by on the street, guests in your bed-and-breakfast, or passengers coming and going from your bus. Say to yourself, *Ah, there's another one*, and then return your attention to observing your breath. The same applies to positive thoughts, such as *This is wonderful*, *It's exactly what I need*, or *This will be a great help*. Over time, relating to our thoughts in this way, whether they're positive or negative, helps us remember that we don't have to be controlled by any of our thoughts unless we choose to be.

Mindful Breathing with Other Sensations

Now that you're familiar with mindful breathing, you can combine it with awareness of other sensations. Let's go back to the introductory exercises and add mindful breathing. This creates an exercise known as "breathing with" (Williams et al. 2007). You've been breathing with the rest of your experiences all your life, but perhaps you've never been mindfully aware of it.

These exercises may seem odd and artificial at first. Please be patient. This is a skill that requires practice. With experience, you'll see that it's worth the effort.

EXERCISE: Breathing with Sensations in Your Hand

Put your hand on a surface and observe the sensations, as you did before. Notice the feelings in each of your fingers, your thumb, the back of your hand, and your palm. Take your time.

Now expand your awareness to include your breath as well as your hand. Your attention may shift back and forth between your hand and your breath. This is okay. If it's helpful, think of your attention as a spotlight. It can be narrowly focused on just your hand or just your breath, or it can be expanded to include both. Experiment and observe what happens. If your mind wanders off, gently bring it back. Practice patience and open-mindedness.

After you've practiced this a few times, try putting your hand in other locations and breathing with the sensations: on your head, on your abdomen, under running water, in a glove, and so on.

EXERCISE: Breathing with Sounds and Sights

Take a few moments to become aware of sounds. Settle into a nonjudgmental, curious attitude about sounds as best you can. Notice their qualities. Observe the silences between sounds.

Now expand your awareness to include your breath. Practice breathing with the sounds. Your attention may shift back and forth between breathing and sounds. This is okay. If your focus narrows to only sounds or only breathing, see if you can expand it to include both.

Now try breathing with sights. Choose something to look at, perhaps a tree outside your window. Observe the leaves and branches. Notice their colors, shapes, and movements in the breeze. Expand your attention to include your breath. Continue to observe the tree while also noticing your breathing.

EXERCISE: Breathing with Routine Experiences in Daily Life

Try breathing with the sensations you feel while sitting at your desk, holding on the phone, riding in an elevator, walking down a hallway, and so on. During meetings, conversations, or household chores, see if you can notice your breath in the background without ignoring the task at hand or tuning it out.

* *Ethan's Experience with Mindful Breathing in Stressful Circumstances* *

Mindful breathing is especially useful for coping with the stresses of daily life. Ethan, an accountant who spends many hours working at a computer and is prone to tension headaches, provides a good example. Here's his description of mindful breathing while having a headache:

I had a tension headache this week while sitting in my office at work. My head, neck, and shoulders were really hurting. I was upset and kept thinking about why I get headaches and how much they interfere with everything.

Then I realized this wasn't helping. I closed my door, turned off the light, set the timer in my phone for ten minutes, and sat quietly. First I focused on my breathing and tried to ignore the headache. That didn't work. The headache was too strong to ignore.

Then I tried focusing directly on the headache, but that felt worse. I got caught up in thinking about how bad it was. So then I focused on my breathing without trying to ignore the headache. I was aware of both. When thoughts came along, I noticed them but didn't obsess as much.

I noticed my breathing was faster at first and slowed down after a while. I could feel myself getting more relaxed even though my head still hurt. I was less bothered by having a headache.

After ten minutes the headache was a little better. I did some stretches my doctor had showed me, took a painkiller, and went on with my work. The headache gradually faded away.

At first, Ethan found it difficult to balance his attention. Focusing only on the headache wasn't helpful; neither was trying to ignore it. Expanding his attention to include his breath and the headache helped him stop ruminating and choose constructive behavior (stretching, medication) for dealing with his headache.

Ethan's experience illustrates important points about exercises that involve "breathing with." This isn't a method of suppressing or avoiding an unpleasant experience; rather, it helps us stay present with difficult circumstances in a constructive way.

* Jill's Story, Continued *

Let's return to Jill, the young woman with the phobia of thunderstorms. Jill practiced mindful observation exercises, starting with mindful breathing for five minutes each day while sitting in a chair. At first it made her nervous and uncomfortable. She felt strangely breathless, as if she couldn't get enough air. She cut back to two minutes each day. Over the course of two weeks, she became accustomed to observing her breath and extended the time to ten minutes per day. During rainy weather she practiced on the sofa in her basement. When her heart raced and her stomach tightened, she practiced breathing with these sensations. Her breath began to feel familiar and comforting.

Then she began to observe rainy weather through a closed window. She observed the rain falling and forming puddles, watched the trees swaying, and listened to the wind. When she noticed her heart pounding, she breathed with these sensations for a few moments and then resumed looking out the window. In time, she was able to watch through an open window, noticing the feel and smell of the air and hearing the raindrops hit the ground. Later, she ventured onto her front porch to observe the rain.

For several weeks, there were no thunderstorms. Then a storm arose suddenly in the middle of the night. Jill awoke in a panic and hurried downstairs to the basement. In her usual way, she turned on the TV, wrapped herself in a blanket, and huddled on the sofa. After a few minutes, she realized that this might be a good opportunity to practice mindful observation. *No*, she told herself. *That would be too difficult.*

Then she realized *That would be too difficult* was a thought. She remembered her long-term goal: to participate in craft fairs, rain or shine. She turned down the volume on the TV just enough so she could hear the thunder. Her heart pounded. She observed the sensations and breathed with them.

After a few minutes she turned off the TV and continued to listen to the thunder. She felt anxious and shaky but realized she could observe the sensations in her body while continuing to listen and breathe. After a few minutes, she slowly walked up the stairs, keeping the blanket wrapped around her for comfort. At the top of the stairs, she saw a flash of lightning through a window. A loud boom sounded. She turned quickly and started back down, but she stopped herself after five or six steps. She sat on the stairs for a few minutes, observing her breathing and body sensations while gazing into the basement.

As the storm continued, Jill slowly made her way up into the living room and watched through a window. She checked in regularly with her breathing. She noticed urges to return to the basement but didn't act on them, although several times she put the blanket over her head for a few moments. As the storm subsided, she went out on her front porch and listened to the fading thunder and the gentle rain. Her body felt weak and tired, yet she was excited about her progress. She went inside and rewarded herself with a snack before going back to bed.

Jill realized that breathing with her anxiety symptoms (a racing heart and shaky sensations) helped her see that she could tolerate them while working toward her goal of not avoiding the storm. Knowing that her behavior didn't have to be controlled by the weather gave her a feeling of strength and helped her let go of self-criticism.

Jill continues to practice mindful observation during storms. At night she lies in bed and listens. During the day she watches through a window or carries on with whatever she's doing. She's begun to practice mindful observation of the weather while driving and no longer speeds during storms.

EXERCISE: Keeping Track of Your Mindful Observation Practice

The following worksheet will help you keep a record of your practice of mindful observation. First you'll find an example from Jill, followed by a blank worksheet for your own use. Make copies so you can practice for several weeks. Start by using the mindful breathing recording on the website for this book (http://www. newharbinger.com/29033). Then see if you can incorporate mindfulness of breathing and body sensations into your normal daily life.

WORKSHEET: Mindful Observation Practice Log

Your name: Jill

Day	Exercises practiced	Comments
Thursday	Did ten minutes of mindful breathing with a recorded exercise.	Felt relaxing, getting used to it.
Friday	Mindfully observed blue skies, sunshine.	Felt fine, nice weather today.
Saturday	Observed rain from the living room window and practiced breathing with the nervous feelings.	Felt nervous but didn't go to the basement.
Sunday	Mindfully observed my neighbors' two puppies playing in their backyard.	Very enjoyable.
Monday	Did ten minutes of mindful breathing. Observed the cloudy sky while driving.	Driving was hard. I was tempted to race home but didn't.
Tuesday	Observed rain through an open window for twenty minutes while practicing mindful breathing.	Breathing while watching rain is getting easier. My heart doesn't race as fast.
Wednesday	Did mindful breathing in a staff meeting. I was nervous about a possible storm in the afternoon.	Worried about getting home before the storm started. Breathing helped me concentrate during the meeting.

WORKSHEET: Mindful Observation Practice Log

Your name: _____

Day	Exercises practiced	Comments

Chapter Summary

- Mindful observation can help free us from the psychological traps described in part 2 of the book: rumination, avoidance, emotion-driven behavior, and self-criticism.

- Mindful observation means looking closely at present-moment experiences, both internal to the body and mind (thoughts, emotions, and sensations) and in the external world.

- Mindful observation means letting go of judgments and criticism as best we can, and staying present with whatever we observe.

- Mindful breathing is a useful tool for staying focused on the present moment. It prevents rumination and avoidance and helps with choosing constructive behavior in stressful circumstances.

CHAPTER 9

Mindful Observation with Labeling

We can become aware of judgment… Start by simply noting "judging"
when it arises—and noting it softly, like a whisper, not like a baseball bat.

—Joseph Goldstein and Jack Kornfield

Imagine that you wake up one morning with a runny nose, a sore throat, a headache, and fatigue. *Oh no!* you think. *I'm getting a cold. It feels like a bad one. I don't have time to be sick now. I have too much work to do. This is terrible!* You're tempted to stay in bed, but you dread the consequences of taking the day off: meetings you'll miss, money you won't earn, people you'll inconvenience, and so on. You tell yourself you'll have to carry on as usual, but then you realize how exhausted you'll be by the end of the day. You worry about getting even sicker. Your stress and a nxiety increase. All of these thoughts and feelings occur within a minute or two of waking up.

The inner world of thoughts and feelings is a busy place. We all have constant streams of sensations, emotions, thoughts, and urges passing through our minds and bodies. If we're not mindfully aware of them, we may act on them in unhealthy ways. We may ruminate and criticize: *Why do I always get sick at such bad times? It must be stress. I should be able to handle things better.* Or we may ignore our symptoms and press on at full speed, making ourselves sicker and spreading germs among family, friends, and coworkers. We may avoid constructive actions, such as going to the doctor or rescheduling some of our commitments. Malaise and stress may make us short-tempered in ways we regret.

Mindful observation is the key to handling situations like this, but it's very difficult when the inner world is swarming with unpleasant thoughts, emotions, sensations, and urges. Learning a new skill, mindful labeling, can help. Labeling is simply the act of naming what you're observing. In this chapter, we'll explore how to use labeling to enhance the ability to be mindful of the present moment and respond to it constructively.

One-Word Labeling

Let's consider four labels for things that happen in the body and mind: "sensation," "thought," "urge," and "emotion."

- A *sensation* is a physical feeling in the body, such as aching, tingling, tension, or the pounding of your heart.

- A *thought* is a string of words that passes through the mind, such as *I can't do anything right, That went well, Something bad is going to happen*, or *What's the weather like today?* For now, include mental images and memories in the "thought" category.

- An *urge* is an impulse, temptation, or desire to do something, such as scratch your nose, have a drink, or shout at someone.

- An *emotion*, as discussed previously, is a combination of sensations, thoughts, and urges. Emotions are complex, but they can be labeled with a single word, such as "anger," "happiness," or "sadness."

EXERCISE: One-Word Labeling of Sensations, Thoughts, Emotions, and Urges

Here's a quiz that will help you practice using these labels. In each blank, write whether the item is a sensation (S), thought (T), emotion (E), or urge (U). The first few are filled in as examples. Answers are provided at the end of the chapter.

__T__	1. Why is he being so rude?	_____	9. Sadness.	_____	17. I have too much work to do.
__E__	2. Anger.	_____	10. Temptation to stay in bed.	_____	18. Temptation to quit.
__S__	3. Pounding heart.	_____	11. Heaviness in chest.	_____	19. Churning in stomach.
__U__	4. Temptation to yell.	_____	12. I shouldn't feel like this.	_____	20. Anxiety.
_____	5. I hope no one saw me.	_____	13. Trembling in legs.	_____	21. Frustration.
_____	6. Heat in face.	_____	14. I'm making a mess of things.	_____	22. Why hasn't she called?
_____	7. Embarrassment.	_____	15. Impulse to leave.	_____	23. Impulse to check messages.
_____	8. Impulse to hide.	_____	16. Dread.	_____	24. Disappointment.

EXERCISE: Mindful Breathing Meditation with One-Word Labeling

Now that you're familiar with the labels, try using them in a meditation exercise. This exercise is a variation of the mindful breathing meditation in chapter 8. Just as before, sit in a relaxed but alert posture. If you prefer, lie on a comfortable surface. Read through the instructions carefully before doing the practice, then set a timer for five to ten minutes and begin. If you like, you can use the recording of this exercise on the website for this book (http://www.newharbinger.com/29033). Try this practice several times over the next week or two.

✳ ✳ ✳

To begin, settle into a posture that's relaxed yet alert. Gently close your eyes or gaze at a neutral spot. Focus your attention on the movements and sensations of your breath. Allow your breath to flow at its own pace and rhythm without trying to change it.

When you're ready, expand your attention to include whatever you notice within your mind and body. Use these words to label what you observe: "thought," "emotion," "sensation," or "urge." Say the word silently to yourself. Here are some examples:

What you observe	What you say to yourself
Itching, aching, heat, cold, pressure, tension…	"sensation"
An urge to scratch, stretch, move, quit…	"urge"
Boredom, irritation, sadness, contentment…	"emotion"
This is silly, I can't do this, What's the point…	"thought"
This is great, This is so interesting, I love these exercises…	"thought"
What's for lunch? What time is it? I need a nap…	"thought"
Memory, image, daydream, fantasy…	"thought"
Something from the outer world, like a sound or scent	"sound" or "scent"
Something that's hard to label	"hmm"

Don't try to force anything, just label whatever appears. As best you can, use a gentle tone for your mental labeling.

Use the plural (for example, "sensations" or "thoughts") if you notice several experiences in the same category at once.

After you've said the label silently to yourself, continue with mindful observation. Breathe with whatever you observe.

If you get confused about what to do, focus on your breath. Label it by saying "in" and "out" as you inhale and exhale. When you feel ready, resume labeling your thoughts, emotions, sensations, and urges.

Remember to keep an attitude of friendly curiosity. Practice patience, kindness, and interest. Let go of judgments and criticism as best you can.

✳ ✳ ✳

What did you notice? Like all meditation exercises, this one can be relaxing and enjoyable, challenging and unpleasant, or relatively straightforward. The goal isn't to feel a particular way; the goal is to observe and label the happenings in the inner world, whether they're pleasant, unpleasant, or neutral. Here are some common concerns that come up during this exercise.

Dealing with Urges

Many people feel inhibited about acting on urges that arise, as if it would be unmindful to scratch an itch or stretch an achy muscle. Acting on urges can be part of the exercise. After you've labeled the urge, observe it closely and with interest. If you act on it, observe how it feels to do so. Notice the sensations afterward.

If you have an urge to stop the exercise, perhaps because you find it boring, silly, or a waste of time, remember that boredom is an emotion and that *This is silly* and *This is a waste of time* are thoughts. The purpose of the exercise is to observe emotions and thoughts as they come and go. See if you can refrain from acting on the urge to stop the exercise until the timer sounds. Instead, observe the urge to quit. Notice what it feels like, where you feel it in your body, and if it changes over time. As best you can, refrain from judging yourself for having this urge.

If you're in severe discomfort or distress and it would be unkind to yourself to continue, stop the exercise and do what you need to do to take care of yourself. But don't give up; return to the exercise another time.

Handling Uncertainty About Labels

It's easy, but unhelpful, to get overly involved in thinking about the labels themselves. You may have felt unsure of what label to use. Perhaps you observed something that didn't seem to fit one of the labels. The next time you practice, just say "Hmm" to yourself when this happens and return to observing. "Hmm" is shorthand for "I don't know what this is" or "This doesn't seem to fit." If you get caught up in thinking about the labels, notice that you're having thoughts. Silently say "thoughts" and gently return to observing.

Wanting Different Labels

The words used here are helpful but not required. If you notice mental images or pictures, try using "image" as one of your labels. If you'd like to distinguish memories from other experiences, use "memory" as one of your labels. You could use more than four labels, although using more than five or six might make the task too complex. Experiment with different labels to find the ones that work best for you.

One-Sentence Labeling

Much of the time, we assume that our thoughts and feelings are true and important. We think we should take them seriously and act on them. Sometimes this is helpful. If you wake up feeling anxious and thinking, *I have an important meeting at 2 p.m. and I'm not prepared; I should spend the morning getting organized*, these thoughts and feelings may guide your behavior in useful ways. On the other hand, if you wake up feeling anxious and thinking, *The meeting is going to be a disaster; there's no point in trying*, these thoughts and feelings may guide you to do something you'll regret later, like calling in sick or avoiding constructive preparation.

The purpose of mindfully labeling thoughts and feelings is to recognize that they're distinct from the person who's having them (Hayes 2005). You are not your thoughts and feelings; they are visitors in your guest house or passengers on your bus. They come and go while you remain yourself. You don't have to believe them or do what they say unless you choose to.

A short sentence is sometimes more effective than a single word for reminding us to take this perspective. A particular type of sentence works best. Here are some examples:

- "I'm having feelings of anxiety."

- "Here is a memory."

- "A feeling of sadness has come up."

- "I'm having thoughts about being incompetent."

- "This is a sensation."

- "I'm feeling an urge to eat."

- "An angry feeling is here."

- "I'm noticing butterflies in my stomach."

- "I'm having shaky sensations in my legs."

- "Troubling thoughts are in my mind."

- "A feeling of embarrassment has arisen within me."

- "I'm noticing worries about my health."

- "I'm feeling a temptation to leave work early."

- "I have an urge to yell at my spouse."

The structure of these sentences may seem odd or unnatural to you, but there's a good reason for constructing them this way. It helps us remember that we *have* thoughts, emotions, sensations, and urges, but they come and go—they're visitors. They don't have to define or control us. We can choose what to do while these visitors are swirling around in our minds. So when you catch yourself using sentences such as "I'm an idiot" or "I can't stand this," try rephrasing them as "The thought that I'm an idiot has come to my mind" or "I'm feeling a strong urge to get out of here." With practice, it will become more natural.

EXERCISE: Mindful Breathing Meditation with One-Sentence Labeling

To practice using sentences to label your experience, repeat the previous meditation exercise; but this time, label whatever you observe with a mindful sentence:

- "I'm noticing an ache in my knee."

- "I'm feeling an urge to stretch my neck."

- "I'm having thoughts about tomorrow."

- "A feeling of boredom has come up."

Remember to use a gentle, friendly, nonjudgmental tone. Do this exercise several times over the next week or two. Compare one-word labeling and one-sentence labeling to see which is more helpful for you.

Mindful Labeling in Daily Life

When you're comfortable with mindful labeling using words or sentences, try practicing in daily life. Here are two examples, from Dan and Michelle.

Dan enjoys indoor rock climbing at a climbing wall in a local fitness center. After learning about mindful labeling, he wrote this account of a session:

Yesterday during my climbing session I decided to attempt a harder route than usual. I tried twice and fell. As I got ready to try again, the thought I can't do this came into my head. I felt discouraged and almost gave up. Then I remembered the labeling exercise and said to myself, "A feeling of doubt has come up." I took a good look at the route and considered whether it was really too advanced for me. I decided to try again, even though I felt a bit doubtful. I fell a couple more times but eventually was able to finish the route. That felt great.

I learned that it makes difficult tasks easier if I allow thoughts to be thoughts and don't let them stop me from persevering. Using the labeling skill helped me realize that I didn't have to give up even though I had doubts.

Michelle, a university student, is struggling with her required statistics course. She wrote this description of mindful labeling while doing her homework:

I was doing my statistics homework and I thought, I'm never going to understand this. I felt anxious about failing my statistics class. My stomach was churning. My friends were going out and I was really tempted to join them. I remembered to label all of this: "thought," "emotion," "sensation," "urge." I kept working until I finished my homework, but I wasn't sure I really understood it.

I was about to go out and join my friends, but I felt uneasy. I observed the feeling. It helped to put it into words. I actually said out loud, "I still have worries about statistics." So I e-mailed the teaching assistant to make an appointment. Then I felt a lot better and went to find my friends.

Both Dan and Michelle found that mindful labeling helped them become aware of their thoughts and feelings and take constructive action. Without mindful labeling, Dan would have followed his urge to give up on the challenging climb, and Michelle wouldn't have taken steps to clear up her confusion about statistics.

More About Emotion Labeling

Emotions can be particularly difficult to label. They're complex experiences with several components: thoughts, sensations, and urges (Barlow et al. 2011). We're capable of feeling a wide variety of different emotions, and sometimes we feel several at once. If you're ever uncertain about which emotion you're feeling, you're not alone.

The following table provides general information about the most common categories of emotion and the typical thoughts, sensations, and urges that go with them. Your emotions may fit these descriptions, but remember that everyone has their own emotional style. Your genetics, background, and learning experiences have influenced how you feel your emotions.

Emotion category	Specific emotions	Typical thoughts	Typical sensations	Typical urges
Sadness	Depression	*This is awful.*	Heaviness	Withdraw
	Disappointment	*I'm so sad.*	Fatigue	Isolate self
	Grief	*I really miss…*	Hollowness	Give up
	Hurt	*This is hopeless.*	Emptiness	Lie around
	Sorrow	*Things never work out.*	Lump in throat	Ruminate
Anger	Annoyance	*I hate…*	Face flushing	Yell, curse
	Frustration	*I can't stand…*	Jaw clenching	Attack
	Irritation	*How dare they…*	Neck tense	Pound fist
	Rage	*It shouldn't be this way.*	Fists clenching	Slam door
	Resentment	*This isn't fair.*	Heart pounding	Throw things
Fear	Anxiety	*This will go badly.*	Racing heart	Flee
	Dread	*I'm going to get hurt.*	Sweaty hands	Avoid
	Nervousness	*I can't manage.*	Trembling	Freeze
	Panic	*I'm in danger.*	Tension	Pace
	Terror	*I'll be rejected or criticized.*	Jitteriness	Plea for help
Shame and guilt	Embarrassment	*I'm a loser.*	Blushing	Hide or withdraw
	Humiliation	*I made a terrible mistake.*	Sinking feeling	Criticize self
	Regret	*I shouldn't have…*	Ache in stomach	Avoid
	Remorse	*I'm stupid (silly, crazy).*	Tension	Apologize
	Self-disgust	*I've disappointed people.*	Heaviness	Make amends
Happiness	Cheeriness	*This is wonderful.*	Lightness	Jump for joy
	Contentment	*I'm so excited.*	Energy	Shout or laugh
	Delight	*I love…*	Flushing	Talk or hug
	Elation	*I'm really pleased.*	Bubbly feeling	Raise arms
	Gladness	*Couldn't be better.*	Bouncy feeling	Clap hands

If you find it difficult to label your emotions, start with the general categories as your labels: happy, sad, angry, fearful or anxious, ashamed or guilty. Focus on the specific thoughts, sensations, and urges you're feeling. In time, you'll become more familiar with more specific terms for emotions.

* *Tina's Story* *

Tina, age twenty-eight, is learning mindfulness skills to help with her problems with angry behavior. When Tina was growing up, her parents spent most evenings drinking in bars and were hungover most mornings. By the time she was nine years old, Tina was trying to prepare meals, wash clothes, and get herself and her younger brother to school on time. Her parents showed no appreciation for Tina's efforts and criticized her severely for minor shortcomings, such as leaving dirty dishes in the sink. When she showed any signs of distress, they told her to stop complaining.

Tina learned to criticize herself and to expect criticism from others. She never learned to label her emotions. Now, as an adult, she just says she's upset whenever anything is bothering her. She thinks she should be able to control her feelings, but she's easily angered and tends to lose her temper and then berates herself. She works as a waitress and gets irritable when the restaurant is crowded. She's lost two jobs because of angry outbursts with customers or coworkers.

Tina worked hard on mindful observation and labeling of thoughts, sensations, emotions, and urges. She realized that in any situation where she might be criticized, her strongest emotion is fear. For example, if the kitchen at the restaurant where she works is slow, she fears that her customers will be angry with her for providing poor service. She ruminates about how unfair this is; it's not her fault that the cooks are slow. Her rumination leads to feelings of anger and urges to lash out. If her customers ask when their meals will arrive, she snaps at them and then feels disgusted with herself.

However, mindful observation with labeling is helping Tina understand what she's thinking and feeling. Here are the labels she uses the most:

- "Feeling nervous."

- "I'm worried that this customer is getting angry."

- "I'm annoyed with the kitchen."

- "Fear of getting blamed."

- "I have an urge to yell at someone."

As a result of learning to recognize when she expects criticism, is fearful that others will be angry with her, or has urges to snap at people, Tina's ability to control her temper is much better. Mindful observation with labeling gives her a moment to decide what to do. She was recently complimented by her boss for politely handling a frustrated customer whose dinner arrived later than he desired.

Tina's emotions are completely understandable, given her childhood experiences. But she's extremely judgmental of them, telling herself that her thoughts and feelings are wrong, bad, and inappropriate, and that she's weak and immature for feeling them. We'll return to Tina's story after we consider how to work with judgments of our own thoughts and feelings.

Working with Judgments

Do you say things like the following to yourself?

- *It's stupid of me to be so anxious.*

- *It's ridiculous that I'm still sad. I should be over it by now.*

- *It's idiotic of me to get so angry.*

- *It's crazy how my heart is pounding.*

- *It's silly of me to worry about such a trivial thing.*

- *I'm such a failure. I can't speak in a meeting without shaking.*

- *It's wrong of me to feel this way.*

- *I can't believe I'm jealous. It's so immature.*

- *I shouldn't be thinking about this. It's a sign of weakness.*

- *I'm too emotional. I shouldn't get so worked up.*

If these statements sound familiar, you're observing and labeling your thoughts and feelings, but you're also judging them, and yourself, as bad or wrong in some way. This is harmful for two reasons.

Judgment of Thoughts and Feelings Increases Emotional Suffering

It's painful and difficult to have unpleasant memories or worries in your mind, to feel urges to do things you know you'll regret, or to feel scared, sad, or embarrassed. If you tell yourself you shouldn't be having those thoughts and feelings—that it's bad, wrong, silly, crazy, or immature—you create more negative emotion.

Judgment of Thoughts and Feelings Makes It Harder to Act Wisely

As discussed in chapter 5, emotions occur for reasons and serve useful purposes: they tell us important information and motivate us to take action to solve problems. If you tell yourself that your emotions are a sign of weakness or failure, you miss the messages they're trying to send and you are less able to respond in a helpful way.

Mindful Labeling of Judgments

It's impossible to get rid of judgmental thoughts completely; they will always pop into our minds. As discussed in chapter 4, suppressing unwanted thoughts often backfires. Fortunately, we can learn to work with judgments effectively. If you practice the following skills, you may have fewer judgmental thoughts. And when they do come up, you won't take them so seriously and they'll have less power over you.

EXERCISE: Observing Judgments During Mindful Breathing

Continue to practice mindful breathing with one-word labeling and include "judgment" as one of your labels. Every time you notice criticism or disapproval of your thoughts or feelings, label it by saying "judgment." Remember to use a friendly tone.

EXERCISE: Observing Judgments in Daily Life

Watch for judgments that come up during ordinary activities. When you spot one, label it by saying, "Ah, judging" or "There's a judgmental thought." If you notice many judgments in a short period, say, "I'm noticing a lot of judgments" or "Judgmental thoughts are in my mind." Don't forget the friendly tone.

EXERCISE: Watching Out for Judging Your Judgments

Once you start paying attention to judgments, it's easy to criticize yourself for having judgmental thoughts. Within a few seconds, you might notice an emotion, judge the emotion, judge the judgment, and judge yourself for making judgments, as in the following sequence:

1. *I'm noticing a feeling of anger.*

2. *Well that's ridiculous! It's stupid to get angry about such a trivial thing.*

3. *Oops, that was a judgment. I shouldn't be making judgments.*

4. *This is terrible! I'm hopeless. I'll never learn this.*

If you notice a sequence of thoughts like this, adopt a patient attitude with yourself. Take a few mindful breaths. Then, mindfully observe and label whatever the judgment was about. If you were judging an emotion, thought, sensation, or urge, observe and label it, as you did before:

127

1. *Okay, "lots of judgmental thoughts."*

2. *Let me take a few breaths (in…out…in…out…)*

3. *What do I notice now?*

4. *"Warm face," "tense hands"…*

5. *Keep observing and breathing.*

EXERCISE: Labeling Your Judgments Creatively

In previous chapters, we've already touched on whimsical ways to label judgmental thoughts. Here's a quick review of different ways you might label them:

As people passing by

> *Oh, there's Mrs. Judgment.*

> *Mr. Criticism is making his morning rounds.*

As tapes playing in your mind

> *The "I'm too emotional" tape is playing again.*

> *This is the "I can't do anything right" tape.*

As a radio playing in your mind

> *Ah, I'm tuned in to the "I'm a loser" station again.*

As guests in your bed-and-breakfast

> *The critical guests have returned for another visit.*

As passengers on your bus

> *It seems I've picked up some very judgmental passengers today.*

Feel free to experiment and come up with your own creative ways of labeling your judgmental thoughts.

Distinguishing Preferences from Judgments

When we observe our inner workings, we often notice feelings of aversion and dislike. These feelings aren't judgments; they're preferences. Adopting a nonjudgmental attitude doesn't mean that you have to stop disliking things. It's perfectly okay to have preferences, even strong ones. Don't try to get rid of your likes and dislikes. Instead, observe them. When you read, eat, or do anything else, notice what you find enjoyable or unpleasant. Observe any tendency to judge your reactions. Practice accepting the preferences and letting go of the judgments.

Preference: *I like mysteries better than biographies.*

Judgment: *I have poor taste in books.*

Preference: *I really don't like sushi.*

Judgment: *I must be crazy. People rave about it.*

Preference: *I don't like horror movies. They make me tense and give me insomnia.*

Judgment: *I shouldn't be such a wimp.*

Sometimes preferences are difficult to manage. For example, if you prefer high-fat, sugary foods over fruits and vegetables but you'd like to lose weight, you may need to eat in ways that are inconsistent with your preferences. Judging yourself for your likes and dislikes probably won't help. Instead, acknowledge the difficulty; it's part of being human. Be kind to yourself and eat mindfully (more on mindful eating in the next chapter). In time, you may become more tolerant of fruits and vegetables—perhaps you'll even enjoy them. But even if you don't, your ability to choose foods consistent with your goals is likely to improve.

EXERCISE: Restating Judgments as Mindful Labels

On the following pages, you'll find a worksheet that will help you practice mindfully restating judgments. There are three versions of the worksheet. The first provides instructions. The second is an example from Tina. After spending some time practicing nonjudging with the mindful breathing exercise, she learned to say "judgment" or "That's a judgmental thought" whenever she criticized herself for feeling afraid or angry. Then she used the worksheet to practice rephrasing her judgments. As she began to let go of judging, she was better able to think of constructive ways to handle situations in the restaurant, such as checking politely with the kitchen staff about when a meal would be ready, telling customers what the kitchen staff said, and offering complementary desserts to people whose orders took a long time to arrive.

After Tina's example, you'll find a blank version for your own use. Make several copies so you can use it as many times as you like.

WORKSHEET: Restating Judgments as Mindful Labels

Remember to maintain an attitude of friendly curiosity.

Day and time	What was the situation?	What thoughts, emotions, sensations, or urges did you notice?	What was your judgmental thought?	Restate your judgment as a mindful label in three different ways.
When did the judgmental thoughts occur?	Where were you? What was going on? Were other people involved?	Briefly note what you observed in your body and mind.	Write it down exactly as it appeared in your mind, or as closely as you can remember.	Examples: 1. That's a judgment. 2. I'm having self-critical thoughts. 3. The "I'm irrational" tape is playing again.

WORKSHEET: Restating Judgments as Mindful Labels

Your name: Tina

Remember to maintain an attitude of friendly curiosity.

Day and time	What was the situation?	What thoughts, emotions, sensations, or urges did you notice?	What was your judgmental thought?	Restate your judgment as a mindful label in three different ways.
Saturday, 9 p.m.	The restaurant was really crowded. I snapped at a coworker in the kitchen because my customers' food was taking a long time and they were impatient for their dinner.	Thoughts: It's not fair, not my fault the kitchen is slow. Emotions: Afraid the customers might get angry and walk out. Sensations: Tense neck and shoulders. Urges: To quit this job.	It's ridiculous that I get so worked up. I should be able to stay calm.	1. Judgment. 2. Self-critical thoughts are here. 3. The "I'm out of control" tape is playing again.
Thursday, 7 p.m.	A customer kept changing his mind after he'd ordered his meal. I had to tell the kitchen and they were annoyed.	Thoughts: This customer is an idiot. Emotions: Irritation. Sensations: Teeth clenching, heart pounding. Urges: To tell the customer to make up his mind or go somewhere else.	I'm not cut out for waitressing. I'm too impatient for this job.	1. Those are judgments. 2. Self-critical thoughts have come up. 3. Judgmental passengers are on my bus.

WORKSHEET: Restating Judgments as Mindful Labels

Your name: _____

Remember to maintain an attitude of friendly curiosity.

Day and time	What was the situation?	What thoughts, emotions, sensations, or urges did you notice?	What was your judgmental thought?	Restate your judgment as a mindful label in three different ways.

Letting Go of Labeling When It's Not Necessary

Mindful labeling has many benefits. It helps us learn to identify thoughts, sensations, emotions, and urges; encourages us to remember that they're visitors to the mind; and reminds us to pause to observe them before deciding whether and how to act on them.

In time, as your mindfulness skills develop, you'll realize that labeling isn't always necessary. It's a bit like learning to play the piano. At first, it may be helpful to label the notes or chords. Eventually, labeling can be dropped. For skilled players, labeling interrupts the flow of the music. This doesn't mean that they're playing mindlessly, with their attention focused elsewhere. Rather, they're participating with awareness in the ongoing activity of playing the piano.

In daily life, it's often enjoyable or helpful to focus our full attention on something we're doing without labeling the experience. Playing a game or a sport, working on a project, singing a song, or having a conversation can feel satisfying when we're fully engaged and not distracted or self-conscious. Labeling can get in the way. In the next chapter, we'll explore exercises that cultivate the ability to participate in activities with awareness.

Chapter Summary

- Mindful observation with one-word labeling is helpful for staying focused on the present moment, especially when the moment includes a multitude of sensations, thoughts, emotions, and urges swirling around in the mind.

- Labeling with nonjudgmental sentences helps us remember that thoughts and feelings are temporary experiences that pass through the mind. We don't always have to believe them, take them seriously, or act on them, although we can if we choose to do so.

- Judgmental labeling increases emotional suffering and makes it more difficult to act wisely in difficult situations. Although it's impossible to completely get rid of judgmental thoughts, there are many ways of rephrasing them so that they're less harmful.

- Labeling isn't always necessary. Practice enough to be familiar with labeling and its benefits. Then remember that mindful observation can be practiced with or without labeling.

ONE-WORD LABELING OF SENSATIONS, THOUGHTS, EMOTIONS, AND URGES

Answers

__T__ 1. Why is he being so rude?	__E__ 9. Sadness.	__T__ 17. I have too much work to do.
__E__ 2. Anger.	__U__ 10. Temptation to stay in bed.	__U__ 18. Temptation to quit.
__S__ 3. Pounding heart.	__S__ 11. Heaviness in chest.	__S__ 19. Churning in stomach.
__U__ 4. Temptation to yell.	__T__ 12. I shouldn't feel like this.	__E__ 20. Anxiety.
__T__ 5. I hope no one saw me.	__S__ 13. Trembling in legs.	__E__ 21. Frustration.
__S__ 6. Heat in face.	__T__ 14. I'm making a mess of things.	__T__ 22. Why hasn't she called?
__E__ 7. Embarrassment.	__U__ 15. Impulse to leave.	__U__ 23. Impulse to check messages.
__U__ 8. Impulse to hide.	__E__ 16. Dread.	__E__ 24. Disappointment.

CHAPTER 10

Acting with Awareness

There are some people who eat an orange but don't really eat it. They eat their sorrow, fear, anger, past, and future.

—Thich Nhat Hanh

Think back to the last time you washed the dishes. If you were washing them mindfully, you may have noticed the sound of the water splashing, the scent of the dishwashing liquid, the light reflecting off the plates, or the sensations and movements of your body as you worked. On the other hand, you might have been washing the dishes without paying attention, while thinking of other things.

Mindfulness teachers refer to the second way as automatic pilot. Just as a plane can fly itself while the pilot does something else, our bodies can do many things while our minds are elsewhere. We eat while reading or watching TV. We walk or drive while planning the day or daydreaming. We cook, clean, and get the kids ready for bed while preoccupied with the future or the past.

Much of the time, being on automatic pilot causes no serious harm. The ability to function automatically is often valuable. We can look for road signs or talk to passengers while driving automatically. Planning your day while walking to work might be a constructive use of time. The dishes may get perfectly clean even if you're daydreaming, listening to music, or talking with someone while you wash them.

On the other hand, we can make mistakes on automatic pilot. We forget things we intended to do, such as buying groceries on the way home from work. We act habitually, perhaps walking toward an old office after moving to a new one. Sometimes we do serious or even deadly harm. Numerous accidents have been caused by people driving on automatic pilot while talking on their phones. And we miss countless moments from our lives, each of which, in its own way, might have been interesting, beautiful, enjoyable, important, or meaningful: the sunset as we take out the garbage, the taste of an interesting food, or a child's laughter as he splashes in the tub.

Research shows that people who spend less time on autopilot are happier and more satisfied with life. In one famous study, several thousand adults of all ages were contacted by phone at random intervals and asked three questions:

- What were you doing just now?

- Were you focused on it or thinking of something else?

- How happy were you feeling?

Participants were consistently happier when they were focused on what they were doing, regardless of what it was (Killingsworth and Gilbert 2010). There are probably several reasons for this. Awareness of the present moment keeps us from falling into the psychological traps discussed in part 2 of the book: rumination, avoidance, emotion-driven behavior, and self-criticism. It allows us to make wise decisions in difficult situations. It helps us appreciate life's small but precious moments.

This doesn't mean we should never function on autopilot. That would be an unrealistic goal. With practice, however, we can learn to be more aware of what we're doing in the present. It's well worth the effort. Once we've developed the ability to act with awareness, we can choose when to pay attention and when to go on autopilot. The exercises in this chapter will cultivate this ability. We'll begin with mindful eating and walking. Then we'll consider two common ways of operating in modern life: multitasking and rushing.

EXERCISE: Eating Raisins Mindfully

An exercise that involves eating raisins (Kabat-Zinn 1990) is used by many mindfulness teachers. Its purpose is to help you practice mindful awareness of eating, a routine activity that we all do every day, often without noticing much about it. To do this version (inspired by Segal, Williams, and Teasdale 2002), you'll need two raisins.

As you prepare to do this exercise, imagine that you're an explorer from outer space visiting Earth. Like all explorers, you take a strong interest in everything you encounter. At the moment, you've encountered these small wrinkly objects. As best you can, adopt an attitude of open-minded interest and curiosity about them as you do the exercise.

* * *

To begin, set a raisin gently in the palm of your hand and look at it closely. Notice its shape, size, and color. Notice how the light reflects off of it. Observe the wrinkles and the variations of color. Roll it around and look at it from different sides. Pick it up with your thumb and forefinger and turn it around slowly, looking at it from all angles. Hold it up to the light. Observe everything there is to see about it.

Set it back in the palm of your hand and observe the feel of it sitting there. Notice its weight and the sensations where it touches your palm. Rub it gently with a finger and notice the texture. Pick it up again and observe the feeling of it between your finger and thumb.

Hold it under your nose and inhale gently. Notice the aroma. If smelling it leads to sensations in your mouth or stomach, observe them.

Associations, memories, and thoughts may arise. If so, notice them without judgment as best you can. If you like, use labels such as "thoughts," "memories," or "images." Then gently return your attention to observing the raisin.

Hold the raisin close to your ear. Gently squish it around between your thumb and forefinger, noticing if it makes any sounds.

Return to looking at it for a few moments. If you're having thoughts or feelings about the raisin or the exercise, notice them and return to observing the raisin.

Slowly bring the raisin up to your mouth. Notice the sensations in your arm as you do this.

Gently touch the raisin to your lips. Observe the sensations you experience. Notice if anything happens in your mouth as you do this.

Put the raisin in your mouth, setting it on your tongue. Observe what happens.

Experiment with moving the raisin around in your mouth. Put it into one cheek, then the other one. Notice the sensations and texture.

Position the raisin between your upper and lower teeth. Slowly bite down on it, observing what happens to its texture. Notice the taste and sensations in your mouth.

Slowly chew the raisin, observing the movements, tastes, textures, and sensations. Notice how the raisin changes as you chew.

Notice when you first feel an urge to swallow. Pause and observe the urge.

When you choose to swallow, observe the movements and sensations as you do so.

Notice what happens next. Observe as any remaining bits of raisin are cleared from your mouth.

When the raisin is gone, notice the aftereffects: tastes, sensations, thoughts, images, memories, or emotions.

Repeat with another raisin.

What the Raisin Exercise Reveals About Acting Mindfully

The raisin exercise illustrates several important points about doing routine activities mindfully.

We Notice Details We Usually Overlook

When we pay attention to something we normally do automatically, we notice many things we haven't observed before, even though they've been present all along. Here are some comments about this from members of a mindfulness-based stress reduction (MBSR) class:

- *I never looked closely at a raisin before. It wasn't very appealing. It looked dry and wrinkly and sort of ugly. If I were a Martian, I might not think of eating this thing.*

- *When I first put the raisin in my mouth, it seemed pretty tasteless. But after I bit down on it there was a lot of flavor. I was surprised how much flavor one little raisin could have. Usually I eat a handful all at once and don't notice the taste that much.*

- *I never tried to listen to a raisin! At first I thought that was ridiculous, but then I actually heard some little sounds.*

The Mind Has a Life of Its Own

It's normal for the mind to wander during this exercise. Memories, plans, thoughts, and emotions may arise. Chains of associations can take us on journeys through time. Here are more observations from the MBSR class:

- *I remembered making oatmeal raisin cookies with my sister when we were young. That was a pleasant memory and I thought about making some cookies this weekend. Then I started thinking about what I need to buy—raisins, oats, and I wasn't sure what else. I was trying to remember my mother's old recipe and wondering if I have it written down somewhere. Then suddenly I remembered to focus on the raisin.*

- *I had a mental image of a vineyard I visited last summer. I was thinking about how the grapes are so juicy on the vine and how they get all dried up and shriveled when they're turned into raisins.*

- *Eating the raisin reminded me that I didn't have time for dinner because my boss wanted me to stay late. I barely got here on time, and I'm hungry and annoyed. I started thinking about all my problems with my job. It was hard to focus on the raisin.*

- *I've never liked raisins and I didn't want to eat this one. I ate it anyway. I still don't like them, but it wasn't terrible. I didn't mind it as much as I thought I would.*

- *We spent so much time looking at the raisins that I got sort of attached to mine. Then it seemed cruel to eat it. I told myself that was silly.*

Paying Attention Enhances Both Pleasant and Unpleasant Experiences

If you like raisins, you may have noticed that eating them mindfully made the experience more enjoyable than usual. The same thing happens with other pleasant experiences in daily life; they're more vivid, rich, and intense if we're paying attention.

What if you don't like raisins? The benefits of mindful attention to unpleasant experiences are less obvious but just as important. Our usual reactions to unpleasantness often lead us into psychological traps, like the MBSR participant who got caught up in ruminating about her job and the one who criticized herself for getting attached to her raisin. If we're mindfully aware of unpleasantness, rather than trying to avoid it, we often find that we can tolerate it more easily than we thought. We can choose wisely how to respond.

EXERCISE: Variations on Mindful Eating

Here are a few other mindful eating exercises to try:

- Mindfully eat a food that you like very much, such as chocolate or ice cream. Practice savoring the pleasant flavors, textures, and sensations.

- Mindfully eat a food that you don't like, perhaps one you've avoided for a long time. As best you can, practice nonjudgmental observation of the taste, the texture, and your feelings of aversion. The point is not to torture yourself; it's to practice mindfulness of an unpleasant but harmless experience.

- Mindfully eat something that you eat often but isn't very healthy—something with artificial ingredients or high levels of fat, sugar, or salt.

- Eat mindfully during your usual meals and snacks.

* Scott's Experience with a Burrito *

Scott, who works for a landscaping service, tried mindful eating with a lunch he has quite often, a steak burrito. As you can see from his description of the experience, approaching his usual lunch mindfully helped him appreciate the food more and also helped him notice when he was full:

After a long morning of planting and trimming trees, I stopped for a steak burrito for lunch. I eat them a lot, but never mindfully. Usually I'm looking over the schedule for my afternoon jobs. First I noticed how large the burrito was and how eager I was to start eating it. Next I smelled it. My mouth watered, my stomach rumbled, and I felt really hungry. Then I took a bite. I noticed all the delicious tastes and textures. The rice was soft and chewy and somewhat sweet. The onions and peppers had strong flavors. They were soft and slid around in my mouth. The salsa was cool, wet, and smooth. The chunks of steak were coarse and rough on the outside but rare and juicy on the inside. I also noticed the heat from the spices. My nose was running and my forehead was sweating.

I enjoyed this so much that my mind hardly wandered at all. Just once I thought about the work I needed to do after lunch. The most surprising thing was that I got full more quickly than usual and didn't finish the burrito. Normally I eat the whole thing.

* Alison's Experience with Cookies from a Vending Machine *

Alison, an administrative assistant at a hospital, has a tendency to eat unhealthful snacks at work. She found that paying attention to these snacks helped her realize that she doesn't like them and would prefer to eat something else:

I have a bad habit of eating unhealthy snacks from the vending machine at work. One day this week I bought a packet of cookies. I've eaten these cookies many times, and I thought I liked them. But this time I decided to eat them mindfully, and I was very surprised. I didn't like them at all. The first one tasted like chemicals, and the texture was unpleasant. At first it was dry and gritty, and then as I chewed, it felt slimy in my mouth. I couldn't believe it. I ate another one to be sure, and it was just as bad. I looked closely to see if they were moldy, but they looked normal. I threw the rest away.

This was very interesting, so I experimented with mindfully eating other things from the vending machine. I realized most of it tastes like chemicals and isn't very enjoyable. Now I feel much more motivated to bring healthier snacks to work.

* *Judy's Experience with Breakfast and the Newspaper* *

Judy, a retired schoolteacher, tried eating breakfast mindfully. Although she decided not to stick with this over the long term, she noticed some benefits, and she also noticed that she has a choice about when and whether to eat mindfully:

> *Normally I read the newspaper while eating breakfast, but this week I tried eating mindfully and reading the paper later. At first, it was interesting to really taste my cereal and toast, but after a couple of days I decided to go back to eating while reading the paper. I don't think I'm missing much. I eat the same thing every morning, and I enjoy reading the paper while I eat.*
>
> *I did notice an effect of mindful eating. My attention now seems to switch to my food more often, just for a few moments. I appreciate the flavor of the toast, which is made from very nice bread from a local bakery. So I'm enjoying it a bit more, even though I still read the paper while eating.*

* *Jason's Experience with a Dirt-Flavored Jelly Bean* *

Jason, a university student learning about mindfulness in a psychology class, experimented while eating something he found disgusting. While the food remained disgusting, he learned an important lesson about how to approach unpleasant experiences:

> *My friend Thomas had some Harry Potter jelly beans so we experimented with eating nasty flavors mindfully. When I put the dirt-flavored one in my mouth, I was bracing for an unpleasant experience but at first it wasn't bad, just smooth and not much taste. Then I bit down on it and the flavor flooded my mouth. I had a strong reaction of disgust and a powerful urge to spit it out. I grimaced and tried to get my tongue away from it. Then I thought, Wait, this won't kill me. Let me just notice this. I chewed it mindfully before swallowing it, although much faster than with the raisin. It was definitely unpleasant, but very interesting in a strange way.*
>
> *In the end, I decided this was a good way to practice observing things I don't like. In other situations, there's a risk of doing things I'll regret later when I encounter something unpleasant. This taught me I can slow down and think about what to do. I don't have to react right away even when I have a really strong urge to avoid something.*

EXERCISE: Mindful Walking

Mindful walking is another common way to practice awareness of present-moment behavior (Kabat-Zinn 1990). To practice this version (inspired by Segal, Williams, and Teasdale 2002), you'll need a place where you can walk slowly back and forth without a destination: for example, across a room, yard, or garden. Choose a place where you won't be concerned about anyone observing you.

As in the raisin exercise, imagine that you're an explorer from another planet. For your visit to Earth, you've taken on human form. This is your first experience with walking in a human body, so you're very curious about it.

* * *

Begin by standing still. Allow your arms to hang loosely at your sides, or gently clasp your hands in front of your abdomen. Take a few mindful breaths. Observe the sensations in your body.

. While continuing to stand, see if you can direct your attention to your feet. You don't have to look at them; instead, look softly ahead in the direction you'll be walking. Notice the sensations in your feet as you stand. Feel your weight as they support you. Notice their contact with your shoes, your socks, the ground, or the floor.

Slowly shift your weight onto one leg. Allow the other knee to bend and the heel to come off the floor. Move this foot slowly forward through the air and set your heel down a short distance in front of you.

Slowly shift your weight forward, observing as your front foot lowers to the ground and the heel of the back foot lifts up. Pause here. Notice how your weight is balanced. Feel the sensations in your feet and legs.

Bring the back foot up and slowly move it forward through the air, setting your heel down just in front of you.

Continue to walk very slowly across the space you've chosen. As best you can, notice the sensations in your feet and lower legs as you walk.

Experiment with silent labels: "lifting," "moving," "placing," "shifting." Labeling helps some people stay focused; others find the labels a nuisance. Try it both ways.

When you reach the other side of the space you've chosen, stand still again. Notice your breath and the sensations throughout your body.

Slowly turn around. Observe the complex movements involved in turning around. Then slowly walk back the other way.

When your mind wanders, gently bring it back to focusing on walking.

If you observe judgmental thoughts about this exercise, feeling awkward or silly, losing your balance, your mind wandering, or anything else, briefly label them ("judgments") and return your attention to walking.

* * *

You can vary this exercise by walking at a normal pace or quickly. Experiment with observing your arms and hands, your body as a whole, or your breath. Try turning your attention outward to the sights and sounds in the environment.

In all its forms, mindful walking is a type of meditation, so practice allowing the present moment to be as it is and simply observing it. You don't have to get anywhere. You have no goals except to observe the experience.

Mindful Walking in Ordinary Life

In daily life we usually have a destination and prefer to walk at a normal pace. Yet we can still walk mindfully. Here are some comments about mindful walking in daily life from members of a mindfulness class:

- *Normally when I'm walking to a meeting in another building, I have my phone in hand to check e-mails and send texts. I decided to walk mindfully, without looking at my phone. I realized how much goes on in that five-minute walk. There were smells I'd never noticed before, like hot concrete, exhaust from cars, and that vague but fresh outdoor smell. I also realized how quickly I tend to walk—in a rush and absorbed in my own world. I walked more slowly and noticed how much more relaxed my shoulders and neck felt, as well as my breathing. I had some difficulty letting thoughts pass through, but focusing on my senses helped bring me back to the present moment.*

- *I tried mindfully walking to my car after work. It was difficult. I could only walk about three steps mindfully before I was off in some other world worrying about my day. I got very frustrated with myself and thought I was doing it wrong. Then I realized those were judgments. My mind continued to wander off, and I kept bringing it back to focusing on my steps. I tried to let go of the criticism and just refocus on walking.*

- *I practiced mindfulness while walking my dog. I could feel my feet rolling along and hear the dog making click-click noises with her claws on the sidewalk. There were so many things to notice that I had trouble deciding what to focus on. I realized it worked best to choose one, like the feel of the breeze on my face. After a while I switched to hearing the sounds, and a bit later I went back to feeling my body moving.*

Like any meditation exercise, mindful walking can be pleasant or unpleasant, easy or difficult. Judgmental thoughts and negative emotions may arise. This is all okay. The point isn't to feel a particular way, but to observe whatever is happening.

EXERCISE: Doing Daily Activities with Awareness

You can do virtually anything mindfully. We've looked at eating, walking, and washing the dishes mindfully. Here's a list of other possibilities:

- Brushing your teeth

- Taking a bath or shower

- Petting or brushing your dog or cat

- Loading or unloading the dishwasher

- Loading or unloading the washing machine or dryer

- Folding laundry or ironing

- Mowing the lawn or weeding the garden

- Cooking

- Singing, playing an instrument, dancing, or exercising

- Any craft or hobby (sewing, painting, woodworking, and so on)

Start by doing one of these activities mindfully every day, then gradually add more. In time, you'll become skillful at recognizing when you're on automatic pilot and redirecting your attention to the present moment—if you choose to do so.

Multitasking

One of the members of the mindfulness class mentioned earlier noticed that it's sometimes pleasant to do two things at once:

> *Last night I washed the dishes mindfully. I felt the warm water swirling around my hands and heard the dishes clattering. I even heard the bubbles popping, which I'd never noticed before. It was pleasant and peaceful, and I enjoyed being in the moment. But there's a radio show I like to listen to while I wash the dinner dishes. It's part of my evening routine. Does this mean I'm not being mindful?*

The short answer is "not necessarily." It's sometimes possible to be mindful of doing two things at once. Next time you engage in this sort of multitasking, observe what's happening with your attention. You'll probably notice that it shifts back and forth. You may be absorbed in the radio show while washing the dishes automatically, or attending fully to the dishes and losing track of the radio show. There may be moments when you're aware of both, and other moments when you're aware of neither because you're thinking or daydreaming.

EXERCISE: Awareness of Multitasking

The following worksheet will help you tune in to your tendency to multitask. Remember to be nonjudgmental of all these experiences. If you like to wash the dishes on autopilot while listening to the radio, you may find that this is enjoyable and does no harm. Or perhaps you'll choose to broaden your attention to include aware-ness of both. The more you practice mindfulness, the more you'll recognize where your attention goes. Then you can direct it as you choose.

There are four versions of the worksheet. The first contains instructions. It's followed by two examples from Anna, who is married and has nine-year-old twin girls. She and her husband, John, both have full-time jobs. Anna is a social worker, and John is a lawyer. Although their marriage and family life are happy, Anna finds it difficult to manage the demands of full-time work and involvement in their daughters' activities. She wants to do less multitasking, but she can't see how to meet her responsibilities without doing several things at once. Because doing several things at once is very common, Anna filled two worksheets on a single day.

After Anna's examples, you'll find a blank version for your own use. Make copies so you'll always have a blank worksheet available.

WORKSHEET: Awareness of Multitasking

Remember to maintain an attitude of friendly curiosity.

Day and time	What two or more things were you doing at the same time?	Pleasantness (1–5)	Advantages	Disadvantages
When did this example of multitasking occur?	Write down two or more behaviors or activities you were trying to do simultaneously.	Was it pleasant to do these things at the same time? Rate your experience on a scale of 1 to 5. 1: very unpleasant 2: somewhat unpleasant 3: neutral 4: somewhat pleasant 5: very pleasant	What were the advantages of doing these things at the same time?	What were the disadvantages of doing these things at the same time?

WORKSHEET: Awareness of Multitasking

Your name: Anna

Remember to maintain an attitude of friendly curiosity.

Day and time	What two or more things were you doing at the same time?	Pleasantness (1–5)	Advantages	Disadvantages
Tuesday 7 a.m.	Giving the girls their breakfast and talking to John about plans for this evening.	3. Neutral.	Both had to be done, and there's not much time in the morning.	Felt a bit rushed, but no real problems.
Tuesday 7:45 a.m.	Driving the girls to school and quizzing them on their spelling words for a test today.	5. It was fun; we all enjoyed it.	The girls wanted to review. It made them feel confident about the test.	Have to be careful to pay attention to driving.
Tuesday 8:15 a.m.	Walking from car to office checking e-mail on my phone.	2. Stress level rose as I started thinking about the demands of the day.	Getting a head start on what I have to do when I get to my office.	Not watching where I'm going. I don't really accomplish much.
Tuesday 10:30 a.m.	Answered a phone call while driving to a home visit with a client.	3. Neutral.	The call was important. It was about something I needed to know for the home visit.	I almost ran a red light. I know phone calls while driving are dangerous.
Tuesday noon	At work, eating a sandwich while writing a report.	1. Very irritating. Constantly had to stop typing to pick up the sandwich. Hard to concentrate.	Report had to get done, and I had to eat.	Made me feel grumpy, rushed, and disorganized.

145

WORKSHEET: Awareness of Multitasking

Your name: Anna

Remember to maintain an attitude of friendly curiosity.

Day and time	What two or more things were you doing at the same time?	Pleasantness (1–5)	Advantages	Disadvantages
Tuesday 1:30 p.m.	At work, writing a report while helping a new staff member learn her job. She kept coming into my office with questions.	1. I felt annoyed every time she interrupted, but it's my job to train her, and her questions were good.	Both needed to get done.	I kept losing track of what I was trying to write and felt scattered and inefficient.
Tuesday 6:30 p.m.	Cooking dinner with John and talking about the day.	5. Nice way to spend time together.	Dinner gets made and we talk to each other.	None that I can think of.
Tuesday 7:30 p.m.	Washing dishes while listening to the radio.	5. It felt relaxing and I like the radio show.	Enjoyable way to wash the dishes.	I guess I'm not fully present with the dishes, but they get clean.
Tuesday 8 p.m.	At home, trying to catch up on paperwork for work and also be available for the girls' homework questions.	2. Frustrating. I like helping my kids with homework but felt pulled in two directions.	Both needed to get done.	Never felt really focused. I kept losing track of what I was doing with paperwork.
Tuesday 10 p.m.	John and I folded laundry together while watching TV. The girls were in bed.	4. Enjoyable, peaceful.	The laundry needed folding, and John and I need relaxation time together.	I wish I had time for TV without having to do a chore at the same time.

WORKSHEET: Awareness of Multitasking

Your name: _____

Remember to maintain an attitude of friendly curiosity.

Day and time	What two or more things were you doing at the same time?	Pleasantness (1–5)	Advantages	Disadvantages

The Pros and Cons of Multitasking

Research shows that some forms of multitasking are enjoyable or useful, others are neutral or harmless, and some are unpleasant or risky. Activities that don't require much mental effort, such as walking, eating, listening to music, watching TV, and simple chores, can often be combined (Spink, Cole, and Waller 2008).

When two tasks require concentration, like writing a report and answering a supervisee's questions, it's impossible to do them simultaneously. Instead, your attention shifts back and forth. Every time you switch, you lose your train of thought, and it's hard to get back on track. It's inefficient and can make you feel stressed and disorganized (Crenshaw 2008).

Some forms of multitasking are dangerous. Studies show that driving while using a phone is just as dangerous as driving while intoxicated, and hands-free phones are no better (Strayer and Drews 2007). As you experiment with mindful awareness of multitasking in your daily life, please don't drive while using a phone. It's not worth risking your life or anyone else's.

*   Anna's Experience with Awareness of Multitasking   *

After observing her experiences with multitasking for a week, Anna decided to change some of her behavior, starting with working during lunch. She found that taking fifteen minutes just for eating was more productive than trying to eat and work at the same time. After enjoying her lunch, she then could concentrate more efficiently on her work. She also stopped using her phone during the short walk from her car to her office. Instead, she practiced mindful observation of her surroundings and felt more refreshed when she entered her building.

Next, she considered her daughters' homework time. Her top priority was to encourage them to work independently but to be available when they had questions. So she decided to do less mentally demanding activities during that time, such as household chores or light reading, rather than tasks that required focused concentration. This made her daughters' interruptions less stressful.

Multitasking at work was more challenging. Anna scheduled regular meetings with her supervisees and asked them to save their questions for these meetings as much as possible. This gave her a little more uninterrupted time for tasks that require sustained concentration, like writing reports.

Final Thoughts on Multitasking

"Multitasking" is a term that originated in the world of computers. It refers to jobs done by central processing units. In daily life, "multitasking" is hard to define. What counts as a task? When you wash the dishes, you're standing at the sink, keeping your balance, holding a plate with one hand, wiping it with the other, watching the traces of food disappear, and discerning when it's clean. Is this multitasking, or are you just washing the dishes?

From the perspective of mindful awareness, it doesn't matter. The point is to practice nonjudgmental observation of your behavior in the moment. Some behaviors can be combined; but trying to do too many things at once can be unpleasant, stressful, inefficient, or even dangerous. Observe your own experience with openness and curiosity, and see for yourself.

Once you understand acting with awareness, you can choose how to direct your attention. If you choose to eat your breakfast automatically while reading the newspaper, that's perfectly fine. Try it both ways. Eating your breakfast mindfully and reading the paper later might be more satisfying—or not. Or it might change from day to day. Pay attention, and you'll discover what works for you.

Mindful Rushing

Many mindfulness exercises are done slowly, for good reason: it's easier to observe the present moment with openness and interest when we're not rushing. On the other hand, this creates the mistaken impression that we have to be slow to be mindful. People in mindfulness classes often say they didn't have time to be mindful in their daily lives because they were in a hurry.

However, it's possible to practice mindfulness while doing things quickly. If you only have a few minutes to walk to a meeting in a distant building, try walking as quickly and mindfully as you can. Notice the movements of your body as you stride along. Observe your breathing and the air rushing by. Notice your surroundings. Observe your thoughts. Are you criticizing yourself for being late? Ruminating about how you're always late? Worrying about what will happen if you're late? Acknowledge the thoughts briefly by labeling them ("Ah, thoughts and worries are here") and then return your attention to walking quickly with awareness.

Try this any time you're in a hurry. If you have ten minutes for lunch, eat mindfully and quickly. Notice the sensations, tastes, and movements. Acknowledge your thoughts and emotions and return your attention to eating mindfully.

Flow

Many studies show that immersing yourself in whatever you're doing, so that you're totally focused on it, creates a state called flow (Czikszentmihalyi 1990). When we're in flow, we feel strong, alert, engaged, and in control. Some activities are so enjoyable and absorbing that they naturally lead to flow. But we can experience flow in whatever we're doing, no matter how tedious, if we pay full attention to it. Here's a description by Jon Kabat-Zinn, a leading mindfulness teacher, of mindfully cleaning the stove while listening to jazz (1994, 205):

> Cleaning became dancing, the incantations, sounds, and rhythms and the movements of my body merging, blending together, sounds unfolding with motions, sensations in my arm aplenty, modulations in finger pressure on the scrubber as required, caked remains of former cookings slowly changing form and disappearing, all rising and falling in awareness with the music. One big dance of presence, a celebration of now. And, at the end, a clean stove.

The message is clear: Acting with awareness provides us greater happiness and satisfaction than proceeding on automatic pilot, even when we have to do something potentially tedious or unpleasant, like clean the stove. And mindfully doing two things at once, like listening to music while cleaning, can enhance the experience.

But what if you have to do something that's more challenging, stressful, scary, or painful than cleaning the stove? Acting with awareness will help, as will another useful skill: acceptance of the fact that it's difficult. "Acceptance" is a tricky term, and it's easily misunderstood. In the next chapter, we'll explore the nature of mindful acceptance and how it helps with difficult experiences.

Chapter Summary

- Acting with awareness, or paying attention to what we're doing while we're doing it, is an important mindfulness skill. It makes us happier and helps us avoid psychological traps.

- Mindful eating and mindful walking cultivate the ability to pay attention to what we're currently doing. We can also practice mindful awareness with most of the routine activities of daily life.

- Sometimes it's useful or enjoyable to mindfully do two things at once, such as washing the dishes while listening to music.

- If activities require mental effort and concentration, multitasking can be stressful, inefficient, or even dangerous. Practicing mindful observation of any tendency to multitask can help us make wise decisions about it.

- Rushing is often stressful. Acting with awareness while doing things quickly can reduce the degree of stress.

CHAPTER 11

Acceptance and Willingness

It takes a huge amount of fortitude and motivation to accept what is—
especially when you don't like it—and then to work wisely and effectively
as best you possibly can with the circumstances you find yourself in.

—Jon Kabat-Zinn

A large group of smokers interested in quitting volunteered for an experiment about coping with cravings (Bowen and Marlatt 2009). After abstaining from cigarettes for at least twelve hours, they reported to a university classroom. While sitting at a desk, each person opened a pack of cigarettes, took one out, placed it between his or her lips, and brought a lighter to it without igniting it. This created strong urges to smoke.

Depending on which group they were in, participants practiced one of two strategies for coping with the desire to smoke. For about twenty minutes, half practiced mindful acceptance of their urges: closely observing their sensations, thoughts, and emotions without trying to change or get rid of them; feeling the urges without judgment or self-criticism; and watching the urges ebb and flow like waves without fighting or giving in to them. The other participants did what they normally do when resisting urges: they tried to ignore them or distracted themselves.

For the next seven days, everyone kept track of their moods, smoking urges, and the number of cigarettes they smoked. The groups didn't differ in their moods—all the smokers felt the normal ups and downs of daily life. Nor did they differ in urges to smoke—everyone continued to feel those urges. But those who had practiced mindful acceptance during the experiment smoked fewer cigarettes. They'd learned to feel their moods and urges without yielding to them by lighting up.

Several other studies have shown a similar pattern:

- Chocolate lovers were asked to carry a transparent box of chocolates with them for forty-eight hours without eating any. Those who practiced mindful acceptance of urges ate less chocolate than those who tried to distract themselves (Forman et al. 2007).

- Patients at a clinic for chronic back pain attempted difficult bending and stretching exercises. Some practiced mindful acceptance of the pain; others tried to control or prevent the pain. Both groups found the exercises equally painful, but the mindfulness group completed more of them (Vowles et al. 2007).

- People with anxiety and depression watched an upsetting scene from the classic film *The Deer Hunter*, in which captured soldiers in Vietnam are forced to play Russian roulette. Everyone found it very distressing. However, those who practiced mindful acceptance of their emotions during the film recovered more quickly afterward than those who tried to suppress or control their emotions (Campbell-Sills et al. 2006).

Understanding Acceptance

Acceptance of unpleasant feelings means observing them without judgment and allowing them to take their natural course, rather than trying to change or get rid of them. At first, this may not sound like a good idea. In Western society, we're trained to believe that feeling bad is unnecessary and that we should be able to avoid it if we use the right strategies. But as the studies described above show, trying to control or get rid of thoughts and feelings often causes more trouble than allowing them to come and go in their own way and time. Although that seems paradoxical, accepting unpleasant thoughts and feelings has two important advantages over trying to avoid or escape them:

First, it keeps us out of the psychological traps that make matters worse: rumination, avoidance, emotion-driven behavior, and self-criticism. In fact, we may recover more quickly after an emotional experience if we accept the feelings as they arise.

Second, acceptance of thoughts and feelings helps us perform important but challenging behavior, such as refraining from smoking or doing painful but necessary exercises. Engaging mindfully in goal-consistent behavior, even when it's stressful and uncomfortable, is called willingness (Orsillo and Roemer 2011). To pursue our deepest values, such as love and friendship, satisfying work, caring for our health, or contributing to the community, we often have to do uncomfortable things—express controversial opinions, allow our work to be evaluated, learn new skills that we perform clumsily at first, tell people how we feel about them, or resist temptations. If we accept the reality that we're going to feel awkward, uncomfortable, or tense, and allow these feelings to come and go while focusing on our goals, we'll be more willing to do the things that matter most.

Willingness doesn't mean forcing yourself to do things while trying to suppress or deny the discomfort and criticizing yourself harshly. Telling yourself, *I'm such a coward; I've got to do these exercises; just ignore the pain*, is not willingness. Statements like *There's no denying these exercises are painful. It's unfortunate that I need to do them. Let me do the best I can, keeping in mind that it will be worth it in the end* reflect a willing stance.

In this chapter, we'll explore how to cultivate mindful acceptance of thoughts and feelings, especially the unpleasant and unwanted ones, so they'll cause less suffering and less interference with our willingness to do what matters.

* Susan's Story *

Susan is forty-six years old. She's married, has two teenage sons, and works full-time as a bookkeeper. She's struggled with intermittent depression since her early twenties. For the last several months, she's had difficulty falling asleep. She lies in bed ruminating about how bad she feels and how little she's contributing to the household. Most mornings she's fatigued but forces herself to go to work. After work, she feels exhausted and lethargic and spends her evenings watching TV. Her husband cooks dinner and washes the dishes. Susan used to attend her sons' athletic events and band concerts with pride and enthusiasm, but now she's lost interest and makes excuses not to go. Then she feels guilty about not being a good mother.

Susan knows she'd feel better if she exercised regularly. But every time she thinks of going for a walk, she feels tired, fat, discouraged, and embarrassed. *Not today*, she tells herself. *I really don't have the energy.* Each evening, as bedtime approaches, she feels regretful and guilty. *I've got to do better tomorrow*, she thinks, but each day the pattern is the same.

Susan's doctor referred her to a weekly mindfulness class for people with depression. During the first session, the teacher led the class in a body scan exercise.

EXERCISE: Practicing Acceptance with the Body Scan

The body scan is a meditative exercise used in many mindfulness programs to cultivate flexible, nonjudgmental awareness of bodily sensations (Kabat-Zinn 1990). It involves lying comfortably or sitting in a chair, focusing your attention on different parts of the body, and observing the sensations. Breathing helps you stay in the present and accept the moment as you find it. Here are some important points about practicing the body scan (this version inspired by Segal, Williams, and Teasdale 2002):

- You're not trying to achieve any particular state by doing a body scan. You may get relaxed, or you may not. You may enjoy it, or you may not. You may feel many sensations in your body or only a few. All of these experiences are perfectly okay. Your goal is to focus your attention on each part of the body in turn, bringing your awareness to whatever is happening in each moment and accepting it as it is.

- See if you can refrain from judgments about whether your body and its sensations are good or bad, right or wrong. You're not trying to change your body or how it feels. You're not trying to create sensations or get rid of them. Instead, allow your body to feel just as it feels in each moment. As best you can, adopt an attitude of friendly curiosity and interest about the sensations in your body, as if you were an explorer in new territory. If you notice judgmental thoughts, simply note and label them ("Ah, thinking") and gently return your attention to observing the sensations.

- Your mind will wander off. This is normal. The goal is not to rid your mind of thoughts. When you notice that your attention has drifted, gently bring it back to observing sensations in the body without criticizing yourself.

- You may feel urges to change your position, stretch a muscle, scratch an itch, or rub an ache. Observe the urge closely for a few moments. See if you can adopt a curious and open-minded attitude about the nature of the urge. Where exactly do you feel it? What does it feel like? Are the sensations changing or staying the same? If you decide to act on the urge, do so with mindful awareness. Observe how it feels to move, stretch, scratch, or rub. Notice how your body feels afterward.

- You may have feelings of boredom, restlessness, worry, impatience, and so on. This is normal. It doesn't mean you're doing the exercise wrong or that it isn't working. As best you can, notice these feelings without judging them or yourself as good or bad. Gently return your attention to sensations in the body.

- You may also feel relaxed, calm, or peaceful. If so, practice mindful observation of these feelings and remember that they aren't the goal. The goal is simply to observe whatever appears. All feelings come and go. None are right or wrong.

Before you begin, read through the following instructions carefully. Most people find it easier to practice the body scan while listening to a recording. A twenty-minute recording for the body scan can be found on the website for this book (http://www.newharbinger.com/29033).

Find a place where you can lie on your back on a comfortable surface, such as a bed, carpet, or mat. If you prefer, practice while sitting in a chair, with your feet flat on the floor, your back supported, and your hands resting in your lap. Wear loose, comfortable clothes. Use a sweater or a blanket to stay warm if you like.

It's best to minimize interruptions. If you live with others, ask them not to disturb you. Silence your phone.

Beginning

To begin, settle into your position. If you're lying on your back, allow your arms to rest alongside your body, palms up, and let your feet fall away from each other. If you're sitting in a chair, place your feet comfortably on the floor and rest your hands in your lap. Gently close your eyes and allow the body to become still.

Next, bring your attention to the breath going in and out of your body, however that's happening in your body right in that moment. Notice the sensations in your abdomen as you breathe—rising and falling, expanding and contracting. There's no need to change your breathing in any way. Just notice it as it happens, one breath after another. Continue for a few minutes. When your mind wanders off, gently return to observing your breath.

Feet

Shift your attention down to your feet. Observe them both together or one at a time, whichever you prefer. Notice any sensations. If your feet are warm, cold, itchy, or sweaty, observe that. Notice contact with your shoes, socks, or the floor. Direct your attention throughout your feet: toes, heels, soles, skin, muscles. If you don't feel anything in your feet, notice the absence of sensation. Don't try to make your feet feel different; just observe how they feel. See if you can refrain from judging the sensations as good or bad, right or wrong.

Legs

Shift your attention to your legs. Slowly move your attention through your ankles, lower legs, knees, and thighs. Notice sensations of contact with your clothes, the floor, or the chair. Observe sensations on the skin and within the muscles. If you're thinking about your legs (for example, *too fat*, *too thin*, or *too short*) rather than observing them, let go of the thoughts and return to feeling the sensations as best you can.

Expand your awareness to include your legs, feet, and breath. Your attention may shift back and forth a bit. This is okay. Observe what happens. If you like, imagine that when you breathe in, the breath flows into your legs and all the way down to your feet. Then imagine it flowing all the way back up when you breathe out.

Torso

Shift your attention to your torso. Move your attention slowly through your hips, pelvis, lower back, and lower abdomen. Gradually move up through your back, chest, and shoulders. Take your time and notice all the sensations, on the surface and deep inside. If you find yourself thinking about or judging this area of the body (for example, *unattractive*, *weak*, or *flabby*), gently return to feeling the sensations that are present.

Expand your awareness to include your torso and your breathing. Observe the sensations in your torso while staying aware of your breathing in the background. If you like, imagine that your breath flows into different parts of the torso, such as the hips, back, or shoulders.

Arms and Hands

Slowly move your attention through your arms and hands, noticing all sensations that are present. If you can't feel anything in a particular spot, notice the absence of any sensation there. Let go of judgmental thoughts and simply observe the sensations. If your mind wanders off, gently bring it back.

Expand your awareness to include your breathing. See if you can observe the sensations in your arms and hands while staying aware of your breathing in the background. If you like, imagine that when you breathe in, the breath travels down through your arms and out to your hands. When you breathe out, imagine it traveling the other way.

Neck, Head, and Face

Shift your attention slowly up your neck, feeling all sensations there. Move your awareness into your head. Explore all the regions of your face, taking an interest in any sensations that are present. Allow your attention to include both your breath and your head.

Whole Body

Expand your awareness to include your breath and your entire body. Let go of expectations about how your body and breath should be. Accept them as they are right now. When you're ready, resume your normal activities. See if you can keep some of this mindful awareness going as you move on with your day.

✳ ✳ ✳

It's important to practice the body scan regularly. You won't see much benefit from doing it just once or twice. Try to make time to do this exercise every day for a week or two. Some people prefer to practice early in the morning, before the demands of the day have set in. Others prefer the evening. There is no right or wrong time; any time that works for you is fine.

How the Body Scan Fosters Mindful Acceptance

The body scan provides intensive practice of mindful acceptance of the present moment as it is. Consider the many things that you can accept while doing the body scan: physical discomfort, sleepiness, noises, thoughts and feelings about the exercise, and thoughts and feelings more generally.

Physical Discomfort

Aches, pains, itches, feeling too warm or too cold, and other forms of physical discomfort provide an excellent opportunity to practice friendly interest and acceptance of bodily sensations as you breathe with them and allow them to be as they are. This doesn't mean you have to resign yourself helplessly and passively to feeling uncomfortable. Instead, you're practicing willingness to open up to whatever comes along. If you feel an urge to do something about discomfort, such as change your position or put on a sweater, observe the urge and accept its presence, as if it were a passenger who has boarded your bus. If you decide to act on the urge, do so with nonjudgmental awareness.

Sleepiness

Falling asleep during the body scan is common. If you fall asleep, it isn't a failed practice; you'll probably notice that you spent some of the time sleeping. On the other hand, you'll get more benefit if you stay awake. When sleepiness arises, see if you can observe the sensations of sleepiness with acceptance and interest. If you consistently fall asleep while practicing, try doing the body scan sitting up or with your eyes open, or experiment with different times of day. Perhaps the body scan is telling you that you're sleep deprived.

Distracting Noises

Many people mistakenly believe that meditative exercises require peace and quiet. In fact, noise can be part of the practice. If unpleasant sounds are present, practice accepting them as they are—not in a white-knuckled, clenched-teeth way, but with friendly interest, as best you can. If a dog is barking, observe the sounds. You don't have to be passive or helpless: For example, if it's your dog and the neighbors will be annoyed, it might be wise to bring the dog in. See if you can do the whole thing mindfully: getting up, walking to the door, opening the door, calling the dog, closing the door, returning to your spot, sitting or lying down, and resuming the body scan.

If you're frustrated or angry about sounds you can't control, observe your thoughts and feelings. Remember, you're practicing nonjudgmental acceptance of *everything* that comes up, including noises, distractions, and negative thoughts and emotions. Note their presence and gently return your attention to the body scan as best you can. The goal isn't to make yourself like the sounds or to banish them from your mind; it's okay to hear them, not like them, and not like your reactions to them. Practice acceptance of the entire experience.

Thoughts and Feelings About the Body Scan

It's common and normal to feel bored and restless or to have thoughts like *This is silly; I don't see the point.* Your goal is to recognize these experiences for what they are: emotions (boredom, impatience), thoughts (*I don't like this exercise*, *This won't help me*), and urges (desires to quit and do something else). Observe and accept them without letting them control your behavior. Labeling will help. Say to yourself, "Ah, those are thoughts (*or emotions, or urges*)." You're cultivating one of the most important skills to be learned from practicing mindfulness: willingness to do something important even when it feels unpleasant. Don't give yourself a hard time about not liking it. It's okay to dislike it. Disliking is a normal feeling that comes and goes.

Thoughts and Feelings About Other Things

Everyone's mind wanders. The goal isn't to stop your mind from wandering. Instead, observe when it wanders and gently bring it back. If your mind wanders to painful problems or memories and negative emotions arise, notice what's happening. If you're getting swept up in thoughts—for example, *She had no right to treat me that way* or *The meeting is going to be terrible*, label the experience by saying to yourself, "Angry thoughts are in my mind" or "A feeling of anxiety is here." Then return your attention to the body scan. If you're using a recording, listen closely to what the voice on the recording is saying and follow its instructions as best you can.

* Susan's Experience with the Body Scan *

Susan practiced the body scan nearly every day after the first session of her mindfulness class. She didn't like it at first. Rumination and self-criticism flooded her mind. She kept thinking about all the things she hadn't been doing lately, especially household tasks like cooking and participating in her sons' activities. She had strong urges to stop the body scan and do chores instead. "It's strange," she said during the second meeting of the class. "When I'm watching TV in the evenings, I know I should work on the laundry or empty the dishwasher, but I can't make myself do it. But during the body scan, I have urges to jump up and do these things. I feel guilty just lying there."

Susan's teacher assured her that these feelings are normal and common and encouraged her to persist with the body scan, noticing urges, thoughts, and feelings without being carried away or controlled by them, and gently returning her attention to the sensations in her body.

During the second week of daily body scans, Susan began to notice that she occasionally enjoyed them. At the third session of her mindfulness class, she told her teacher, "I'm starting to see that I don't have to do what my thoughts and feelings tell me to do. If I suddenly have an urge to empty the dryer, I notice that it's an urge. I focus on how it feels in my body and make a mental note to empty the dryer later." Here's how Susan described one especially notable practice:

My younger son, Tim, who's thirteen, was practicing the clarinet in his room while I was doing the body scan downstairs. He was working on a difficult piece. I heard squawks and wrong notes. I realized it's been ages since I talked with Tim about how it's going in band, what music they're working on, and whether he's enjoying it. I started thinking about what a bad mother I've been. But I didn't go down that road in my mind. I firmly told myself to come back to my body. I observed the sinking feeling in my stomach and breathed with it. Then I started listening to the clarinet again, and I realized Tim was making progress with the difficult passage. I felt happy and proud of him. I wanted to jump up and tell him how good he sounded. Of course, that was also a distraction, so I focused on my body and noticed sensations that were part of the happy feeling. I felt lighter. There was an uplifting feeling in my chest.

For the last few minutes, my mind was alternating between the body scan and the clarinet, but I kept coming back to the body scan until I finished it. I learned that I can keep going with things that are important, even if distracting thoughts and feelings come to my mind. And if I don't get caught up in obsessing and ruminating, I'm more aware of things around me, like what's going on with my kids.

Why It Makes Sense to Focus on the Body

To understand why the body scan is helpful, let's look closely at what happens to Susan when she wakes up on a typical morning: First she notices a feeling of fatigue. Immediately she has thoughts about it: *I didn't sleep well. Today will be terrible. I'll be so exhausted. Why does this keep happening? I hate feeling this way. What's the matter with me? Why can't I be normal?* This is rumination and makes her feel worse. Then she tells herself not to think about it. *Come on. Get going. You're wasting time,* she tells herself harshly, and she forces herself out of bed. The self-critical tone adds to her feelings of unworthiness. She showers and dresses in a bad mood, then goes into the kitchen for coffee and a quick breakfast. Her sons appear at about this time with their minds on the school day ahead. She'd like to have a cheerful word with them before they leave for the bus stop, but she's preoccupied and misses the moment. She drives to work lost in thoughts about how badly things are going.

Now let's see how Susan's experience changes as she learns to direct more mindful attention to her body: Susan wakes up and notices a feeling of fatigue. She quickly scans her body, noting sensations of heaviness in her arms, legs, and chest. She takes a few mindful breaths, imagining her breath traveling through her arms and legs. A thought appears: *Why am I always so tired?* She recognizes that it's a thought and says to herself, *I don't need to get sucked into rumination. I've been a bit depressed lately. Tiredness is part of it.* Gently she stretches her arms and legs, observing the sensations and noticing that she feels slightly more wakeful though still rather blue. *What do I need?* she asks herself. *A quick shower and a healthy breakfast, and maybe a walk after dinner tonight for some exercise.*

Feeling more willing to engage with the day, she gets out of bed, feeling the cool floor under her feet. As she follows her morning routine, she's aware of feelings of fatigue and sadness, but she doesn't ruminate or criticize herself. She also notices many other things, such as the soap and water on her body in the shower, the warmth from the hair dryer, and hot coffee moving down her throat. She chats briefly with her sons, says, "Have a good day!" and drives to work, feeling her hands on the steering wheel and observing her surroundings.

Emotions have strong bodily components. Depression includes physical sensations of fatigue and heaviness that can trigger unhealthy behavior and thinking patterns, especially when we're not paying attention. Observing what's happening in her body helps Susan recognize her emotions as they come and go without falling into the traps of rumination and self-criticism. She hasn't gotten rid of all the unpleasant feelings; rather, she's expanded her awareness to make room for them while treating herself with kindness and doing things she values.

What If the Body Scan Is Intensely Difficult and Unpleasant?

If you experience very strong negative emotions or traumatic memories during the body scan, you may feel that this practice is too difficult. Before giving up on it, consider the following options.

Gentle, compassionate persistence can overcome many difficulties. Experiment with practicing for shorter periods, with your eyes open, or sitting up rather than lying down. You might scan only your legs and feet one day, and your torso another. See if you can find a way to be kind to yourself without abandoning this exercise.

Alternatively, if the body scan is a serious obstacle, postpone working with it for now and try again later. Meanwhile, use the approaches in chapter 10 to practice awareness of the body with mindful walking or mindfulness of other routine activities, such as showering or bathing, brushing your teeth, combing your hair, standing in line, cooking, shopping, or emptying the trash. In addition to the obvious parts of the body, see if you can observe your feet while combing your hair, the opposite hand as you brush your teeth, or your abdomen while standing in line.

If you've suffered traumatic experiences or are susceptible to intense negative emotions, consider working with a mental health professional who has knowledge of mindfulness-based treatments. An experienced teacher can help you overcome difficulties with the body scan and find ways to benefit from it.

EXERCISE: Practicing Acceptance and Willingness in Daily Life with Mindful Pausing

Mindful pausing is a way to apply the skills learned from the body scan to ordinary life. The goal of mindful pausing is to step out of automatic pilot, bring mindful awareness into the present moment, and see what the situation requires. Mindful pausing has several steps. Use the acronym SOBER to remember them, as outlined below:

- **S: Stop or slow down.** Say to yourself, *Okay, let's pause for a moment* or something similar. Adjust your posture and let it reflect your intention to be open to the present moment: Straighten your spine a bit, aligning your head directly over your neck. Lower your shoulders and relax your jaw.

- **O: Observe.** What's happening right now in your body and mind? Notice sensations, thoughts, emotions, and urges. It may be helpful to label them—for example, *Tension in my shoulders... Heaviness in my chest... A feeling of anger is here... Self-critical thoughts are racing around... Feeling sad and stressed... Wishing I could leave work early.*

- **B: Breathe.** Observe the sensations as your breath goes in and out. Focus your attention just on breathing as best you can. When your mind is pulled away, gently bring it back to breathing. Experiment with silent labeling or counting—for example, *Breathing in 1...breathing out 1...breathing in 2...breathing out 2...,* and so on. Take at least two or three mindful breaths, or five or ten if you have enough time.

- **E: Expand your awareness.** Observe your body as a whole, including your sensations, posture, and facial expression. Focus gently and kindly on uncomfortable sensations. Breathe with them and allow them to be as they are. Say something along these lines to yourself: *Let me just notice this, It's okay for me to feel this,* or *It's already here. Let me go ahead and feel it.*

- **R: Respond mindfully.** As best you can, choose wisely what to do. In some situations, the wisest option is to allow a situation or feeling to run its natural course. In other situations, you may need to take action. Mindful pausing will help you remember what you care about and discern what the situation requires.

✻ *Susan's Experience with Mindful Pausing* ✻

Mindful pausing allowed Susan to realize what she was feeling and thinking and how her thoughts and feelings were controlling her behavior. One day just as she came into the house after work, her son Tim reminded her that he had a band concert that evening. Her immediate feeling was dread, and her first impulse was to say she was too tired to go. But she held back. "Oh," she said, standing by the door and looking at Tim.

Silently, she reminded herself to pause. She observed feelings of fatigue and irritation—with herself for forgetting the concert and with Tim for not reminding her. She also noticed a desire to collapse into the recliner and watch TV. *But I do that every night, and I don't feel any better,* she thought. She stood up a little straighter, took a breath, and observed her body standing in the hall, still wearing her coat, holding her purse and keys, her feet aching in her work shoes.

"Mom," said Tim. "Are you okay?" She looked into his concerned face, realizing she'd been staring at him for several seconds. "Yes," she said, with a bit more energy. "Let's have an early supper so we can all get to the concert." Mindfully, she set down her purse, hung up her coat, and changed her shoes. She and her husband organized a quick meal. Susan noticed that everyone seemed cheerful, and she felt a little happier herself.

In the car on the way to the concert, a feeling of exhaustion came over her. She observed her breath for a few moments and allowed her body to sink into the car seat while her husband drove and the kids chattered in the back. *The concert is important to Tim,* she told herself. *He wants me to be there. I might even enjoy it.*

To her surprise, Susan did enjoy the concert. The band played well, several of the parents chatted with her afterward, and her family seemed very pleased that she was there. Mindful pausing helped Susan behave consistently with something she cares about: participating in her kids' activities. She accepted the presence of unpleasant emotions and sensations and willingly went to the concert.

EXERCISE: Developing an Ongoing Practice of Acceptance and Willingness

Make a commitment to practice acceptance and willingness more often, then use the following worksheet to keep a record of your experiences. There are three versions of the worksheet. The first provides instructions. The second is an example from Susan. After the example, you'll find a blank version for your own use. Again, make copies of the blank version so you can use it repeatedly.

WORKSHEET: Acceptance and Willingness Log

Remember to maintain an attitude of friendly curiosity.

Day and time	In the service of these values and goals…	I practiced mindful acceptance of these thoughts and feelings…	And willingness to do these behaviors or activities…
When did this example occur?	What were the important values and goals you were pursuing? (For a review of values and goals, revisit chapter 7.) General categories: Work Family Other relationships Self-care, health Contributing to others or the community	What did you observe in your body and mind? General categories and examples: Body sensations (aching, fatigue) Thoughts (*I don't feel like doing this, This is going to be terrible*) Urges (desires or impulses to do something) Emotions (sadness, anger, fear) Other (images, memories) **Important note:** Acceptance doesn't mean you liked, wanted, or approved of your thoughts and feelings; it only means that you acknowledged them and allowed them to come and go on their own without letting them control your behavior.	What did you do that was consistent with your values and goals? **Important note:** Willingness means that you went ahead with behavior consistent with your values and goals. It doesn't mean that doing so necessarily felt good. You may have felt anxious, sad, fatigued, discouraged, frustrated, angry, or otherwise. However you felt is okay.

161

WORKSHEET: Acceptance and Willingness Log

Your name: *Susan*

Remember to maintain an attitude of friendly curiosity.

Day and time	In the service of these values and goals…	I practiced mindful acceptance of these thoughts and feelings…	And willingness to do these behaviors or activities…
Saturday 9 a.m.	*Taking better care of myself by getting exercise*	*I thought, I'm too fat and out of shape. There's no point. It will be embarrassing. I felt heavy and tired, wanted to stay inside, had a sense of dread, and felt gloomy and discouraged.*	*Went for a walk around the neighborhood. Observed sensations of walking and my surroundings. Spoke to a couple of neighbors who were out walking.*
Thursday 5:30 p.m.	*Being a good mother by being involved in my kids' activities*	*I thought, I'm too tired to go to Tim's concert tonight. He should have reminded me so I'd be prepared. I felt fatigued and irritated. I wanted to stay home.*	*Got a quick dinner ready. Went to Tim's band concert. Enjoyed it more than I thought I would.*
Monday 2 p.m.	*Being a good employee by being helpful to others at work*	*Felt nervous, anxious. My heart was beating fast and I had a trembly feeling. I thought people would get bored or confused.*	*Gave a training session for my coworkers on how to use a new software program.*

WORKSHEET: Acceptance and Willingness Log

Your name: _____

Remember to maintain an attitude of friendly curiosity.

Day and time	In the service of these values and goals...	I practiced mindful acceptance of these thoughts and feelings...	And willingness to do these behaviors or activities...

*   *Susan's Story Continued*   *

By practicing the body scan and mindful pausing, Susan learned some important lessons. Behaving consistently with her values and goals is satisfying, and she doesn't have to feel any particular way to get started. When she feels blue, discouraged, tired, and unmotivated, she can turn her attention to the sensations in her body, observe her breath, accept her thoughts and emotions as they ebb and flow, and choose wisely what to do. Although she finds it difficult to do things when she feels discouraged, fatigued, or nervous, it's also empowering. It gives her a feeling of inner strength to realize that her thoughts and feelings don't have to control her behavior.

As Susan works toward greater willingness to behave consistently with her values and goals, she'll have to be careful to avoid a big pitfall: taking a harsh, self-critical attitude. Forcing herself to do things, telling herself she's an idiot or a failure if she doesn't, and mentally beating herself up is inconsistent with a mindful, accepting attitude and will lead to rumination, avoidance, and worsening mood.

Like Susan, most of us find it difficult to treat ourselves compassionately, and it's even harder if we've struggled with anxiety, depression, and other problems. In the next chapter, we'll explore how self-compassion and mindfulness work together to help us accept ourselves as human beings while building the life we want.

Chapter Summary

- Acceptance of thoughts and feelings is an important mindfulness skill. It means observing our thoughts and feelings and allowing them to run their natural course without trying to suppress them or get rid of them in unhealthy ways.

- Willingness means going ahead with behaviors and activities that are important to pursuing our values and goals even when doing so is difficult and uncomfortable.

- Practicing the body scan cultivates acceptance and willingness. When difficult thoughts and feelings arise, mindful observation and acceptance of sensations in the body help keep us out of the psychological traps discussed in part 2 of the book: rumination, suppression and avoidance, emotion-driven behavior, and self-criticism.

- Mindful pausing gives us time to see clearly what's happening in the mind and body and choose wisely what to do. Sometimes the wise choice is to allow difficult feelings and situations to run their natural course. At other times, we need to take action. Keeping our important values and goals in mind helps us choose meaningful and satisfying behavior.

CHAPTER 12

Self-Compassion

True mindfulness is imbued with warmth, compassion, and interest.
—Christina Feldman

The importance of compassion has been recognized since ancient times. Most of the world's religions teach that compassion, kindness, and caring for others are essential virtues. Modern scientists believe that compassion is a part of human nature that evolved because it helps us survive: communities in which people care for each other are more likely to provide a healthy environment for future generations (Germer and Siegel 2012).

Most definitions of compassion include both feelings and actions: empathy and concern for people who are suffering, and working to alleviate suffering (Gilbert 2009). Acting with compassion can be difficult. It requires awareness of others' pain, along with willingness to stay present and try to help, even when turning away would be easier and more comfortable. Despite the difficulties, most people agree that we should aspire to treat others with compassion whenever possible.

We tend to be less convinced that we should be compassionate toward ourselves (Germer 2009). We fear that self-compassion will make us lazy and undisciplined, that it's selfish, or that we don't deserve it (Neff 2003). As a result, we're often harsh and unkind to ourselves during difficult times, blaming and criticizing ourselves in ways that would seem cruel if directed toward others. However, research shows that self-compassion is much healthier than self-criticism, and that practicing mindfulness makes us more self-compassionate (Neff 2011). In this chapter, we'll explore the nature of self-compassion and the benefits of treating ourselves kindly.

*   *Dana's Story*   *

Dana is worried about her weight. She's usually on a diet and has many personal rules about foods to eat and to avoid. Like most dieters, she often has a paradoxical reaction when she eats a food she's denying herself: rather than returning immediately to her diet plan, she eats more of the forbidden food.

This happens because eating food that's usually off limits triggers self-critical thoughts and feelings of regret, shame, and inadequacy. Dana tells herself she's hopeless, has no self-control, and might as well eat more. The forbidden food is comforting and temporarily distracts her from her difficulties in living up to her goals. This may sound irrational, but it's a surprisingly common pattern. The same thing happens with people trying to cut back on drinking or smoking. If you've ever behaved this way, you're not alone.

Dana (whose story is adapted with permission from Adams and Leary 2007) volunteered for a study at the local university. She was told it was about eating while watching TV; in reality, it was about the effects of self-compassion on eating sweets. When Dana arrived, the researcher asked her to sit alone in a room and eat a doughnut while watching a video. Dana's heart sank; she tries to avoid doughnuts because of the fat and sugar. But she complied. When she finished watching the video, the researcher entered the room and said, "You might wonder why we picked doughnuts to use in the study. It's because people sometimes eat unhealthy, sweet foods while they watch TV. But several people have told me they feel bad about eating doughnuts in this study, so I hope you won't be hard on yourself. Everyone eats unhealthily sometimes, so I don't think there's any reason to feel bad about it. This small amount of food doesn't really matter anyway."

This message was designed to help the participants adopt a self-compassionate attitude: recognizing that eating unhealthy food is common, refraining from excessive self-criticism, and taking a balanced perspective on the situation. After hearing this statement, Dana felt a bit better. *She's right*, Dana thought. *It was just one doughnut, and not a very large one. That's not so bad. I can eat healthy the rest of the day.*

Then the researcher brought three bowls of candy into the room along with a form for rating their taste, texture, appearance, and aroma. She asked Dana to taste the candies, complete the rating form, and then fill out some questionnaires. "You can eat as much of the candy as you like while you're working," she said. "I'll be in the next room. Come and tell me when you've finished all the forms."

All of the participants in this study were concerned about their weight. Half of them, including Dana, heard the compassionate message after eating the doughnut. The others weren't given this reassurance. The real purpose of the study was to find out which group would eat more candy during the taste test. Previous studies had shown that a diet violation, such as eating a doughnut, tends to weaken self-control, causing people to eat more candy than they would otherwise. In the current study, researchers were interested in whether encouragement to adopt a self-compassionate attitude would make a difference.

The results were clear. Those who weren't given the compassionate message showed the typical pattern: they were more distressed about eating the doughnut, reported more self-criticism about it, and ate more candy during the rest of the experiment. Those who had been encouraged to be self-compassionate were less upset and less self-judgmental, and ate less candy. Dana's experience was consistent with this pattern: She was tempted by the candy, but she ate only slightly more than necessary to complete the taste test.

After Dana had finished the taste test and questionnaires, the researcher explained the real purpose of the study. Dana was intrigued. "After you told me not to be hard on myself about the doughnut, it felt easier to resist the candy," she told the researcher. Dana was starting to realize what the study confirmed: a self-compassionate attitude helped people with weight concerns eat less of a tempting but unhealthy food.

* George's Story *

George (whose story is adapted with permission from Kelly et al. 2010) has been a regular smoker for ten years. He's extremely self-critical about his failure to quit, often berating himself for his lack of self-discipline. He volunteered for a study about ways to reduce smoking and was assigned to a group that learned self-compassion skills. During a forty-five-minute session, the researcher guided him through several activities:

First they discussed the self-compassionate approach to smoking reduction, which has the following elements:

- Understanding of how difficult it is to quit

- Wisdom about what's best for one's long-term well-being

- Strength to cope with setbacks

- Nonjudgment when failures occur

- Warmth in relating to oneself

Next, George visualized adopting these qualities and wrote himself a letter from the perspective of a compassionate person:

I'm really glad you're taking steps to help yourself feel better in the long run. Making this decision is difficult and brave, and I know it's hard for you. I'd like to help you get through the difficult moments. It will be stressful, but let's try to tolerate the short-term pain to feel healthier in the long run. This is hard. Giving up cigarettes is a huge loss. Let's focus on smoking reduction as one of the kindest things you can do for yourself.

Then George practiced what to say to himself from a self-compassionate perspective when faced with urges to smoke:

I know you really want this cigarette. I feel how hard this is for you. Let's focus on your long-term well-being. To feel better and be healthier, let's try to resist this cigarette in spite of how hard it is. I know you can do it, and in time you'll be grateful that you did.

George felt skeptical but agreed that for the next three weeks he would give these skills his best effort. He reread the self-compassionate letter every day and talked to himself in a self-compassionate way whenever he felt an urge to smoke. He kept detailed records of the cigarettes he smoked. The control group kept the same records but didn't learn about self-compassion. Over the three-week period, the self-compassion group smoked substantially fewer cigarettes. The difference was greatest for people like George, who were extremely self-critical prior to the study. Once again, self-compassion was more effective than self-criticism in helping people change an unhealthy habit.

At the end of the three weeks, George met with the researcher to turn in his forms and discuss the study. "I have to admit I'm surprised," he said. "I really thought this was silly. I thought I had to beat myself up to make any progress at all. But I've been doing that for years and I'm still a smoker. During these last three weeks I've cut way back. If I keep this up, I might be able to quit completely."

The Many Benefits of Self-Compassion

Most research studies are short-term. George practiced self-compassion for three weeks. Dana was encouraged to be self-compassionate on a single occasion. Studies of people who are naturally self-compassionate or who have practiced self-compassion for months or years show that a general attitude of self-compassion has many benefits (Neff 2012). For example, self-compassionate people are less likely to become depressed. They feel the normal ups and downs of daily life and have sad thoughts and feelings when misfortunes occur. But they ruminate less, and they don't try to suppress their feelings; they weather emotional storms with acceptance and equanimity, and without descending into depression (Kuyken et al. 2010).

Self-compassionate people are also less likely to develop anxiety disorders, especially if something traumatic happens to them. They're less angry and hostile. In addition, they're less perfectionistic, have less fear of failure, and are more open to growth and learning. When they encounter awkward or embarrassing situations, they keep their emotional balance and a healthy perspective (Neff 2011).

Concerns About Self-Compassion

When people are encouraged to practice more self-compassion, certain concerns tend to arise. The following ones are especially common.

"Isn't Self-Compassion Selfish?"

People often feel they should focus primarily on others' needs, rather than their own. However, studies using brain scans show that the same area of the brain is activated whether people are compassionate toward themselves or others (Davidson 2007). This may explain why self-compassionate people also show more concern for others: they're more compassionate in general. Before criticizing someone, they're more likely to imagine how they'd feel in that person's place (Neff and Pommier 2013). In romantic relationships, they're more supportive of their partners, less aggressive and controlling, and more respectful of their partner's opinions (Neff and Beretvas 2013).

People in the helping professions, such as doctors, nurses, therapists, and the clergy, are susceptible to compassion fatigue and burnout—forms of emotional exhaustion brought on by working with people who are suffering. Research shows that self-compassion reduces burnout, making it easier to continue practicing compassion toward others (Barnard and Curry 2012). People who take good care of themselves, accept negative thoughts and emotions as a normal part of their job, and refrain from harsh self-criticism are less likely to become drained, discouraged, and disconnected from the people they work with (Ringenbach 2009). They're also more likely to find satisfaction in their opportunities to make a difference in the world, despite the inevitable stress.

"What If I Don't Feel Kindly or Compassionate Toward Myself?"

George didn't always feel self-compassionate when urges to smoke arose. Sometimes he felt self-critical, self-blaming, and guilty. We don't have to feel kindly toward ourselves in order to behave in a self-compassionate way. When we act with self-compassion, we try to find the wisest and most helpful course of action for the circumstances, regardless of how we're feeling in the moment.

You've probably behaved nicely to others when you were annoyed with them and thought they didn't deserve it, perhaps because you value treating people with decency and respect. If you value treating yourself in the same way, a principle discussed in chapter 7 applies: behaving consistently with important values doesn't have to depend on the feelings that are present in any particular moment.

EXERCISE: Practicing Self-Compassion When It's Difficult

If you're feeling undeserving of self-compassion because you've made mistakes, hurt someone, or caused harm, gently experiment with the following approach.

Remind yourself that everyone makes mistakes, hurts others, and causes harm now and then.

Remember that guilt and remorse are built into human nature. Their purpose is to motivate us to apologize, make amends, and correct our mistakes as best we can. They're useful emotions if we handle them constructively. Mindfulness and self-compassion help us do this.

Observe your thoughts and emotions without judgment, including thoughts such as *I don't deserve compassion*. Remember that this is a thought.

Observe the sensations in your body. Breathe with them.

Ask yourself, *What really matters to me in this situation? What behavior is consistent with my values and goals?*

Remember that constructive self-criticism can be helpful, but that you're more likely to behave consistently with your values and goals if you're not consumed with excessive self-criticism. (For a review of constructive criticism, revisit chapter 6.)

What Self-Compassion Is and Isn't

If you're a highly self-critical person, self-compassion may seem nearly impossible. It's important to understand that self-compassion is a set of skills that anyone can practice. In the rest of this chapter we'll explore how to cultivate these skills. First, here's a summary of what self-compassion is and is not.

Self-compassion includes…	Self-compassion does not include…
Seeing situations clearly, including our own mistakes. This requires mindful observation and keeping a balanced perspective.	Ignoring our mistakes and weaknesses or giving ourselves false praise.
Recognizing that pain, hardships, failures, and inadequacies are part of being human. Everyone experiences them.	Wallowing in self-pity. While pitying ourselves we tend to forget that many others have similar problems or suffer in their own ways.
Caring for ourselves with kindness and understanding because we're human, not because we're above average or special.	Judging ourselves, either positively or negatively, or evaluating whether we're superior or inferior to others.
Constructive, persistent efforts to change behaviors or correct mistakes that are causing harm.	Being lazy, self-indulgent, or undisciplined.

Five Ways to Cultivate Self-Compassion

The cultivation of self-compassion skills takes practice. Here are five effective techniques.

Practicing the Mindfulness Exercises You Already Know

Research shows that people who consistently practice mindfulness become more self-compassionate (Shapiro et al. 2005). This isn't surprising. As we've seen, mindfulness includes a kind, openhearted, and friendly attitude toward ourselves, especially when we're having painful thoughts and feelings. The mindfulness exercises described in previous chapters will help you develop your self-compassion skills. This will be good for your mental health.

Basic Self-Care

Eating a nutritious diet, exercising regularly, and getting enough sleep are among the kindest things you can do for yourself. You'll still have negative emotions, but there's a good chance they'll be less intense and won't last as long if you're well nourished and rested. You'll cope with them better because you'll have more energy for practicing the mindfulness skills you've been learning. You'll think more clearly and make wiser decisions. You may also feel more positive emotions.

Don't try to overhaul your health habits all at once. Behavior change takes time and patience. Start with small goals, like eating a healthier breakfast, going for a walk after dinner, or going to bed at a reasonable hour. Gradually add other healthy behaviors. Remember to apply the mindfulness skills you've learned to eating and exercising. If you have trouble sleeping, the following suggestions may help:

- **Sleeping environment**

  - Use a good mattress and pillow.

  - Keep the room dark, quiet, and at a comfortable temperature.

- **Eating, drinking, and exercise**

  - Eat regular, nutritious meals.

  - Don't go to bed hungry.

  - Avoid heavy or greasy foods before bed. A light snack is okay.

  - Avoid caffeine and alcohol in the evenings. Drink other liquids in moderation.

  - Exercise regularly, but not within three hours of bedtime.

- **Time spent in bed**

  - Don't spend extra time in bed. If you need seven hours of sleep, spend seven hours in bed.

- Use your bed only for sleeping and sex. Read, eat, and watch TV elsewhere.

- Go to bed and get up at roughly the same time every day.

- **If you can't sleep**

  - Get up, go to another room, and do something quiet and relaxing, like read a book (not an exciting one). Don't watch TV or use a computer; the bright screen may induce wakefulness. When you feel sleepy, go back to bed.

  - Put the clock where you can't see it. Clock-watching during the night can cause frustration and worry, which interfere with sleep.

  - Practice mindful acceptance of not sleeping.

Savoring

Imagine going to an excellent restaurant, ordering your favorite dish, eating it mindfully, and relishing the moment while focusing your attention on the delicious flavors, aromas, and textures. This is savoring. The alternative is to eat mindlessly while checking your messages, reading, talking with someone, or thinking of other things.

Now imagine that you've just won an award at work. You've received a glowing letter from your supervisor praising your performance and telling you that your name will be added to the plaque in the main hall. Savor this by allowing yourself to bask in your good feelings.

Some people are wary of savoring. They think that it will bring on bad luck, that they don't deserve their good fortune, that it's unseemly to enjoy things too much, or that they can't live up to the high standard they somehow attained on this unusual occasion (Peterson 2006). However, research shows that people who consistently enjoy and appreciate their positive experiences are happier, more optimistic, and less likely to be depressed than people who don't (Bryant 2003). Savoring is an excellent way to be kind to yourself.

Use your mindfulness skills to practice savoring. When you have a pleasant experience, observe it closely and allow the good feelings to flow. If you're having a delightful time at a gathering of family or friends, be present and enjoy it to the fullest. If you've finished a difficult piece of work and you're pleased with how it turned out, relish the feelings of pride and satisfaction. When doubtful thoughts arise, such as *This won't last, I can't expect things to keep going this well*, or *That was just good luck; I don't really deserve this*, label them as thoughts and gently return your attention to enjoying the moment while it lasts.

Self-Soothing

Self-soothing is a way of being gentle and kind with yourself when you're under stress and feeling upset. It focuses on the five senses (Linehan 1993b). Instead of waiting for pleasant experiences to come along, intentionally seek out simple comforting experiences and attend to them mindfully to help yourself through difficult moments. Here's an example: Robin is a fifty-two-year-old woman who found a lump in her breast.

She had a biopsy and then had to wait for three days to learn the results. She practiced self-soothing during that time and wrote this account of her experiences:

Waiting for the results of the biopsy was very difficult. I continued to go to work, but in the evenings it was hard to keep myself from obsessing and worrying. I tried to eat healthy, but I was so anxious I didn't have much appetite. I decided that self-soothing might help. I tried all kinds of things. I don't like the winter cold, so I focused on warm things.

One evening I took a hot bath with some scented bath oil and listened to my favorite music. I savored the sensations, sounds, and smells. My mind went back to thinking about cancer at times, but I kept bringing it back. I drank tea and hot chocolate, and I ate soup and toast made from my favorite bread. I tried to eat and drink everything mindfully. I watched entertaining movies with my husband, Jerry, while snuggling in a soft quilt. Jerry put it in the dryer for a few minutes first so it was nice and warm. We also made fires in the fireplace and I watched the flames, listened to the crackling sounds, and smelled the smoky scent. I mindfully petted our cat a lot. He has a big soft tummy and a wonderful purr. That was very comforting.

Self-soothing made those three days a little easier. Staying in the present was difficult at times but much better than dwelling on the fear and uncertainty for endless hours. On the fourth day I learned that I have an early-stage cancer that can be treated successfully in most people. I'll continue being kind to myself while I go through the treatment.

Self-soothing isn't a form of avoidance or suppression; you're not denying that you're in a difficult situation and feeling upset, nor are you avoiding constructive behavior that might solve the problem. Self-soothing is a way to be self-compassionate when you have a stressful problem that can't be solved right away. It helps you be aware of the present moment without ruminating, obsessing, or behaving rashly. It puts you in a better frame of mind for taking wise action when you can.

Here are some suggestions for self-soothing with each of your five senses (inspired in part by Linehan 1993b and Neff 2011); you may have other ideas that would work well for you:

- **Eating, drinking, or cooking**

  - See the colors, textures, and shapes of the food and its arrangement on the plate.

  - Hear any sounds: chopping, sizzling, fizzing, bubbling, and so on.

  - Smell the aromas and taste the flavors.

  - Notice the temperature, texture, and weight of the food and the feel of utensils, cups, or glasses.

- **Being out in nature or in a park**

  - See the trees, flowers, wildlife, or waves if you're near water.

  - Hear the breeze, birds, waves, other people, or passing cars.

  - Smell the air, flowers, water, and so on.

- Feel the ground under your feet, the air and sun on your skin, or the texture of tree trunks.

- **Being out in your neighborhood or in a city**

  - See houses, trees, gardens, or people passing.

  - Hear the sounds.

  - Smell any scents in the air.

  - Feel the ground under your feet.

- **Listening to music you enjoy**

  - If you're at a live performance, see the musicians playing.

  - See images that the music brings to mind.

  - Hear the instruments, melodies, and harmonies.

  - Feel the rhythm if you like, and move to the beat.

- **Being indoors**

  - Watch a fire in the fireplace. Hear the crackling sounds and smell the smoke.

  - Take a bath or shower, feel and hear the water, and smell the soap or shampoo.

  - Wear your most comfortable clothes and feel the texture on your skin.

  - Put flowers around your house—see their colors and shapes, and smell their scents.

The key to self-soothing is to do it mindfully. Closely observe whatever you see, hear, smell, taste, or touch. Savor it. When your mind wanders off, gently bring it back without criticizing yourself.

Self-soothing doesn't have to be time-consuming. If you don't have time for a long bath or sitting in front of a fire, think about ways to make your regular environment more soothing. Photos or pictures, plants or flowers, background music, a more comfortable chair—all can provide brief soothing moments at home or work. Some people find that self-affectionate behavior, such as placing your hand over your heart or gently stroking your own arm, is soothing.

Self-Validation

Validation is a kind and helpful way of practicing mindful acceptance of thoughts and feelings. It involves observing thoughts and feelings without judgment and recognizing that they're understandable given the circumstances, even if they seem irrational on the surface. We can validate either ourselves or other people. In the following example, Tony validates his daughter, who's frightened of a bee:

I was driving with my eight-year-old daughter, Lindsey, in the backseat, and suddenly she started screaming hysterically that there's a bee in the car. I pulled over and waved the bee out the window. Lindsey was wailing that she didn't want to go to the hospital again. I was confused because she's never been in the hospital. But then I remembered that last year we were on a trip and Lindsey got an insect bite just under her eye. We put ointment on it, but it was uncomfortable and everywhere we went people asked what happened to her eye.

So we took her to a clinic. It wasn't a hospital, but maybe Lindsey remembers it that way. She didn't like being there. She was afraid she'd get an injection. The doctor said it was an insect bite and gave us more ointment, and eventually it went away. I'd forgotten all about it but Lindsey remembered.

So I said, "I understand the bee scared you because you ended up at a clinic that time when everyone was looking at the bug bite under your eye. That was no fun." That helped her settle down, so then I said, "Let's figure out what you can do if a bee gets in the car again." Lindsey said she could open the window and she could tell me. She thought she'd be able to stay calmer next time.

Tony's behavior is a good example of validation. He communicated to Lindsey that her emotional reaction was understandable in the circumstances. His behavior was kind, considerate, and constructive. It helped Lindsey feel calmer and make a plan for what to do on future occasions. Tony loves Lindsey deeply, but he didn't *feel* very compassionate during this incident; he was impatient with the delay and irritated with Lindsey for making such a fuss. However, he *behaved* in a kind and compassionate way because he values being a supportive parent. Many psychologists believe that children who grow up with validating adults learn healthy ways of managing upsetting situations and negative emotions.

Lindsey's reaction to the bee seemed irrational and out of proportion at first. Tony had to think for a moment before it made sense to him. As discussed in previous chapters, emotions may seem illogical on the surface, but they usually make sense for the following reasons (Linehan 1993b):

- **Emotions are built into human nature; we have them because they serve useful purposes.** Lindsey's emotional reaction was a way of communicating her fear and motivating her father to take action to help her.

- **Normal learning and conditioning processes have a big impact on our emotional reactions.** Lindsey has learned from experience to associate small flying insects with uncomfortable bites or stings and scary medical environments.

- **Brain and body chemistry influence how we feel our emotions.** Some people naturally have intense, easily triggered emotions, whereas others are less sensitive. Lindsey may have an intense emotional temperament. If so, validation and learning constructive ways to handle upsetting situations will be especially important for her.

- **Temporary conditions also influence how we think and feel.** If we're tired, hungry, sick, or in pain, we're more susceptible to strong negative thoughts and emotions. Perhaps Lindsey was tired or hungry that day.

Validation isn't just for children. Research shows that it makes difficult tasks less stressful for adults. In one study, students attempted several sets of challenging mental arithmetic problems (Shenk and Fruzzetti 2011). During rest periods, the researcher conversed with them about how it felt to work on the problems.

For half of the participants, the researcher made validating comments, like "It really is hard to do math problems without pencil and paper" or "Most of the other participants felt the same way you do." For the other participants, the researcher was invalidating, saying things like "I don't understand why you would feel that way" or "They're just math problems. There's no point in getting frustrated." Those who were invalidated got more and more annoyed and stressed as the study went on, and their heart rates went up. Those who were validated stayed calm, and their heart rates went down.

Validating ourselves is just as important as validating other people, though sometimes more difficult. Here's an example of self-validation from Joel, who works in a frozen yogurt shop:

> *I got to work and found that the guy I was supposed to be working with had called in sick. This meant that I had to do the work of two people all day. I was angry and wanted to take care of only my own responsibilities. Then I felt guilty for thinking that way and told myself I had a bad attitude. Then I remembered to self-validate. My feelings were totally normal and understandable for that situation. Instead of judging myself, I considered the consequences of acting on my wishes. I realized that if I only did my own tasks, my boss would be upset with me, and for good reason. I decided to take care of everything that needed doing as best I could. I didn't want to jeopardize my job or my reputation as a good worker. It was a hard day, but I was able to keep things going pretty well on my own. I stayed focused on what I needed to do and didn't obsess about the situation. I felt proud of myself at the end of the day.*

Joel's self-validation was kind and constructive. It helped him stop criticizing himself for having normal thoughts and feelings. He accepted them as understandable, didn't dwell on them, and willingly took on the tasks consistent with being a responsible employee—one of his important values.

How to Validate Your Thoughts and Feelings in Difficult Situations

Self-validation includes several steps. It combines self-compassion skills with mindfulness skills you already know: mindful observation and labeling, accepting the reality of a situation, and mindful pausing. When you talk to yourself in the ways recommended here, see if you can use a kind and sympathetic tone.

Step 1. Mindfully Observing and Labeling

First you have to recognize when you're having a difficult or stressful experience. It may be helpful to pause and label it, using words that feel natural. Here are some examples:

- *I'm having a difficult (painful, upsetting) moment.*

- *This is a tough (unpleasant, stressful) situation.*

Take a few moments to observe your thoughts and feelings without judging them or judging yourself for having them.

Step 2. Recognizing That This Is a Common Human Experience

Remind yourself that everyone goes through difficult and painful situations, has unpleasant thoughts and feelings, and does things they regret. These experiences are part of life. Here are some examples:

- *Everyone has difficulties at some point.*

- *Problems are a normal part of life.*

- *Everyone makes mistakes.*

- *I'm not the only one who…*

Step 3. Expressing Kind Understanding

Remember that your thoughts and feelings are a result of your brain and body chemistry, your previous learning experiences, and the current situation. They make sense in their own way, even if they seem irrational on the surface. Here are a couple of examples of what you might say to yourself:

- *It's understandable that I'm feeling this way.*

- *This isn't surprising for this situation.*

When Your Thoughts and Feelings Don't Seem to Make Sense

Remember that thoughts and feelings are visitors. We don't always understand how our visitors come to us. Don't ruminate or obsess about where your thoughts and feelings came from or criticize yourself for not knowing this. Observe them with interest and openness. Practice mindful acceptance of them, and of yourself for having them.

Think about how you would behave toward a friend whose bed-and-breakfast was suddenly overrun with strange and unexpected guests, some of whom were rude, loud, and unpleasant. Practice treating yourself with the same consideration. For example, perhaps you might say to yourself, *My goodness, what a lot of strange, unpleasant visitors. How can I be helpful in this situation?*

The Value of Self-Validation

Self-validation is useful in several ways. It helps us feel better and see situations more clearly. It helps us get out of psychological traps, including rumination, avoidance, and emotion-driven behavior. It puts us in a better position to make wise choices about what to do in difficult situations. And if there's nothing we can do, it helps us accept the reality of the situation without doing something that makes matters worse.

EXERCISE: Practicing Self-Validation

Practicing self-validation can help us think of wise ways to deal with troubling or unpleasant situations. We don't have to feel self-compassionate before we can self-validate; validation is a skill that we can use anytime, regardless of the feelings that might be present. The key is to remember to use it. This improves with practice. The following worksheet will help you practice.

There are three versions of the worksheet. The first provides instructions. The second is an example from Susan, the woman from the previous chapter who has two teenage sons and is susceptible to self-criticism and depression.

After the example, you'll find a blank version for your own use. Again, make copies of the blank version so you can use it repeatedly. One pointer: When utilizing the steps for self-validation outlined above, use the skills that are helpful. If recognizing common humanity doesn't help in a particular situation, omit it. (But do try it again in another situation.) If your thoughts and feelings don't seem understandable and it feels false to say that they are, practice mindful acceptance of having puzzling or confusing thoughts and feelings.

WORKSHEET: Self-Validation

Remember to maintain an attitude of friendly curiosity.

Day and time	What was the situation?	What did you say to validate your experience?	Did self-validation help? If so, how?
When did this example of self-validation occur?	What was going on? What sensations, thoughts, urges, or emotions did you observe? Did you catch yourself falling into any psychological traps? Ruminating Trying to avoid something Acting on your emotions in a way you might regret later Criticizing yourself harshly	Using your own words, describe how you used the three steps outlined above. Here are some examples. Labeling mindfully: This is… …a difficult (painful, upsetting) moment. …a stressful (unpleasant, tough) situation. …a moment of suffering. …really hard. Recognizing your common humanity: Pain (difficulty, stress) is part of life. I'm not the only one who feels this way in situations like this. Expressing kind understanding: It's understandable that I feel this way, given the circumstances. My feelings are normal (to be expected, not surprising) for this situation.	Did self-validation help you see the situation more clearly? Did you feel better able to handle the situation wisely? Did it help you out of a trap?

WORKSHEET: Self-Validation

Your name: *Susan*

Remember to maintain an attitude of friendly curiosity.

Day and time	What was the situation?	What did you say to validate your experience?	Did self-validation help? If so, how?
Monday, 6 a.m.	I woke up, felt fatigued and depressed, didn't want to get out of bed, and started thinking about what's wrong with me.	"This is a difficult moment. No one likes feeling like this. I've been a bit depressed lately. Tiredness is a normal part of depression."	Kept me from ruminating about why I'm so fatigued. Helped me focus on what I needed: a hot shower and a good breakfast.
Tuesday, 6 p.m.	I was grocery shopping after work and suddenly remembered I was supposed to pick up my son Chris at soccer practice. I called to tell him I'd be fifteen minutes late. I felt guilty and told myself what a bad parent I am.	"It's natural to be upset about forgetting, but my husband usually picks up Chris from soccer. We're very busy and it's understandable to forget something now and then, especially a change in the routine."	Helped me realize that all parents make mistakes. Chris has a phone. If I hadn't remembered, he would have called me. Later, Chris showed me how to program my phone to send me reminders.
Thursday, 3 p.m.	I was using a new software program at work and realized I'd made a mistake and had to repeat two hours of work. I was angry at myself and calling myself an idiot.	"This is a frustrating situation. It's unfortunate I have to repeat this work, but I'm only human. Mistakes are to be expected when working with something new."	Made me realize I needed to take a few minutes to calm down. I went for a walk up and down the hall and did mindful breathing. Then I was able to think about how to correct the error.

WORKSHEET: Self-Validation

Your name: _____

Remember to maintain an attitude of friendly curiosity.

Day and time	What was the situation?	What did you say to validate your experience?	Did self-validation help? If so, how?

Looking Ahead

Having read this far in the book, you've learned about the following mindfulness skills and how to use them:

- Observing and labeling your present-moment thoughts and feelings without judging them or yourself for having them

- Paying attention to what you're doing while you're doing it

- Accepting your thoughts and feelings while acting in ways that are consistent with your long-term goals and values

- Treating yourself with compassion

These skills are an excellent collection of useful tools for managing the moments of your life, whether they're painful or joyful, easy or difficult. We've looked at the skills separately, but they all work together. The next chapter includes several exercises that will help you bring everything together—one exercise each for sensations, thoughts, emotions, and urges. They're a little more advanced than the previous exercises, but the skills you've learned will help you work with them.

Chapter Summary

- Self-compassion is an important mindfulness skill. It means treating ourselves kindly during times of stress and unhappiness; remembering that pain, failure, and struggles are part of the common human experience; and keeping a mindful, balanced perspective on the situation and our feelings.

- Self-compassion is good for our mental health. It reduces the risk of depression and anxiety and helps us see more clearly what to do in difficult situations. We're more likely to behave consistently with our values and goals when we're self-compassionate than when we're harshly self-critical.

- Self-compassion is a set of skills that anyone can practice. Mindfulness includes a self-compassionate attitude. Basic self-care, including eating healthfully, exercising, and getting enough sleep, makes self-compassion easier.

- Self-compassion can also be practiced with savoring, self-soothing, and self-validation.

PART 4

Putting It All Together

CHAPTER 13

Exercises for Combining the Skills

Let me embrace thee, sour adversity, for wise men say it is the wisest course.
—William Shakespeare

Imagine that you're hiking toward a beautiful mountain. The mountain represents something of great value to you; reaching it is an important and meaningful personal goal. As you get closer, you discover that a stinky, mucky swamp lies between you and the mountain. This is annoying and disappointing. Your map shows no swamp.

To get a better view, you climb a tree. From there, you see that if you want to reach the mountain, there's no way to avoid the swamp. You also notice a supply shop not far away. You proceed to the shop for advice.

The shopkeeper confirms that there's no way around the swamp but offers rubber boots, insect repellent, bottled water, food, and a map drawn by a previous traveler showing the easiest way through. You stock up on these supplies and head into the swamp.

Navigating Adversity with Mindfulness

We all encounter swamps as we pursue our goals (Hayes, Strosahl, and Wilson 1999). Mindfulness makes it easier and less unpleasant to get through them. Picture yourself in the swamp, using the mindfulness skills you've learned so far.

Acceptance and Willingness

Accepting that you have to cross the swamp and that it's likely to be unpleasant, you focus on what you need to do. Acceptance doesn't mean that you have to wallow in the swamp or take the most difficult path. You can use all the help that's available to get through as quickly and comfortably as possible. Once you've prepared as best you can, you willingly walk into the swamp—knowing that you're likely to get wet, dirty, bitten by insects, and tired—because reaching the mountain is important to you.

Mindful Observation

You pay close attention to your surroundings, observing the terrain and how it corresponds to the hand-drawn map. You observe your physical sensations, noticing when you feel hungry, thirsty, or tired and pausing to eat, drink, or rest. You find that mindfulness of sounds adds a touch of pleasantness to the journey: birds chirp, frogs croak, the breeze rustles in the swamp grass. When you spot a bird, a frog, or a dragonfly, you take a few moments to really see it before walking on. You notice that your footsteps make interesting noises. The swamp smells unpleasant at first, but you observe without judgment and begin to appreciate the variety of scents.

Acting with Awareness

You walk with awareness of walking, noticing the sensations as your body moves and sensing the swampy ground under your feet. When you stop for a snack, you eat and drink mindfully, appreciating the tastes and textures of the granola bars, dried fruit, and water. When your mind gets absorbed in angry thoughts (*Why is this swamp here? Why wasn't it on my map? This isn't fair! I shouldn't have to do this!*), you acknowledge the feelings of frustration, observe the sensations, and shift your attention back to walking mindfully. You pull your camera out of a pocket. Taking photographs helps you be mindful of the colors, shapes, textures, and patterns in this unusual environment.

Self-Compassion

You recognize that everyone has unexpected setbacks while pursuing meaningful goals, and that no one likes crossing stinky swamps. You realize that your annoyance, disappointment, and aversion to the swamp are normal and understandable. You refrain from self-criticism about feeling this way. You help yourself constructively, as best you can, pacing yourself and using your supplies.

Combining Mindfulness Skills to Work with Difficult Situations

The preceding chapters discussed mindfulness skills separately, but in many situations it's helpful to use all of them simultaneously: observing present-moment experiences with a nonjudgmental and self-compassionate attitude; accepting them as they are; willingly taking wise actions even when it's difficult; and acting with awareness. The rest of this chapter describes four exercises that combine these skills: one each for sensations, thoughts, emotions, and urges. These exercises can help you with the most difficult situations you face. You may find them more challenging than earlier exercises, but the skills you've learned will help you use them effectively.

EXERCISE: Working with Sensations Through Mindful Movement

Many mindfulness exercises, like the breathing meditation and the body scan, invite us to sit still. Stillness helps us observe our sensations, thoughts, emotions, and urges—coming and going, rising and falling—without reacting to them in impulsive ways. Stillness cultivates strength, equanimity, and mindful presence.

On the other hand, we also need ways to practice mindfulness while our bodies are moving. Much of life isn't conducted while sitting still, and our bodies are healthier if they move around regularly. Chapter 10 explored mindful walking, which cultivates mindful awareness during an ordinary daily activity that we often do mechanically. To sharpen awareness of body sensations, many mindfulness programs also include gentle movements and stretches, a practice popularized in mindfulness-based stress reduction (Kabat-Zinn 1990).

The exercise described below (inspired by Williams et al. 2007 and Williams and Penman 2011) involves a series of movements and stretches. However, the specific movements are less important than the attitude you bring to the exercise. Mindful movement is a way to combine the skills explored in previous chapters: observing without judgment, acting with awareness, acceptance, willingness, and self-compassion. It's an opportunity to let go of goal setting and problem solving. There are no standards for how far you should stretch or how long you should balance. As best you can, adopt an attitude of friendly curiosity and acceptance of your body and its sensations while doing these movements. Before beginning the exercise, consider the following points:

- This exercise is done in a standing position. Choose a place where you can stand comfortably and gaze straight ahead without getting too distracted. You need room to raise your arms straight out to your sides.

- It's important to take care of yourself. Recognize your limits and don't push yourself beyond them. Refrain from anything that doesn't feel appropriate for you to do. If you have physical limitations that might make it unwise for you to do these movements, consult with your doctor before trying them.

- The purpose of this exercise is not to achieve any particular goals other than awareness and acceptance of the body in each moment. You're not trying to strengthen the muscles, give them a workout, or get the body into shape. You're just noticing sensations and allowing them to be as they are, without judging them or yourself as good or bad.

- Don't do anything that causes pain. Other sensations, such as trembling, tingling, pulling, or stretching (within reasonable limits) are normal. Practice observing them mindfully. What do the sensations feel like? Where do you feel them? Are they changing or shifting? Are they pleasant, unpleasant, or neutral? See if you can adopt an attitude of friendly curiosity.

- Notice your reactions to the sensations. Judgmental thoughts about your body may arise, such as how it looks; how strong, fit, or flexible it is; or how well it's doing these movements. Remember that this is a mindfulness exercise, not a competition or a performance. Don't stand in front of a mirror. As best you can, let judgmental thoughts pass by like clouds in the sky, and return your attention to observing the sensations. If you have emotions or urges, observe them mindfully, focusing on how they feel in your body.

- The movements are designed to be practiced slowly, with full awareness of all the sensations that arise. Spend as much time as you like with each movement. There are no time limits.

- Remember that the mind will wander. When your attention drifts away, gently bring it back, as best you can, to observing the sensations. Let go of judgmental thoughts about the wandering mind.

- Read through the following instructions and look at the accompanying illustrations to understand what you're being invited to do. Then you can refer to the instructions or pictures as you go along. If you prefer, the website for this book (http://www.newharbinger.com/29033) has a recording of the exercise.

Standing

Stand with your feet about hip-width apart, back reasonably straight but not stiff, shoulders relaxed, arms hanging loosely at your sides, gazing straight ahead. Feel the sensations in your body as it stands. Notice your feet on the floor and the movement of your breath. Notice any subtle movements as you keep your balance.

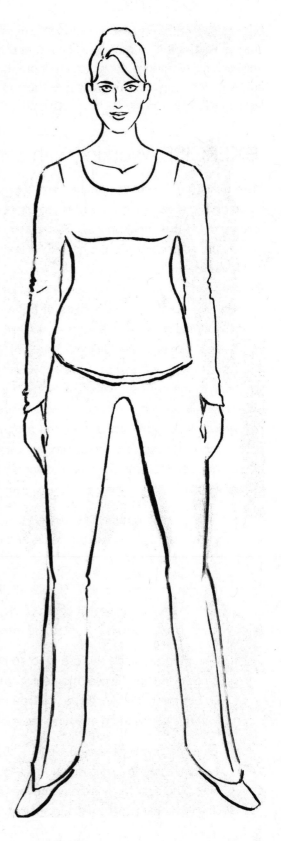

Head Tilts

Slowly tilt your head to the right. Your eyes and nose continue to face forward; your right ear comes closer to your right shoulder. Feel the sensations this produces. Tilt only as far as your head wants to go. Gently explore your limit. Breathe in and out. When you're ready, slowly bring your head back to vertical. Breathe. Now tilt your head to the left in the same way. Breathe in and out. Feel the sensations. Slowly return to vertical. Practice friendly curiosity about whatever you notice.

Head Turns

Slowly turn your head to the right so that your chin comes closer to your right shoulder. Turn only as far as your head wants to go. Carefully explore your limit. Pause here, feel the sensations, and breathe in and out. When you're ready, come back to the starting position, head facing forward. Now slowly turn your head the other way, so that your chin comes closer to your left shoulder. Feel the sensations. Breathe in and out. Turn back to the starting position, head facing forward. Pause and observe the sensations. Allow thoughts to come and go.

Shoulder Rolls

Slowly move your shoulders forward and then up toward your ears, squeezing them gently. Move your shoulders softly toward the back and then down to the starting position. Breathe in and out. Repeat, moving slowly and feeling all the sensations as your shoulders go around. Pause at the starting position. Next, try coordinating with your breath. Inhale while moving your shoulders forward and up, and exhale while moving them back and down. Repeat the cycle at the pace of your breath as many times as you like.

When you're ready, pause at the starting position and then switch directions. Inhale while your shoulders move back and then up; exhale while they move forward and then down. Repeat as many times as you like, slowly and gently, observing and accepting the sensations as they are. Refrain from anything that feels painful or unsuitable for your body. Pause in the starting position.

Raising Arms Halfway

As you inhale, slowly raise your arms to the sides until they're parallel with the floor and your fingers are pointing toward the walls. Flex your wrists so that your fingers point up. Feel the sensations, accepting them as they are and breathing with them. Now bend your wrists the other way, so that your fingers point down. Gently alternate hand positions: fingers pointing up, fingers pointing down, pausing to breathe with the sensations in each position. When you're ready, slowly lower your arms to your sides, feeling every sensation on the way down. Pause with your arms hanging loosely. Breathe. Practice acceptance of whatever you feel.

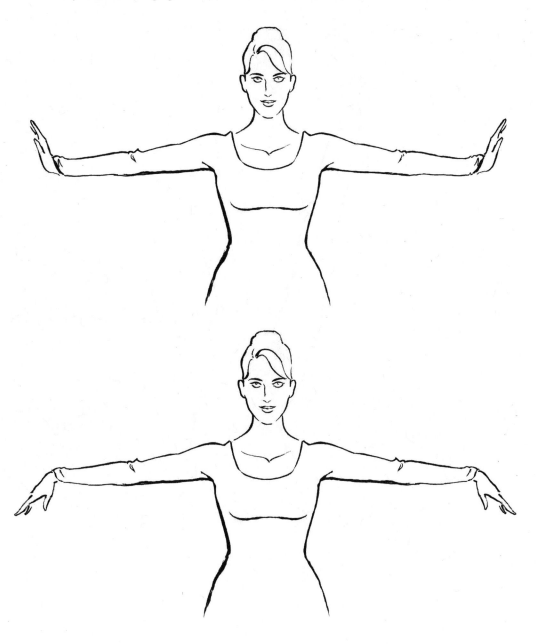

Raising Arms Overhead

As you inhale, slowly raise both arms, keeping your elbows straight, until your hands are over your head and reaching for the ceiling. If you can't reach that high or prefer not to, practice acceptance of what your arms will do. Pause here, feeling the sensations as you hold your arms overhead. If you're willing, tilt your head up so that you can see your hands and the ceiling. Feel the sensations. Remember to breathe. When you're ready, return to looking straight ahead and slowly lower your arms all the way down, feeling every sensation along the way.

Balancing on One Foot

Imagine that your head is at twelve on a clock, your feet at six. Raise your arms just enough that your hands are pointing to four and eight. Gaze straight ahead and stand tall. Shift your weight to your left foot, making your left leg strong and tight. Bend your right knee and raise your right foot slightly off the ground. Balance here if you can. If you prefer, keep your right toes on the ground. Feel the sensations and breathe with them. Practice nonjudgmental acceptance of any wobbling or difficulty keeping your balance.

Now place your right foot back on the floor and shift your weight to the right, making your right leg strong and tight. Gaze straight ahead and stand tall. Bend your left knee and raise your left foot slightly off the floor, or if you prefer, keep your left toes on the floor for balance. Pause here. Breathe with the sensations. Practice willingness to feel whatever is present.

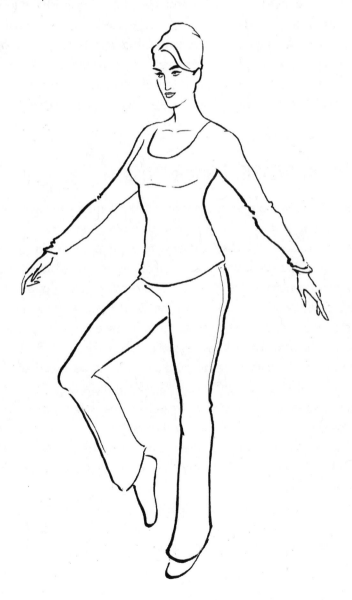

Return to Standing

Return your left foot to the floor, hip-width from the right foot. Distribute your weight evenly across both feet. Stand tall but not stiff. Allow your arms and shoulders to relax. Observe how your body feels after doing these movements.

✳ ✳ ✳

Sometimes mindful movement is pleasant and enjoyable. The movements may be relaxing or soothing, the sensations in the body pleasing or refreshing. Sometimes we feel flexible, stable, mindfully present, awake, calm, and alert. If a sense of well-being arises, mindful awareness helps us appreciate it.

On the other hand, this exercise can be uncomfortable. Muscles may ache, pull, or tremble in ways we don't like. We may have judgmental thoughts about our bodies; feelings of disappointment, frustration, anger, or sadness; or urges to quit or push the body too hard. Observing these experiences with gentle, friendly awareness cultivates mindful acceptance of the constantly changing nature of thoughts and feelings. It helps us choose wisely how to respond. You might choose gentle perseverance—continuing with the exercise while accepting the body's limits and treating it kindly. Or you might discontinue the exercise for now and come back to it later.

EXERCISE: Mindfulness of Thoughts

As discussed in previous chapters, thoughts can feel compelling. When a thought comes to mind, such as *I shouldn't have to cross this stinky swamp; I'll never make it* or *This is going to be horrible*, it's easy to forget that these are thoughts. We often assume that they're important and that we should take them seriously.

Of course, it may be true that the swamp is stinky, that the crossing will be difficult and uncomfortable, and that your arrival at the mountain will be delayed. On the other hand, it may not be helpful to dwell on these thoughts. Mindful observation may reveal that the swamp is interesting and the discomfort can be managed. Crossing the swamp may provide great stories to tell when you finally reach the mountain. And it may build your strength for the next goal that lies beyond the mountain.

If *I'll never make it across this swamp* comes to mind and you believe it without question, you might turn back and never reach your goal. Or you might say, *Well, I have to make it, so I'll just get it over with*, and rush into the swamp without adequate preparation. In that case, you may fail to cross it and fear trying again. But if you say, *Ah, there's a discouraging thought. This swamp looks impossible, but maybe it isn't. Let me consider my options*, you're in a position to gather information that will help you make a wise choice. Maybe it really is too difficult and you need to make a new plan. Or maybe it's worth trying; others have done it, and you can learn from their experiences and prepare.

The Leaves on a Stream exercise (inspired by Hayes 2005) cultivates a mindful perspective on thoughts. This exercise works best if you sit with your eyes closed. Read the following instructions carefully before you begin. Then set a timer for five minutes, close your eyes, and try the exercise. The timer saves you from having to worry about when to stop.

✳ ✳ ✳

To begin, imagine that you're sitting by a beautiful stream passing through a valley. In your mind's eye, sit on a blanket, a rock, or a chair, in sun or shade—wherever you like. Notice that trees overhang the stream. Now and then, a leaf falls into the water and is carried downstream on the surface. Watch the leaves floating by.

Start noticing your thoughts as they arise. As each thought comes up, picture it written on a leaf and watch it float by. If your thoughts take the form of images, put each image on a leaf. The content of the thought doesn't matter. If you think, *I hope my sister is okay*, *I'm worthless*, or *What's for lunch?*, put it on a leaf and watch it float by. If the same thought keeps popping up, place it on a leaf each time, as patiently as you can.

If you notice that your mind has wandered off, gently bring it back to watching the leaves float by. If you find that you've fallen into the stream and have been carried along with your thoughts, gently climb out and resume watching.

Watch for thoughts like *I can't do this exercise* or *This isn't working for me*. Treat these thoughts in the same way: write them on leaves and watch them float by. If they come back, do this again.

Practice acceptance of any thought that comes along. There's no such thing as an unacceptable thought.

As best you can, practice kindness and patience with yourself as you do this exercise.

Variations

If you prefer, use one of the following images to practice mindfulness of thoughts:

- Visualize a parade in which each person is holding a sign. When a thought or mental image comes to your mind, picture it on one of the signs and watch it go by (Hayes, Strosahl, and Wilson 1999).

- Imagine yourself looking up at the sky. Clouds are slowly passing by. When you have a thought or mental image, picture it sitting on a cloud and watch it pass by (Orsillo and Roemer 2011).

✳ ✳ ✳

The purpose of practicing mindfulness of thoughts isn't to get rid of the thoughts or to dismiss all thoughts as unimportant. Leaves, clouds, and marchers in the parade pass by, but a particular thought may reappear, perhaps repeatedly. These exercises teach us to recognize thoughts, particularly repetitive ones, so that we can decide how to respond. If the thought is saying, for example, *Don't forget, the plumber is coming at three o'clock*, you can make a reasonable plan to meet the plumber. If you think *This is going to ruin my whole day*, you can acknowledge the frustration, let the thought pass by, and still make a reasonable plan to meet the plumber.

EXERCISE: Mindfulness of Difficult Emotions

This is a meditative exercise for practicing mindful observation, acceptance, and self-compassion while a troubling situation or problem is in your mind (inspired by Segal, Williams, and Teasdale 2002). It incorporates mindful breathing with awareness of the body while sitting in a quiet, dignified posture. Here's a brief overview of the steps, which are described in detail below:

1. Observing your breath for a few moments

2. Deliberately bringing to mind something that's been distressing you

3. Mindfully observing what happens in your body

4. Breathing with the sensations while allowing them to come and go in their own way and time

Before beginning, consider the following points:

- You don't have to bring to mind your most serious or overwhelming problem. You might think about a minor disagreement you had with someone, a small disappointment, or something that annoyed you.

- This exercise can be uncomfortable. It may be helpful to remember the Guest House metaphor. Think of the troubling problem as an invited guest and make room for it. If you prefer, use the Passengers on the Bus metaphor; you've invited one of the difficult passengers to sit at the front. The goal isn't to change your guests or passengers, but to practice relating to them mindfully, even when they're unpleasant.

- Remember that everyone has difficult thoughts, feelings, and situations. You're not alone in this. See if you can adopt an attitude of warmth and kindness about it, as you would for a loved one with the same problem.

- Watch for the tendency to get caught up in thinking about the troubling situation. Your mind is probably eager to jump into problem-solving mode. This can easily lead to rumination and self-criticism. Instead, gently bring yourself back to mindful acceptance, focusing on sensations in your body and simply observing them without trying to change or fix them.

✳ ✳ ✳

To begin, settle into your sitting posture. Gently close your eyes or gaze downward at the floor in front of you.

Focus your attention on your breath. Observe the sensations and movements as the breath goes in and out of your body. As best you can, follow the breath all the way in and all the way out, allowing the breath to go at its own pace and rhythm without trying to change it.

Expand your awareness to include your body as a whole. Observe the sensations of sitting in the chair and the contact between your feet and the floor. Notice the sensations in your hands.

When you're ready, intentionally bring to mind something that's been troubling you; something difficult that's been going on in your life. If you can't think of anything current, choose something from the past that was stressful or unpleasant. Here are some examples:

- *My son is having trouble making friends at school.*

- *My boss made unreasonable demands today.*

- *I'm worried about my mother's health.*

- *I'm having trouble deciding what to do about…*

- *I regret how I handled…*

Scan your body and notice what happens when this difficulty is in your mind. Does your heart rate change? Do you feel tension or tightness anywhere? Does anything feel warm or cold, heavy or light, tingly or numb? Observe closely, with friendly curiosity. Notice where in the body you feel the sensations and whether they're changing from one moment to the next.

It may be helpful to apply short verbal labels, such as "tension" or "tightness," to the sensations you observe. As best you can, use a gentle, accepting tone as you label.

Expand your awareness to include both the sensations and your breath. If you like, imagine your breath going into the part of the body where you feel the sensations and coming back out from that part of the body.

If judgmental thoughts come up, such as *It's bad* (or *wrong,* or *stupid…*) *to feel this way, I'm such an idiot,* or *I'm not doing this right,* observe and label them ("Ah, judgments") and return your attention to the sensations in your body.

Your body may try to resist or get rid of the unpleasant sensations. Signs of resistance include clenching your fists or teeth, scowling, tensing the abdomen, or bracing your arms or legs against the floor or chair. If you observe these signs, see if you can gently let go of the tension and open up to the sensations, accepting them as they are.

Practice willingness to feel the sensations, allowing them to be just as they are. It may be helpful to remind yourself, *Whatever it is, it's already here. Let me go ahead and feel it.* This doesn't mean you have to like the sensations. It's okay not to like them.

Remember the Guest House metaphor. Think of the sensations as difficult guests who have come to visit. As best you can, be polite to them and make room for them.

Observe your thoughts. Are they racing around looking for solutions? If so, gently thank them for their efforts and return your attention to observing the sensations in your body.

Remember the attitude of friendly curiosity. Without trying to force yourself to feel a particular way, consider being kind. Statements like these may be helpful:

- *Painful feelings are here.*

- *Problems and difficulties are part of life.*

- *May I be kind to myself, as best I can.*

✳ ✳ ✳

This exercise can be challenging. Remember that practicing mindfulness is a way of taking care of yourself; it's not about tormenting yourself or forcing yourself to do things. Caring for yourself sometimes requires a warm and compassionate persistence with things that are difficult. See if you can find a way to work gently with this exercise, perhaps doing only a few minutes at a time. If it feels too intense, shift your awareness to your breath or to sounds in the environment. When you feel ready, shift your attention back to the problem. If it's still too difficult, try again another day.

* *Lydia's Story* *

After learning this exercise for practicing mindfulness of difficult emotions, Lydia used it after a worrisome conversation with her boyfriend. Here's her description of her experience:

Eli and I have been dating for almost a year, and I thought things were going really well. The idea of moving in together has come up a few times but we hadn't made a decision about it. My lease is about to expire, so I brought it up again. Eli didn't seem excited about it. I was surprised and disappointed, and I let the topic drop. We haven't discussed it since then.

This has been bothering me for a week, so I decided to practice bringing it to mind for the exercise. At first it was really difficult. I had a strong sinking feeling in my stomach and my face felt flushed. I felt shaky. A lot of thoughts went through my mind, like Is he about to leave me? Maybe our relationship isn't what I thought it was. I should have seen this coming. I'm not good enough. *I felt angry and also afraid.*

My mind wanted to obsess over these thoughts and replay the conversation with Eli. But I kept coming back to the sensations in my body. Breathing with them really helped. I could let them come and go. It's not a catastrophe to feel these things. After a few minutes, I realized it isn't the end of the world if we don't move in together now. I also realized that I don't really know what Eli is thinking. I decided to discuss it with him this weekend.

Lydia found this exercise difficult but useful. She realized that she could observe her feelings of distress without getting caught in rumination and avoidance. It didn't resolve the situation immediately, but it helped her see it clearly and make a plan.

EXERCISE: Urge Surfing

Mindfulness teachers like to compare thoughts and feelings to waves in the ocean. Depending on weather conditions, the waves vary in size and strength, but they're always present. Nothing can make the ocean completely smooth. Surfing is a skillful way to handle waves. Rather than trying to stop them or getting overwhelmed, we allow them to be as they are and ride them as they rise and fall.

The Wave metaphor is especially useful when we have to manage urges and cravings to do things that we know we'll regret later. Like a wave, an urge starts small, gets stronger and more intense, and then declines. Then another one comes along. Urge surfing is a mindfulness exercise designed to help people with addictions (Bowen, Chawla, and Marlatt 2011), but you don't have to be addicted to anything to benefit from this practice. If you have any temptations or cravings that you give in to more often than you'd like, this will be a helpful exercise.

To prepare, think of a situation in which you feel urges or temptations to do something you'll regret later—something that's inconsistent with your values or goals. For your first experience with this exercise, choose an urge that's not too powerful, yet strong enough that mindful acceptance won't be too easy. Here are some examples:

- Losing your temper or getting into an argument with someone

- Playing computer games instead of working

- Watching a TV show instead of going to bed

- Drinking or eating more than you think you should

- Buying something you can't afford

Before you begin the exercise, consider the following points:

- Practice while sitting quietly. It's helpful to close your eyes so that you can imagine your scenario as clearly as possible. If you'd rather not close your eyes, gaze downward at a neutral point, such as the floor a few feet in front of you.

- If the exercise begins to feel too intense, open your eyes, look around, and move your body a bit. Shift your attention to your surroundings or to your breath. When you're ready, resume the exercise.

- Remember the image of the wave. Your goal is to ride the wave as it grows and then subsides, observing it mindfully and accepting it as it is.

❋ ❋ ❋

Here are the detailed instructions for urge surfing. If you prefer, the website for this book (http://www.newharbinger.com/29033) offers a recording of this exercise.

To begin, sit comfortably in a position that feels relaxed and dignified. For a few moments, observe the sensations of your body in the chair.

Observe your breath and allow it to flow in and out.

Bring to mind the scenario you decided on: a situation that creates urges to do something you'll regret later. Picture the situation in your mind as clearly as you can. Where are you? Is anyone else present?

Imagine the events that lead up to this urge. Picture yourself right at the point where the urge is the strongest but you haven't yet acted on it. Pause here without giving in to the urge.

Notice how your body feels at this point. What sensations are you feeling? Where do you feel them? Are they shifting or fluctuating?

Notice what thoughts are going through your mind. Recognize that they're thoughts and observe them.

Notice what emotions are present. Are you sad, angry, afraid, hurt, embarrassed, or disappointed? Are you happy or excited?

As best you can, be gentle with yourself. Let go of judgments. Remember that urges and cravings are normal human experiences—we all feel them. Allow the urge to be there without trying to change or control it. Observe what it's like to feel the urge but not give in to it. Take your time.

Remember to breathe. The breath is your surfboard. Breathe with the urge and the sensations, thoughts, and emotions.

Linger in this moment in a friendly, interested way. Practice willingness to feel the urge and refrain from the tempting behavior.

Observe: Is there something behind this urge? Something you need or long for? A problem that needs attention?

When you're ready, let go of the scenario you were imagining. Shift your attention back to your breathing. Open your eyes and look around.

* *Nick's Story* *

Nick has a full-time management job and brings work home nearly every day. In forty-five minutes in his home office, he can make more progress than at work, where he's constantly interrupted by employees with questions and concerns. His family wishes he were more involved with them in the evenings, but they've agreed not to disturb him for forty-five minutes after dinner.

Lately, Nick has been playing an online computer game during his evening work time. At first, he limited his game playing to ten minutes and was able to finish most of his other work in the remaining time. But the game has become more engrossing, and his playing time has crept up. Now he often plays for thirty minutes, sometimes more. He's not getting his work done and feels significantly more stressed during the day. Sometimes he extends his work time at home, but his family complains. He hasn't told them about the computer game.

Nick decided to try the urge surfing exercise. Here are his observations after doing it several times:

As I'm about to call up the game on my computer, I'm feeling several things. There's a sense of excitement about starting the game. I feel sort of energized by it. I also feel resentful that I have to work at home. I think, I deserve some free time to do something fun, and it's not fair I have this extra work to do. I've noticed some angry thoughts about various employees who stop by my office so often that I can't get much done at work.

During the last week, I've been able to stick to a rule: I have to finish the work I brought home, and then I can play the game if there's any time left. Urges to play the game come up while I'm working. I try to be mindful of them. At first I didn't believe the urges would get weaker if I just watched them, but it's really true: They're like waves. They go away and then another one comes along. Observing them helps me see that I don't have to act on them.

I'm not sure I can keep to my rule consistently. I think I could solve this problem better if I changed some things at work. I decided to tell my employees that the last hour of the day is off-limits for questions. I'll close my door and use a Do Not Disturb sign. Then I won't have to bring as much work home, and I can be with my family after dinner.

Nick's experience illustrates some important points about urge surfing:

- Urge surfing doesn't get rid of urges. Nick continued to feel urges to play the game. Yet over time, as Nick observes the urges without acting on them, there's an excellent chance they'll become less frequent and intense. Giving in to urges makes them stronger. Trying to suppress or deny them also makes them stronger. Mindful acceptance of urges is the healthy alternative.

- Urge surfing makes urges feel less overwhelming. Once he observed the thoughts, emotions, and sensations, Nick found them less intimidating and felt more confident that he could handle them.

- Sometimes urges are covering up another problem. Nick realized that beneath his urge to play the computer game was resentment about his employees constantly interrupting him at work. He needed to take steps to change this situation. Mindful observation of urges to play the computer game helped him devise a promising plan.

Taking the Practices into Daily Life

The exercises in this chapter invite you to take a few minutes out of your normal routine. You may be wondering how they'll help with daily life, when you may not have time to sit quietly or practice mindful movement before taking action in a troubling situation. These exercises cultivate mindful awareness that can be applied in countless situations:

- They refine our awareness of whatever is happening in the mind and body.

- They help us learn to stop fighting against or struggling with normal emotions and sensations, even when we don't like them.

- They help us remember that problems and difficulties are part of being human and living a full life, that we don't have to respond with harsh judgment toward ourselves, and that kindness and compassion are often more helpful.

- They provide a way to stay out of psychological traps when we're upset. Instead of ruminating about the problem, trying not to think about it, criticizing ourselves for having it, or behaving rashly, we learn that we can face difficulties and respond constructively.

If we practice consistently, we're better prepared for any problematic situation. We're more likely to pause, see the situation clearly, and make a wise choice about what to do. Practicing mindfulness is like strengthening muscles. As the muscles of mindfulness get stronger, our lives become happier and more satisfying.

Most people long for happy, meaningful, and satisfying lives. In the next chapter—the final chapter in the book—we'll return to the topic of happiness and how mindfulness helps us cultivate it.

Chapter Summary

- Although it's helpful to study mindfulness skills separately, as in part 3 of this book, in reality the skills work together.

- The exercises in this chapter cultivate the ability to adopt a mindful perspective when something unpleasant is happening: troubling emotions or thoughts, unwanted urges, or discomfort in the body.

- Each exercise provides the opportunity to combine the skills previously described: observing without judgment, using mindful labels when helpful, acting with awareness, acceptance, willingness, and self-compassion.

- The exercises in this chapter require taking a few minutes out of your daily routine to practice, but the lessons learned can readily be applied to everyday situations and will build strength and skills for handling life in the long term.

CHAPTER 14

Mindfulness and Happiness

Happiness is not a goal, it is a by-product.
—Eleanor Roosevelt

Throughout history, deep thinkers have debated what it means to live a happy, satisfying life (Waterman 1993). Ancient Greek philosophers wrote about two perspectives on happiness that psychologists still study today: one based on pleasure and enjoyment, the other on meaning and purpose (Ryan and Deci 2001). According to the first perspective, a happy life includes mostly positive emotions and more pleasure than pain. The second perspective says that true happiness comes from living in accordance with deeply held values and fulfilling one's inner potential, even when doing so is stressful and uncomfortable.

Mindfulness experts remind us that life is a constantly changing stream of pleasant, unpleasant, and neutral experiences (Brown and Holt 2011). We all have joys and sorrows, successes and failures, gains and losses. Positive emotions come and go. Sometimes we don't achieve our goals. Real happiness, from this perspective, comes from knowing that we can keep our balance and find peace of mind despite changing conditions, just as a mountain remains strong and stable during sunshine and storms.

Fortunately, we don't have to choose a single definition of happiness. We all want joy and contentment, meaning and purpose, and the inner strength to respond wisely to pain and misfortune. Practicing mindfulness cultivates happiness in all of these forms. In this chapter, we'll explore how the mindfulness skills you've learned in this book will help you find the happiness you seek.

Mindfulness and Positive Emotions

In the late 1990s, I realized that if I wanted to understand mindfulness, I should practice it consistently. I started meditating for ten to fifteen minutes each morning, observing my breath and watching my sensations, thoughts, and emotions come and go. I found it relaxing, but at first I didn't see any other effects.

After a few weeks, I realized that I was noticing more pleasant moments during the day. I enjoyed the feel of the air when I stepped outdoors, the colors and shapes of the clouds, the patterns of tree branches against the sky, the sounds of birds or people passing by. The indoor world also seemed richer. Ordinary experiences, like listening to cats purr, chopping garlic and sautéing it in olive oil, and rinsing fruit at the kitchen sink with the sun shining through the window, were more vivid.

My life was already satisfying in many ways, but mindfulness of daily experiences made me feel happier. Research shows that I'm not alone.

A Study of Mindfulness and Enjoyment of Daily Life

For most people, unpleasant events, emotions, and circumstances are more attention grabbing than pleasant ones. We tend to focus on the negative while ignoring the positive. This is especially true for people susceptible to depression. A recent study showed that practicing mindfulness helps us appreciate moments of pleasure and enjoyment in daily life, even if they're fleeting (Geschwind et al. 2011).

For six days, 130 adults with a history of depression wore digital wristwatches programmed to beep ten times a day during waking hours. At each beep, participants completed a short questionnaire about their mood at that moment and the pleasantness of their current activity.

After this six-day period, half the participants completed an eight-week mindfulness program that teaches many of the skills and exercises described in this book. They attended weekly two-hour sessions and were encouraged to practice daily. The other participants, who served as the control group, continued with their normal routines and didn't attend the mindfulness course.

After eight weeks, all participants repeated the six-day procedure with the digital watches, reporting on their feelings and activities throughout each day. Results confirmed the hypothesis: Participants in the mindfulness course showed significant increases in positive emotions, moments of pleasantness, and enjoyment of ordinary activities in their daily lives, while those in the control group showed no change over the eight-week period.

Enjoyment of ordinary activities increases resilience in the face of life's normal ups and downs and helps prevent depression. The participants in this study had experienced severe depression in the past and were at high risk for future episodes. Practicing mindfulness for eight weeks substantially lowered their risk of relapse.

The Benefits of Positive Emotions

We think of positive and negative emotions as opposites, but they're alike in a very important way: they're built into human nature because they can be useful if we handle them constructively (Fredrickson 2001). Pleasant feelings like happiness, contentment, and interest motivate us to explore the environment, participate in valued activities, and bond with others. They increase creativity, openness to new experiences, and receptiveness to feedback. As a result, we gain knowledge, skills, and social support that enrich our lives and help us recover more quickly from stressful events.

Positive emotions don't have to be intense to provide these benefits (Cohn et al. 2009). We don't have to seek out unusual or thrilling activities. We also don't have to get rid of negative emotions. The positive ones are beneficial even as the negative ones continue to come and go. Mindfulness of the simple, momentary pleasures of normal daily life can have a big impact on the overall quality of our lives. This idea is beautifully communicated by the following poem by Linda Pastan (1991).

The Happiest Day

It was early May, I think
a moment of lilac or dogwood
when so many promises are made
it hardly matters if a few are broken.
My mother and father still hovered
in the background, part of the scenery
like the houses I had grown up in,
and if they would be torn down later
that was something I knew
but didn't believe. Our children were asleep
or playing, the youngest as new
as the new smell of the lilacs,
and how could I have guessed
their roots were shallow
and would be easily transplanted.
I didn't even guess that I was happy.
The small irritations that are like salt
on melon were what I dwelt on,
though in truth they simply
made the fruit taste sweeter.
So we sat on the porch
in the cool morning, sipping
hot coffee. Behind the news of the day—
strikes and small wars, a fire somewhere—
I could see the top of your dark head
and thought not of public conflagrations
but of how it would feel on my bare shoulder.
If someone could stop the camera then…
If someone could only stop the camera
and ask me: are you happy?
perhaps I would have noticed
how the morning shone in the reflected
color of lilac. Yes, I might have said
and offered a steaming cup of coffee.

Practicing mindfulness teaches us how to stop the camera and notice the simple joys of daily life.

Mindfulness, Meaning, and Purpose

Of course, not all moments of daily life are full of simple joys. A sense of meaning and purpose can provide a different form of happiness and satisfaction, even when the present moment is stressful or painful. Many psychologists use the term "well-being" for the type of happiness based on meaning, purpose, and fulfilling one's potential. Research on psychological well-being has identified six important components (Ryff 1989):

- **Autonomy:** acting in accordance with your inner standards and preferences, pursuing your goals, resisting social pressures

- **Competence:** having knowledge and skills, managing the demands and responsibilities of daily life

- **Healthy relationships:** having warm, trusting, satisfying relationships; feeling concern, empathy, and care for others

- **Self-acceptance:** understanding and accepting all aspects of yourself, including your strengths and weaknesses

- **Personal growth:** openness to new experiences, learning, and self-improvement; seeking challenges; broadening your horizons

- **Purpose in life:** having goals, direction, and a sense of meaning in life

Cultivating these elements of well-being isn't always pleasant or enjoyable. Standing on our principles and managing daily demands can be stressful. Even the healthiest relationships have awkward, uncomfortable moments. It's painful to face up to our failures and shortcomings, to feel clumsy and nervous while learning new skills. Yet research shows that people who act in accordance with these six elements of well-being have higher overall life satisfaction, fewer symptoms of depression, and higher self-esteem.

Studies also show that practicing mindfulness improves all six elements of psychological well-being (Carmody and Baer 2008; Baer et al. 2008). The same pattern is seen in people who take eight-week mindfulness courses and in people who have meditated for years. The more they practice, the more their well-being improves. Mindfulness makes it easier to act autonomously, with purpose, in ways that lead to personal growth, even though it's sometimes painful to do so. Mindfulness makes us more aware of what's actually happening in the present moment so that we can pursue what really matters and handle difficulties constructively.

I experienced the effects of mindfulness on well-being while writing this book. I was passionate about doing it, and yet it wasn't always pleasant. At times, I felt stressed and discouraged. I had doubts about whether it's any good and fears that I would never finish it. Sometimes I worried about whether readers would like it, avoided writing by doing other things, or criticized myself for writing too slowly or being unclear.

Again and again, mindfulness enabled me to observe what was happening, let go of unhelpful patterns, and redirect my attention to the writing process with acceptance of the difficulties and willingness to keep working at it. This had a big impact on my well-being.

For example, when I wasn't caught in psychological traps, I could think more clearly about what I wanted to say (autonomy) and manage the demands of my life to create time to write (competence).

Willingness and self-compassion helped me stretch my mind, develop new writing skills (personal growth), and work constructively with my strengths and weaknesses as a writer (self-acceptance). Awareness of the writing experience helped me talk about it with friends and develop connections with other authors (relationships). It also kept me focused on my goal: to share my understanding with readers in ways that I hope will be helpful and interesting (purpose).

In exchange for these benefits to my well-being, I was willing to feel tired, stressed, doubtful, and nervous at times. At other times I felt pleased, excited, and energized. Sometimes I felt neutral. All of these feelings came and went, repeatedly, like waves whipped up by the wind on the surface of a lake. Below the surface, where the water was clear and calm, I found great satisfaction in writing this book, no matter how it felt at any given moment.

Mindfulness and Well-Being in Unpleasant Situations

Over the years, to deepen my practice of mindfulness, I've attended several weeklong meditation retreats at the Insight Meditation Society in Massachusetts. Each retreat has seventy-five to one hundred participants and several teachers and is conducted mostly in silence. The daily schedule includes periods of sitting and walking meditation, meetings in small groups for questions and discussion, interviews with teachers, mindful meals, and a talk each evening. The atmosphere is caring and peaceful. It's an excellent way to practice mindfulness intensively.

To keep the price affordable, each participant is given a daily housekeeping task. On one of my retreats, I was assigned to vacuum a long corridor lined with dormitory rooms. The vacuum cleaner was heavy and awkward. On my first day I had trouble steering it and got into a struggle—yanking, shoving, and inadvertently banging it on several people's doors. When I finally finished, feeling sweaty and irritated, I wrestled the vacuum cleaner into its closet and forgot about it.

Late that night, I awoke with a sharp pain in my right shoulder. I didn't understand the source of the pain until after breakfast when I started vacuuming again. I found it necessary to vacuum with my left arm, slowly and gently.

I realized I should vacuum mindfully. As best I could, I let go of judgments, observed the sensations, listened to the sounds, and watched the dirt disappear. I practiced acceptance of the lumbering vacuum cleaner and stopped trying to force it. By acting with awareness, I found a way to move without struggle that got the floor clean and allowed my sore shoulder to heal. Vacuuming this way was slow, but there was no need to hurry. Mindful vacuuming began to feel graceful—a bit like dancing. By the end of the week, I felt peaceful and content while vacuuming.

We're all happier when engaged in rewarding, satisfying activities (Cantor and Sanderson 1999), but for most of us, unpleasant or tiresome tasks aren't entirely avoidable. The question is how to manage them skillfully. Doing these tasks mindfully is often more effective than trying to force things to be different or ruminating about how unpleasant they are. As an experiment, try doing the unpleasant tasks in your life mindfully and notice what happens. See if you can find ways to make them less irksome.

In addition, notice your facial expressions while doing your unpleasant tasks. Are you scowling, frowning, or clenching your teeth? This might be making matters worse. We think of facial expressions as outward signs of our inner states: we scowl because we're frustrated and smile because we're happy. However, research shows that facial expressions also *influence* emotional states by providing information to the brain (Lewis 2012). According to several studies, if you smile, you'll feel a little happier. If you frown, you'll feel more sad and anxious. If you raise your eyebrows, you'll find new facts more surprising. If you wrinkle your nose, you'll find disgusting odors more unpleasant.

EXERCISE: Half Smiling

Half smiling is an exercise that takes advantage of the interesting relationship between facial expression and mood (Nhat Hanh 1976; Linehan 1993b). To practice, start by relaxing your shoulders, neck, and face. Make your facial expression neutral. Now turn the corners of your mouth up gently, just a little, to make a soft, pleasant, relaxed expression that won't tire your facial muscles. Keep your jaw relaxed. Don't freeze your face; allow it to move naturally.

Half smiling creates a facial expression of calm and serenity. It influences your brain so that you *feel* a little more calm and serene. Half smiling won't get rid of your negative emotions, but it will help you accept the present moment with equanimity.

* *Caroline's Experience with Half Smiling* *

Caroline works in human resources at a company that just hired a new manager. Here's what she wrote about her experience with half smiling:

> *A new manager was hired where I work. It's the same woman who was in charge of firing people, including me, from my previous job when the company downsized. Last week we were all notified of a staff meeting to introduce her. I still have a lot of bad feelings about losing my previous job. I know it wasn't this woman's fault, but I really didn't want to go to the meeting.*
>
> *However, it would have been unprofessional to skip it, and I can't avoid her forever, so I decided I was willing to go. I observed my feelings of anger, dread, and reluctance. I told myself it was completely understandable that I felt this way. I also decided to half smile.*
>
> *I got to the meeting room a couple of minutes early. I relaxed my face and shoulders, sat in a dignified posture, and smiled just a little. I looked around and said hello to a few of my coworkers. Then my friend Jane came and sat next to me. She knows how I feel about the new manager. She also knows I'm learning about mindfulness. One day I told her about half smiling and we tried it. It made us giggle.*
>
> *"I was expecting you to be stressed, but you look positively serene," she said.*
>
> *"I'm half smiling," I told her.*
>
> *She stared at me. "Oh, gosh!" she said. "You are, aren't you? I'm so impressed!" This made me chuckle.*
>
> *Then the boss came in with the new manager and introduced her to the staff. The rest of the meeting was routine except for the new manager being there. A few times I reminded myself to keep a pleasant expression without being stiff and unnatural.*
>
> *When I first learned about half smiling, I thought it was fake and insincere, like papering over my true feelings. But it wasn't like that at all. My negative feelings about the new manager didn't go away, but half smiling made me feel a little calmer. It helped me realize that I can handle it if she works here. It gave me a feeling of inner strength.*

Caroline wasn't happy about the new manager, for good reason. But she was pleased with how she handled the situation. She reminded herself of something she values: behaving professionally at work. This helped her resist the temptation to avoid an unpleasant situation by skipping the meeting. Mindfully half smiling helped her feel autonomous, competent, and self-accepting. It showed her that she can have strong feelings of well-being in an unpleasant situation.

Mindfulness and Facing Adversity

No matter how much we practice mindfulness, we can't escape real misfortune and tragedy, such as sickness, loss, rejection, and pain. In this section, we'll consider serious illness—cancer in particular, for several reasons. First, cancer affects many people. In the United States, 46 percent of men and 38 percent of women will be diagnosed with cancer at some point in their lives. Of those, 64 percent will survive for five years or more (Speca et al. 2006). Second, cancer patients face extremely distressing circumstances: difficult and painful treatments, reduced ability to work, disruptions in their family and social lives, and uncertainties about how long they will survive. Third, researchers have studied the benefits of mindfulness for people with cancer.

Being diagnosed with cancer can feel like the end of happiness and well-being. Yet studies show that cancer patients who participate in mindfulness training feel more cheerful, relaxed, and vigorous. Their daily lives feel more interesting. They find more satisfaction in the work they're able to do. Their relationships feel closer and more supportive (Hoffman et al. 2012; Ledesma and Kumano 2009).

Below, you'll find reflections of several cancer patients (reprinted with permission from Mackenzie et al. 2007). All of them completed an eight-week course of mindfulness-based stress reduction at a leading cancer center in Canada and continued to attend weekly sessions afterward, some for several years. Participants ranged in age from forty-three to seventy-seven and had a variety of cancers, including malignant melanoma, Hodgkin's disease, and breast, prostate, and ovarian cancer. They were interviewed for a study of the effects of mindfulness on their mental health:

- *I don't think the disease has gotten to me as stressfully and horribly as it could have. I am a fairly emotional woman. If I hadn't taken mindfulness, I would be a mess.*

- *What the meditation does is give me time to look within. By looking within, that gives me control.*

- *Meditation means taking time out of all the chaos. Meditating gave me the chance to give the chaos some kind of meaning.*

- *It's changed my outlook on life, my relationship to other people, and, most importantly, my relationship to myself. That's the one person I have to deal with every day.*

- *This whole notion of embracing change as the constant—I'd never really thought of it that way before.*

- *The ideas actually have a physical embodiment. That's what is so powerful about this—you don't just read it. It's about how you take those ideas and actually do what you have to do. It's very simple what you have to do. You have to sit, you have to be quiet, and you have to listen to your breathing. That is really beautifully simple.*

- *The way I look at cancer is that once you get through the awfulness it's a very powerful motivator to live your life. I'm grateful I can come up here [to the mindfulness group at the cancer center] and be reminded of that.*

- *I'm a much happier person than I ever thought I could be with the disease.... The program has really transformed my life. I've got a much better life for it.*

Despite having a serious illness, the people in this study found that mindfulness helped them develop many of the elements of psychological well-being: autonomy, personal growth, healthier relationships, and purpose in life. They also felt more positive emotions and fewer negative ones.

Cultivating Happiness

Throughout this book, you've seen that mindfulness contributes to happiness in several ways:

- Mindfulness makes us aware of simple pleasures and momentary joys that are already part of ordinary life but that we often overlook. Savoring these experiences increases our happiness and satisfaction with life.

- Mindfulness cultivates important elements of psychological well-being. It helps us identify and pursue our goals and values, learn and grow, cultivate relationships, accept our strengths and weaknesses, and respond wisely to the inevitable discomforts.

- In some cases, mindful awareness can transform an unpleasant task or situation into a source of contentment.

- Mindfulness can help us find happiness and well-being in the midst of serious adversity.

EXERCISE: The Mountain Meditation

Before ending this book, I offer one more exercise. The mountain meditation, originally developed by Jon Kabat-Zinn (1994) and used in several mindfulness programs, cultivates the inner strength and stability to find various types of happiness—peace of mind, contentment, well-being, even joy—amidst the constantly changing conditions of life. Read through the following instructions carefully before trying the meditation. If you'd like to practice with an audio recording, you'll find one at the website for this book (http://www.newharbinger.com/29033).

❊ ❊ ❊

To begin, sit in a comfortable position that feels relaxed yet alert, with your back relatively straight, but not stiff or tense, and your hands resting comfortably. If you can, allow your spine to be self-supporting, rather than leaning against the back of a chair.

Close your eyes or gaze softly at a spot on the floor.

For a few moments, observe the sensations and movements as the breath goes in and out of your body, allowing the breath to go at its own pace and rhythm.

Now imagine a large, beautiful mountain. It might be a mountain you've seen before, or it might be an imaginary mountain. Picture it as best you can. Notice the mountain's peak, perhaps with snow on it and with rocks showing through the snow. Notice the sides of the mountain. There may be trees growing or sheep grazing, or perhaps the slopes are snow covered. Notice that the base of the mountain is solidly embedded in the earth. The mountain is stable, unmoving, and beautiful.

Imagine that a wizard has granted you a wish, and you wished to become the mountain. Now you are the mountain, and you share its qualities. You are solidly rooted, still, stable, large, dignified, and beautiful. Your head is the top of the mountain and you have a wide view of the surrounding area. Your shoulders and arms are the sides of the mountain, and your lower body is the base, firmly embedded in your chair or the floor. Your spine is straight, just as the mountain seems to reach for the sky yet isn't straining; it is simply being itself.

And now, as you're sitting, notice that during each day, the sun and clouds move across the sky, making patterns of light, shadows, and colors that are constantly changing. As the sun moves below the horizon, the sky becomes dark and stars emerge. The moon may appear. The stars and the moon also move across the sky. Sometimes the moon is full; sometimes it's a slim crescent. Sometimes the stars are numerous and bright; at other times, they're hidden by clouds.

In summer, there may be no snow at all on the mountain, or perhaps there's only snow at the very top or in deep crevices where the sun can't reach it. In the autumn, the trees on the mountain become brightly colored and then gradually lose their leaves, which fall to the ground and turn brown. In winter, the mountain is covered with snow and ice. In spring, flowers bloom all over the mountainsides, leaves emerge on the trees, the birds sing, the snow melts, and the streams are overflowing with melted snow. In any season, the mountain may be covered with clouds, fog, or rain. In any season, there may be violent storms, with powerful wind, lightning, thunder, rain, snow, or sleet.

People may come to look at the mountain. Sometimes they talk about how beautiful, how majestic, or how inspiring it is. At other times, they complain that there are too many tourists on the mountain or that the weather is too cold, cloudy, stormy, or wet to enjoy the mountain that day.

None of this makes any difference to the mountain, which remains beautiful and majestic and strong regardless of the changing conditions. The mountain continues to sit, simply being itself, whether anyone sees it, or whether they like what they see. No matter the season or the weather, the mountain is itself: stable, unwavering, and strong.

Continue to sit and breathe for a few more moments, contemplating the lessons that can be learned from the mountain.

❋ ❋ ❋

Practicing mindfulness teaches us to develop the qualities of the mountain—stillness, rootedness, stability, and simply being ourselves—although many things in our lives are constantly changing. We all have times of light and darkness, calm and storms, intensity and dullness. The thoughts and feelings that we experience, the emotional storms and crises, the periods of joy and excitement are all like weather on the mountain.

This doesn't mean that we ignore the weather, deny it, or pretend it isn't there. We *observe* the weather, in all its variations. We accept the weather for what it is. We know that the mountain is not the weather. The mountain remains, while the weather comes and goes. The mountain continues to be itself.

The image of the mountain can remind us of important aspects of human nature: stability, dignity, balance, presence, stillness. At the same time, people are more complex than mountains. We move around, breathe, talk, see, hear, and feel. Do the mountain meditation in the spirit of exploration and interest and see if it's meaningful to you.

Summing Up and Looking Ahead

Good mental health isn't a matter of what comes to our minds. We all want positive emotions, pleasant thoughts, and urges to do sensible things, and sometimes we have those. But we also have painful emotions, dark thoughts, and destructive urges. What matters is how we respond to them. Do we ruminate, try to suppress or avoid them, give in to destructive urges, or criticize ourselves harshly? These are traps that make matters worse. The alternative is to respond with mindful awareness: observing with friendly curiosity to see what's happening, accepting with compassion the reality of the present moment, and choosing with awareness to do something consistent with what we truly value.

This book has discussed how to use mindfulness skills to respond to stress and difficulties and build a happier, more satisfying life. Now that you've reached the end of the book, you may be wondering how to maintain your new skills. The most important thing is to keep practicing. How to practice is up to you. Having worked your way through this book, you have many options. The following suggestions may be helpful in your journey forward.

Formal Practice

If you can, it's helpful to do formal practices regularly. Formal practice means taking time to do a mindfulness exercise while not doing anything else: to sit quietly and observe your breath, do a body scan, or practice mindful movement. You can use the recordings on the website for this book (http://www. newharbinger.com/29033), or you may find that you no longer need them.

If it's difficult to find time for formal practice, remember that even a very short practice is better than none at all. If you intended to practice but the day got away from you, try practicing for two minutes before getting into bed. Sit quietly and watch your breath or do some mindful neck stretches or shoulder rolls—just for two minutes. You can set a timer. This won't interfere with your sleep; in fact, you may sleep better.

Another option is to practice for short periods during the day. Before you get out of bed, do a short body scan or take five or ten mindful breaths. Look for pauses during your workday when you can do the same.

You also might consider practicing with a group. Look online for mindfulness groups in your area. Or form your own group with friends. Research shows that support and community greatly contribute to maintaining skills over the long term.

Mindfulness of Daily Activities

As you've learned, any activity can become a mindfulness exercise: walking, eating, brushing your teeth, washing the dishes, and more. When you walk, see if at least the first ten steps can be a mindfulness practice. At meals, try eating the first two bites mindfully. Try driving mindfully, without the radio. Wherever you are, observe your surroundings.

Savoring Pleasant Experiences

Mindfulness of ordinary moments of everyday life can improve your overall happiness. Pay attention to life's small, pleasant experiences: the smell of tea or coffee, a child's smile, the sun streaming through a window. Savor them.

Remembering Your Breath

Even if you can't stop what you're doing to sit quietly with your eyes closed, you can direct your attention to your breath throughout the day. Try taking a mindful breath or two at every red light, whether you're driving or on foot. Observe your breath while standing in lines, sitting in waiting rooms, while your computer warms up, or during meetings. When pain, stress, or discomfort arises, breathe with it.

Befriending Your Emotions

Remember that emotions are built into human nature because they serve useful purposes—if we handle them wisely. Instead of ruminating, trying to get rid of them, or criticizing yourself for having emotions, observe what's happening in your body. Breathe with it. Give yourself a little space to decide what to do, if anything.

Remembering That Thoughts Are Just Thoughts

We all have a strong tendency to believe our thoughts. When thoughts like *This is awful*, *I'm an idiot*, or *The future is hopeless* come to mind, remember that they're only thoughts. Labeling them ("Those are thoughts") can be very helpful. This doesn't mean you have to ignore them. Sometimes thoughts are useful. If you act on them, do so with awareness.

Mindful Pausing

When thoughts and feelings are difficult, slowing down, even for a brief moment, often provides enough time to see what's happening—in the situation, your mind, and your body. Taking a mindful breath (or several) gives you a chance to remind yourself of what's truly important and choose what to do. Remember that sometimes the wise choice is to allow a situation to run its natural course.

Remembering the Guest House and the Bus

You are the guest house. Your thoughts and feelings are visitors. You can allow them to be themselves—with acceptance and kindness, and without being controlled by them. Or if you prefer, you can think of your life as the bus, with your thoughts and feelings as the passengers and you as the driver. You decide where to drive. You don't have to control the passengers, and they don't have to control you.

Remember that guest house proprietors and bus drivers need kindness, just like everyone else.

✳ ✳ ✳

Finally, and most importantly, remember that you can start now. As many teachers say, mindfulness is only one breath away. Every moment is an opportunity to start transforming your life.

Resources

Websites: Information About Mindfulness

Center for Mindfulness in Medicine, Health Care, and Society, University of Massachusetts Medical School
http://www.umassmed.edu/cfm

Information about mindfulness-based cognitive therapy (North America)
http://www.mbct.com

Mindful Awareness Research Center, University of California Los Angeles
http://marc.ucla.edu

Information about mindfulness from *Mindful* magazine
http://www.mindful.org

Comprehensive information about mindfulness
http://www.mindfulnet.org

Websites: Insight Meditation Retreat Centers

Insight Meditation Society, Barre, Massachusetts
http://www.dharma.org

Spirit Rock Meditation Center, Woodacre, California
http://www.spiritrock.org

Insight Meditation Retreat Centre, South Devon, United Kingdom
http://gaiahouse.co.uk

Recommended Reading

Bardacke, N. 2012. *Mindful Birthing: Training the Mind, Body, and Heart for Childbirth and Beyond.* New York: HarperOne.

Germer, C. 2009. *The Mindful Path to Self-Compassion: Freeing Yourself from Destructive Thoughts and Emotions.* New York: Guilford.

Harris, R. 2008. *The Happiness Trap: How to Stop Struggling and Start Living.* Boston: Trumpeter.

Kabat-Zinn, J. 1990. *Full Catastrophe Living: Using the Wisdom of Your Body and Mind to Face Stress, Pain, and Illness.* New York: Delta.

Kabat-Zinn, J. 1994. *Wherever You Go, There You Are: Mindfulness Meditation in Everyday Life.* New York: Hyperion.

Kabat-Zinn, J. 2005. *Coming to Our Senses: Healing Ourselves and the World Through Mindfulness.* New York: Hyperion.

Kabat-Zinn, M., and J. Kabat-Zinn. 1997. *Everyday Blessings: The Inner Work of Mindful Parenting.* New York: Hyperion.

Neff, K. 2011. *Self-Compassion: Stop Beating Yourself Up and Leave Insecurity Behind.* New York: HarperCollins.

Orsillo, S., and L. Roemer. 2011. *The Mindful Way Through Anxiety: Break Free from Chronic Worry and Reclaim Your Life.* New York: Guilford.

Salzberg, S. 2011. *Real Happiness: The Power of Meditation.* New York: Workman.

Vieten, C. 2009. *Mindful Motherhood: Practical Tools for Staying Sane During Pregnancy and Your Child's First Year.* Oakland, CA: New Harbinger.

Williams, M., and D. Penman. 2011. *Mindfulness: An Eight-Week Plan for Finding Peace in a Frantic World.* New York: Rodale.

Williams, M., J. Teasdale, Z. Segal, and J. Kabat-Zinn. 2007. *The Mindful Way Through Depression: Freeing Yourself from Chronic Unhappiness.* New York: Guilford.

Books for Professionals

Baer, R. A. 2006. *Mindfulness-Based Treatment Approaches: A Clinician's Guide to Evidence Base and Applications.* Burlington, MA: Elsevier.

Bowen, S., N. Chawla, and G. Marlatt. 2011. *Mindfulness-Based Relapse Prevention for Addictive Behaviors: A Clinician's Guide.* New York: Guilford.

Dimeff, L., and K. Koerner. 2007. *Dialectical Behavior Therapy in Clinical Practice: Applications Across Disorders and Settings.* New York: Guilford.

Eifert, G., and J. Forsyth. 2005. *Acceptance and Commitment Therapy for Anxiety Disorders.* Oakland, CA: New Harbinger.

Germer, C., and R. Siegel. 2012. *Wisdom and Compassion in Psychotherapy: Deepening Mindfulness in Clinical Practice.* New York: Guilford.

Germer, C., R. Siegel, and P. Fulton. 2005. *Mindfulness and Psychotherapy.* New York: Guilford.

Harris, R. 2009. *ACT Made Simple: An Easy-to-Read Primer on Acceptance and Commitment Therapy.* Oakland, CA: New Harbinger.

Hayes, S., V. Follette, and M. Linehan. 2004. *Mindfulness and Acceptance: Expanding the Cognitive Behavioral Tradition.* New York: Guilford.

Hayes, S., K. Strosahl, and K. Wilson. 2012. *Acceptance and Commitment Therapy: The Process and Practice of Mindful Change* (2nd edition). New York: Guilford.

Linehan, M. M. 1993. *Cognitive Behavioral Treatment of Borderline Personality Disorder.* New York: Guilford.

Linehan, M. M. 1993. *Skills Training Manual for Treating Borderline Personality Disorder.* New York: Guilford.

Marra, T. 2005. *Dialectical Behavior Therapy in Private Practice: A Practical and Comprehensive Guide.* Oakland, CA: New Harbinger.

Roemer, L., and S. Orsillo. 2009. *Mindfulness- and Acceptance-Based Behavioral Therapies in Practice.* New York: Guilford.

Segal, Z. V., J. M. G. Williams, and J. D. Teasdale. 2013. *Mindfulness-Based Cognitive Therapy for Depression* (2nd edition). New York: Guilford.

Shapiro, S. L., and L. E. Carlson. 2009. *The Art and Science of Mindfulness: Integrating Mindfulness into Psychology and the Helping Professions.* Washington, DC: American Psychological Association.

Walser, R., and D. Westrup. 2007. *Acceptance and Commitment Therapy for the Treatment of Post-Traumatic Stress Disorder and Trauma-Related Problems.* Oakland, CA: New Harbinger.

Wilson, K., and T. DuFrene. 2008. *Mindfulness for Two: An Acceptance and Commitment Therapy Approach to Mindfulness in Psychotherapy.* Oakland, CA: New Harbinger.

Recordings of Mindfulness Exercises

Recordings by Jon Kabat-Zinn
http://www.stressreductiontapes.com
http://www.mindfulnesstapes.com

Recordings by Mark Williams
http://www.octc.co.uk/product-category/audio

Guided meditations by many teachers, including Tara Brach, Pema Chödrön, Jon Kabat-Zinn, Sharon Salzberg, and Joseph Goldstein
http://www.soundstrue.com

References

Adams, C. E., and M. R. Leary. 2007. Promoting self-compassionate attitudes toward eating among restrictive and guilty eaters. *Journal of Social and Clinical Psychology* 26:1120–1144.

Addis, M., and C. Martell. 2004. *Overcoming Depression One Step at a Time: The New Behavioral Activation Approach to Getting Your Life Back.* Oakland, CA: New Harbinger.

Allen, L. B., R. K. McHugh, and D. H. Barlow. 2008. Emotional disorders: A unified protocol. In *Clinical Handbook of Psychological Disorders: A Step-by-Step Treatment Manual* (4th ed.), edited by D. H. Barlow, 216–249. New York: Guilford.

Averill, J. R. 1975. A semantic atlas of emotional concepts. *Catalog of Selected Documents in Psychology* 5:30.

Baer, L. 2001. *The Imp of the Mind: Exploring the Silent Epidemic of Obsessive Bad Thoughts.* New York: Plume.

Baer, R. A., G. T. Smith, E. Lykins, D. Button, J. Krietemeyer, S. Sauer, E. Walsh, D. Duggan, and J. M. G. Williams. 2008. Construct validity of the Five Facet Mindfulness Questionnaire in meditating and nonmeditating samples. *Assessment* 15:329–342.

Barks, C. 2004. *The Essential Rumi.* New York: HarperCollins.

Barlow, D., K. Ellard, C. Fairholme, T. Farchione, C. Boisseau, L. Allen, and J. Ehrenreich-May. 2011. *Unified Protocol for Transdiagnostic Treatment of Emotional Disorders.* New York: Oxford University Press.

Barnard, L. K., and J. F. Curry. 2012. The relationship of clergy burnout to self-compassion and other personality dimensions. *Pastoral Psychology* 61:149–163.

Baron, R. A. 1988. Negative effects of destructive criticism: Impact on conflict, self-efficacy, and task performance. *Journal of Applied Psychology* 73:199–207.

Bergner, R. M. 1995. *Pathological Self-Criticism.* New York: Plenum.

Blatt, S. J., J. P. D'Afflitti, and D. M. Quinlan. 1976. Experiences of depression in normal young adults. *Journal of Abnormal Psychology* 85:383–389.

Borkovec, T., W. Ray, and J. Stober. 1998. Worry: A cognitive phenomenon intimately linked to affective, physiological and interpersonal behavioral processes. *Cognitive Therapy and Research* 22:561–576.

Bowen, S., N. Chawla, and G. A. Marlatt. 2011. *Mindfulness-Based Relapse Prevention for Addictive Behaviors: A Clinician's Guide.* New York: Guilford.

Bowen, S., and A. Marlatt. 2009. Surfing the urge: Brief mindfulness-based intervention for college student smokers. *Psychology of Addictive Behaviors* 23:666.

Brown, K. W., and M. Holt. 2011. Experiential processing and the integration of the bright and dark sides of the human psyche. In *Designing Positive Psychology: Taking Stock and Moving Forward*, edited by K. M. Sheldon, T. B. Kashdan, and M. F. Steger, 147–159. New York: Oxford University Press.

Brown, K. W., and R. M. Ryan. 2003. The benefits of being present: Mindfulness and its role in psychological well-being. *Journal of Personality and Social Psychology* 84:822.

Brown, K. W., R. M. Ryan, and J. D. Creswell. 2007. Mindfulness: Theoretical foundations and evidence for its salutary effects. *Psychological Inquiry* 18:211–237.

Brozovich, F., and R. G. Heimberg. 2008. An analysis of post-event processing in social anxiety disorder. *Clinical Psychology Review* 28:891–903.

Bryant, F. 2003. Savoring beliefs inventory (SBI): A scale for measuring beliefs about savouring. *Journal of Mental Health* 12:175–196.

Campbell-Sills, L., D. H. Barlow, T. A. Brown, and S. G. Hofmann. 2006. Effects of suppression and acceptance on emotional responses of individuals with anxiety and mood disorders. *Behaviour Research and Therapy* 44:1251–1263.

Cantor, N., and C. A. Sanderson. 1999. Life task participation and well-being: The importance of taking part in daily life. In *Well-Being: Foundations of Hedonic Psychology*, edited by D. Kahneman, E. Diener, and N. Schwarz, 230–243. New York: Russell Sage Foundation.

Carmody, J., and R. A. Baer. 2008. Relationships between mindfulness practice and levels of mindfulness, medical and psychological symptoms and well-being in a mindfulness-based stress reduction program. *Journal of Behavioral Medicine* 31:23–33.

Cohn, M. A., B. L. Fredrickson, S. L. Brown, J. A. Mikels, and A. M. Conway. 2009. Happiness unpacked: Positive emotions increase life satisfaction by building resilience. *Emotion* 9:361–368.

Conway, M., P. Csank, S. Holm, and C. Blake. 2000. On assessing individual differences in rumination on sadness. *Journal of Personality Assessment* 75:404–425.

Crenshaw, D. 2008. *The Myth of Multitasking: How "Doing It All" Gets Nothing Done.* San Francisco: Jossey-Bass.

Czikszentmihalyi, M. 1990. *Flow: The Psychology of Optimal Experience.* New York: Harper and Row.

Davidson, R. J. 2007, October. Changing the brain by transforming the mind: The impact of compassion training on the neural systems of emotion. Paper presented at the Mind and Life Institute Conference, Emory University, Atlanta, GA.

Dunkley, D., R. Masheb, and C. Grilo. 2010. Childhood maltreatment, depressive symptoms, and body dissatisfaction in patients with binge eating disorder: The mediating role of self-criticism. *International Journal of Eating Disorders* 43:274–281.

Ekman, P. 1973. Cross cultural studies of facial expression. In *Darwin and Facial Expression: A Century of Research in Review*, edited by P. Ekman, 169–222. New York: Academic Press.

Evans, D. R., R. A. Baer, and S. C. Segerstrom. 2009. The effects of mindfulness and self-consciousness on persistence. *Personality and Individual Differences* 47:379–382.

Forman, E. M., K. L. Hoffman, K. B. McGrath, J. D. Herbert, L. L. Brandsma, and M. R. Lowe. 2007. A comparison of acceptance- and control-based strategies for coping with food cravings: An analog study. *Behaviour Research and Therapy* 45:2372–2386.

Fredrickson, B. L. 2001. The role of positive emotions in positive psychology: The broaden-and-build theory of positive emotions. *American Psychologist* 56:218–226.

Gámez, W., M. Chmielewski, R. Kotov, C. Ruggero, and D. Watson. 2011. Development of a measure of experiential avoidance: The Multidimensional Experiential Avoidance Questionnaire. *Psychological Assessment* 23:692–713.

Germer, C. K. 2009. *The Mindful Path to Self-Compassion: Freeing Yourself from Destructive Thoughts and Emotions.* New York: Guilford.

Germer, C. K., and R. D. Siegel, editors. 2012. *Wisdom and Compassion in Psychotherapy: Deepening Mindfulness in Clinical Practice.* New York: Guilford Press.

Geschwind, N., F. Peeters, M. Drukker, J. van Os, and M. Wichers. 2011. Mindfulness training increases momentary positive emotions and reward experience in adults vulnerable to depression: A randomized controlled trial. *Journal of Consulting and Clinical Psychology* 79:618–628.

Gilbert, P. 2005. Compassion and cruelty: A biopsychosocial approach. In *Compassion: Conceptualizations, Research, and Use in Psychotherapy*, edited by P. Gilbert, 9–74. London: Routledge.

Gilbert, P. 2009. *Overcoming Depression* (3rd ed.). New York: Basic Books.

Gilbert, P., M. Clarke, S. Hempel, J. Miles, and C. Irons. 2004. Criticizing and reassuring oneself: An exploration of forms, styles, and reasons in female students. *British Journal of Clinical Psychology* 43:31–50.

Goleman, D. 1995. *Emotional Intelligence: Why It Can Matter More Than IQ.* New York: Bantam.

Greenberger, D., and C. A. Padesky. 1995. *Mind Over Mood: Change How You Feel by Changing the Way You Think.* New York: Guilford.

Harman, R., and D. Lee. 2010. The role of shame and self-critical thinking in the development and maintenance of current threat in post-traumatic stress disorder. *Clinical Psychology and Psychotherapy* 17:13–24.

Harris, R. 2008. *The Happiness Trap: How to Stop Struggling and Start Living.* Boston: Trumpeter.

Hayes, S. C. (with S. Smith). 2005. *Get Out of Your Mind and Into Your Life: The New Acceptance and Commitment Therapy.* Oakland, CA: New Harbinger.

Hayes, S. C., K. D. Strosahl, and K. G. Wilson. 1999. *Acceptance and Commitment Therapy: An Experiential Approach to Behavior Change.* New York: Guilford.

Hayes, S. C., K. D. Strosahl, and K. G. Wilson. 2012. *Acceptance and Commitment Therapy: The Process and Practice of Mindful Change* (2nd ed.). New York: Guilford.

Hoffman, C., S. Ersser, J. Hopkinson, P. Nicholls, J. Harrington, and P. Thomas. 2012. Effectiveness of mindfulness-based stress reduction in mood, breast- and endocrine-related quality of life, and well-being in Stage 0 to III breast cancer: A randomized, controlled trial. *Journal of Clinical Oncology* 30:1335–1342.

Kabat-Zinn, J. 1990. *Full Catastrophe Living: Using the Wisdom of Your Mind and Body to Face Stress, Pain, and Illness.* New York: Delacorte.

Kabat-Zinn, J. 1994. *Wherever You Go, There You Are: Mindfulness Meditation in Everyday Life.* New York: Hyperion.

Kasser, T., and R. M. Ryan. 2001. Be careful what you wish for: Optimal functioning and the relative attainment of intrinsic and extrinsic goals. In *Life Goals and Well-Being: Towards a Positive Psychology of Human Striving*, edited by P. Schmuck and K. M. Sheldon, 115–129. Göttingen, Germany: Hogrefe and Huber.

Kelly, A. C., D. Zuroff, C. Foa, and P. Gilbert. 2010. Who benefits from training in self-compassionate self-regulation? A study of smoking reduction. *Journal of Social and Clinical Psychology* 29:727–755.

Keng, S., M. Smoski, and C. Robins. 2011. Effects of mindfulness on psychological health: A review of empirical studies. *Clinical Psychology Review* 31:1041–1056.

Killingsworth, M. A., and D. T. Gilbert. 2010. A wandering mind is an unhappy mind. *Science* 330:932.

Kristeller, J., R. Wolever, and V. Sheets. 2013. Mindfulness-based eating awareness training (MB-EAT) for binge eating: A randomized clinical trial. *Mindfulness.* Published online.

Kuyken, W., E. Watkins, E. Holden, K. White, R. Taylor, S. Byford, A. Evans, S. Radford, J. Teasdale, and T. Dalgleish. 2010. How does mindfulness-based cognitive therapy work? *Behaviour Research and Therapy* 48:1105–1112.

Lassri, D., and G. Shahar. 2012. Self-criticism mediates the link between childhood emotional maltreatment and young adults' romantic relationships. *Journal of Social and Clinical Psychology* 31:289–311.

Ledesma, D., and H. Kumano. 2009. Mindfulness-based stress reduction and cancer: A meta-analysis. *Psycho-Oncology* 18:571–579.

Lewis, M. B. 2012. Exploring the positive and negative implications of facial feedback. *Emotion* 12:852–859.

Linehan, M. M. 1993a. *Cognitive Behavioral Treatment of Borderline Personality Disorder.* New York: Guilford.

Linehan, M. M. 1993b. *Skills Training Manual for Treating Borderline Personality Disorder.* New York: Guilford.

Mackenzie, M. J., L. E. Carlson, M. Munoz, and M. Speca. 2007. A qualitative study of self-perceived effects of mindfulness-based stress reduction (MBSR) in a psychosocial oncology setting. *Stress and Health: Journal of the International Society for the Investigation of Stress* 23:59–69.

McKay, M., and P. Fanning. 1992. *Self-Esteem* (3rd ed.). Oakland, CA: New Harbinger.

McKay, M., J. Wood, and J. Brantley. 2007. *The Dialectical Behavior Therapy Skills Workbook: Practical DBT Exercises for Learning Mindfulness, Interpersonal Effectiveness, Emotion Regulation, and Distress Tolerance.* Oakland, CA: New Harbinger.

Meyer, T., M. Miller, R. Metzger, and T. Borkovec. 1990. Development and validation of the Penn State Worry Questionnaire. *Behaviour Research and Therapy* 28:487–495.

Najmi, S., and D. M. Wegner. 2008. Thought suppression and psychopathology. In *Handbook of Approach and Avoidance Motivation*, edited by A. J. Elliott, 447–459. New York: Psychology Press.

Neff, K. D. 2003. The development and validation of a scale to measure self-compassion. *Self and Identity* 2:223–250.

Neff, K. D. 2011. *Self-Compassion: Stop Beating Yourself Up and Leave Insecurity Behind.* New York: Harper Collins.

Neff, K. D. 2012. The science of self-compassion. In *Wisdom and Compassion in Psychotherapy: Deepening Mindfulness in Clinical Practice*, edited by C. K. Germer and R. D. Siegel, 79–92. New York: Guilford.

Neff, K. D., and S. N. Beretvas. 2013. The role of self-compassion in romantic relationships. *Self and Identity* 12:78–98.

Neff, K. D., and E. P. Pommier. 2013. The relationship between self-compassion and other-focused concern among college undergraduates, community adults, and practicing meditators. *Self and Identity* 12:160–176.

Nezu, A. N., C. M. Nezu, and M. McMurran. 2008. Problem-solving therapy. In *Cognitive Behavior Therapy: Applying Empirically Supported Techniques in Your Practice* (2nd ed.), edited by W. T. O'Donohue and J. E. Fisher, 402–407. Hoboken, NJ: John Wiley and Sons.

Nhat Hanh, T. 1976. *The Miracle of Mindfulness.* Boston: Beacon Street.

Nolen-Hoeksema, S., B. E. Wisco, and S. Lyubomirsky. 2008. Rethinking rumination. *Perspectives on Psychological Science* 3:400–424.

Orsillo, S. M., and L. Roemer. 2011. *The Mindful Way Through Anxiety: Break Free from Chronic Worry and Reclaim Your Life.* New York: Guilford.

Ossorio, P. G. 1990. Appraisal. In *Advances in Descriptive Psychology, Volume 5*, edited by A. Putman and K. Davis, 155–171. Ann Arbor, MI: Descriptive Psychology Press.

Palfai, T. P., P. M. Monti, S. M. Colby, and D. J. Rohsenow. 1997. Effects of suppressing the urge to drink on the accessibility of alcohol outcome expectancies. *Behaviour Research and Therapy* 35:59–65.

Pastan, L. 1991. *Heroes in Disguise.* W. W. Norton and Co.

Peterson, C. 2006. *A Primer in Positive Psychology.* New York: Oxford University Press.

Peterson, C., N. Park, and M. E. P. Seligman. 2005. Orientations to happiness and life satisfaction: The full life versus the empty life. *Journal of Happiness Studies* 6:25–41.

Powers, T., R. Koestner, N. Lacaille, L. Kwan, and D. Zuroff. 2009. Self-criticism, motivation, and goal progress of athletes and musicians: A prospective study. *Personality and Individual Differences* 47:279–283.

Powers, T., R. Koestner, and D. Zuroff. 2007. Self-criticism, goal motivation, and goal progress. *Journal of Social and Clinical Psychology* 26:826–840.

Powers, T., R. Koestner, D. Zuroff, M. Milyavskaya, and A. Gorin. 2011. The effects of self-criticism and self-oriented perfectionism on goal pursuit. *Personality and Social Psychology Bulletin* 37:964–975.

Ringenbach, R. 2009. A comparison between counselors who practice meditation and those who do not on compassion fatigue, compassion satisfaction, burnout, and self-compassion. *Dissertation Abstracts International: Section B: The Sciences and Engineering* 70(6-B):3820.

Robinson, M. S., and L. B. Alloy. 2003. Negative cognitive styles and stress-reactive rumination interact to predict depression: A prospective study. *Cognitive Therapy and Research* 27:275–292.

Ryan, R. M., and E. L. Deci. 2000. Self-determination theory and the facilitation of intrinsic motivation, social development, and well-being. *American Psychologist* 55:68–78.

Ryan, R. M., and E. L. Deci. 2001. On happiness and human potentials: A review of research on hedonic and eudaimonic well-being. *Annual Review of Psychology* 52:141–166.

Ryan, R. M., V. Huta, and E. L. Deci. 2008. Living well: A self-determination theory perspective on eudaimonia. *Journal of Happiness Studies* 9:139–170.

Ryff, C. D. 1989. Happiness is everything, or is it? Explorations on the meaning of psychological well-being. *Journal of Personality and Social Psychology* 57:1069–1081.

Ryff, C. D., and C. L. M. Keyes. 1995. The structure of psychological well-being revisited. *Journal of Personality and Social Psychology* 69:719–727.

Salkovskis, P., and M. Reynolds. 1994. Thought suppression and smoking cessation. *Behaviour Research and Therapy* 32:193–201.

Salzberg, S. 2011. *Real Happiness: The Power of Meditation*. New York: Workman.

Sauer, S. E., and R. A. Baer. 2012. Ruminative and mindful self-focused attention in borderline personality disorder. *Personality Disorders: Theory, Research, and Treatment* 3:433–441.

Segal, Z. V., J. M. G. Williams, and J. D. Teasdale. 2002. *Mindfulness-Based Cognitive Therapy for Depression: A New Approach to Preventing Relapse*. New York: Guilford.

Segal, Z. V., J. M. G. Williams, and J. D. Teasdale. 2013. *Mindfulness-Based Cognitive Therapy for Depression* (2nd ed.). New York: Guilford.

Shapiro, S. L., J. A. Astin, S. R. Bishop, and M. Cordova. 2005. Mindfulness-Based Stress Reduction for Health Care Professionals: Results from a Randomized Trial. *International Journal of Stress Management* 12:64–176.

Sheldon, K. M., and A. J. Elliott. 1999. Goal striving, need satisfaction, and longitudinal well-being: The self-concordance model. *Journal of Personality and Social Psychology* 76:483–497.

Shenk, C. E., and A. E. Fruzzetti. 2011. The impact of validating and invalidating responses on emotional reactivity. *Journal of Social and Clinical Psychology* 30:163–183.

Shipherd, J. C., and J. G. Beck. 2005. The role of thought suppression in post-traumatic stress disorder. *Behavior Therapy* 36:277–287.

Speca, M., L. E. Carlson, M. MacKenzie, and M. Angen. 2006. Mindfulness-based stress reduction (MBSR) as an intervention for cancer patients. In *Mindfulness-Based Treatment Approaches: Clinician's Guide to Evidence Base and Applications*, edited by R. A. Baer, 239–261. San Diego, CA: Elsevier.

Spink, A., C. Cole, and M. Waller. 2008. Multitasking behavior. *Annual Review of Information Science and Technology* 42:93–118.

Strayer, D. L., and Drews, F. A. 2007. Multitasking in the automobile. In *Attention: From Theory to Practice*, edited by A. F. Kramer, D. A. Wiegmann, and A. Kirlik, 121–133. New York: Oxford University Press.

Sukhodolsky, D. G., A. Golub, and E. N. Cromwell. 2001. Development and validation of the anger rumination scale. *Personality and Individual Differences* 31:689–700.

Tangney, J. P., and R. L. Dearing. 2002. *Shame and Guilt.* New York: Guilford.

Trapnell, P. D., and J. D. Campbell. 1999. Private self-consciousness and the five-factor model of personality: Distinguishing rumination from reflection. *Journal of Personality and Social Psychology* 76:284–304.

Treynor, W., R. Gonzalez, and S. Nolen-Hoeksema. 2003. Rumination reconsidered: A psychometric analysis. *Cognitive Therapy and Research* 27:247–259.

Vowles, K. E., D. W. McNeil, R. T. Gross, M. L. McDaniel, A. Mouse, M. Bates, P. Gallimore, and C. McCall. 2007. Effects of pain acceptance and pain control strategies on physical impairment in individuals with chronic low back pain. *Behavior Therapy* 38:412–425.

Waterman, A. S. 1993. Two conceptions of happiness: Contrasts of personal expressiveness (eudaimonia) and hedonic enjoyment. *Journal of Personality and Social Psychology* 64:678–691.

Watkins, E. R. 2008. Constructive and unconstructive repetitive thought. *Psychological Bulletin* 134:163–206.

Wegner, D. M., D. J. Schneider, S. Carter, and L. White. 1987. Paradoxical effects of thought suppression. *Journal of Personality and Social Psychology* 53:5–13.

Whiteside, S. P., and D. R. Lynam. 2001. The Five Factor Model and impulsivity: Using a structural model of personality to understand impulsivity. *Personality and Individual Differences* 30:669–689.

Williams, M., and D. Penman. 2011. *Mindfulness: An Eight-Week Plan for Finding Peace in a Frantic World.* New York: Rodale.

Williams, M., J. Teasdale, Z. Segal, and J. Kabat-Zinn. 2007. *The Mindful Way Through Depression: Freeing Yourself from Chronic Unhappiness.* New York: Guilford.

Wilson, K. G., and T. DuFrene. 2008. *Mindfulness for Two: An Acceptance and Commitment Therapy Approach to Mindfulness in Psychotherapy.* Oakland, CA: New Harbinger.

About the Author

Ruth Baer, PhD, is professor of clinical psychology at the University of Kentucky in Lexington, where she conducts research on mindfulness and teaches mindfulness-based treatments. She is the editor of two books: *Mindfulness-Based Treatment Approaches* and *Assessing Mindfulness and Acceptance Processes in Clients*.

Foreword author Mark Williams, PhD, is professor of clinical psychology at Oxford University, UK. He is a fellow of the Academy of Medical Sciences and a fellow of the British Academy. He is author of many books and articles on the psychology of depression and its treatment, focusing on mindfulness-based approaches.

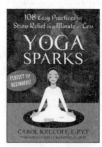